From Elephants to Mice

Animals Who Have Touched My Soul

Dr. James Mahoney

WILEY

Wiley Publishing, Inc.

Howell Book House
Published by Wiley Publishing, Inc., Hoboken, New Jersey

For general information on our other products and services or to obtain technical support please contact our Customer Care Department within the U.S. at (877) 762-2974, outside the U.S. at (317) 572-3993 or fax (317) 572-4002.

Wiley also publishes its books in a variety of electronic formats. Some content that appears in print may not be available in electronic books. For more information about Wiley products, please visit our web site at www.wiley.com.

Library of Congress Cataloging-in-Publication Data:
Mahoney, James, date.
  From elephants to mice : animals who have touched my soul / James Mahoney.
    p. cm.
  Includes bibliographical references and index.
  ISBN-13: 978-0-470-50158-0
  ISBN-10: 0-470-50158-8
  1. Mahoney, James, 1940– 2. Veterinarians—United States—Biography. 3. Animals—Psychology. 4. Human-animal relationships. 5. Animal welfare. I. Title.
  SF613.M3A3 2010
  636.089092--dc22
                        2010002927
Printed in the United States of America

10 9 8 7 6 5 4 3 2 1

Book design by Erin Zeltner
Cover design by Wendy Mount
Book production by Wiley Publishing, Inc. Composition Services

All photos © James Mahoney except page 80 © istockphoto.com/Elemental Imaging, page 82 © istockphoto.com/Michael Stubblefield, and page 108 © Dr. Ben Gasirowski.

To my wife, Marie-Paule, who often showed me the way. She shared everything but sometimes carried the burden alone. It was always a nice burden, though; never a chore. In earlier days she was helped by our three "sparrows," Pádraig, Nathalie, and Christopher, who have since left the nest and carried their compassion with them. Proud and grateful I am of them all!

It is only with the heart that one can see rightly; what is essential is invisible to the eye.

—Antoine de Saint-Exupéry,
The Little Prince

Contents

Acknowledgments

Many of the stories I tell in this book are about the monkeys and chimpanzees I worked with in the confines of the research laboratory. I owe twenty years of gratitude on behalf of the animals to the caregivers, or technicians, as they were proud to call themselves. Without their dedication, love, and compassion, there would be no story to tell, or at least not one that I would wish to tell. To most outsiders, the term *technician* sounds so cold and unfeeling, yet to them it was a badge of honor, a recognition of their aspirations to give the very best of themselves to the animals, never to give them second best. They carried a great burden. When interviewing candidates for openings as animal technicians, I always asked, "How do you feel about using animals in research?" I never selected a person who answered, "I have no problem with that."

I extend a special thanks to Doug Cohn, my veterinary colleague for nine years. We still keep in touch and ask for each other's opinion now and then. I know that he will never set aside the torch of caring.

A special thank you goes to the staff at *Publishers Weekly* who opened a door for me, in particular Reviews Director Louisa Ermelino and Senior Editor Lynn Andriani. Lynn amusingly reported my unintended pun in the magazine, that I was mainly looking for someone who would tell me, "'This is great'" or "As the animal doctor puts it, 'You're barking up the wrong tree.'"

I am indebted to Cynthia Kitchel, Vice President and Publisher at Wiley Publishing, Inc., for taking my proposal. I would also like to thank Wendy Mount, who artistically created the cover for the book.

My deepest gratitude goes to Pam Mourouzis, my editor, someone to whom I have bared my soul. She carried me along when I sometimes started to lose my way, put up with my many typographical errors and genuine misspellings without losing her patience, and was always so cheerful and encouraging.

Then there are the animals, the *crathers,* as my mother used to call them. I thank them for letting me see the other side of life and allowing me to share in their world. I have never taken them for granted.

I hope I don't let any of you down.

Introduction

A Life in Research

For the animal shall not be measured by man. In a world older and more complete than ours, they move finished and complete, gifted with the extension of the senses we have lost or never attained, living by voices we shall never hear. They are not brethren, they are not underlings: they are other nations, caught with ourselves in the net of life and time, fellow prisoners of the splendour and travail of the earth.

—Henry Beston (1888–1968)

It all started in 1977 during a visit I had long planned to the Laboratory for Experimental Medicine and Surgery in Primates (LEMSIP), a primate lab belonging to New York University in upstate New York. There I had a chance encounter with a little chimp who would totally change my life. I don't think I ever knew his name, but he was an impudent-looking little 2½-year-old. He was being led by the hand by a young woman dressed in the typical lab costume: blue cotton surgical scrub suit, disposable face mask hanging below her chin, paper booties, and a bouffant hat that held her long golden hair in place. She had stepped through a doorway in front of me, taking me quite by surprise. I had obviously taken the

1

little chimp by surprise, too, because as he looked up at me he scrunched his face into an expression that clearly said he thought I shouldn't be there. He reached out with a clenched fist and, with all the might he could muster, gave me a backhanded punch behind the knee.

I had never come face to face with a chimpanzee before. Like most people, I had seen chimps in television commercials and in movies, but never in the flesh. *Incredible!* I found myself thinking. *It must be the ultimate experience to work with chimps.* As unrealistic and even arrogant as it seems to me now, I couldn't help thinking to myself that I should try to find a way to convince Dr. Jan Moor-Jankowski, the director of LEMSIP, that he should offer me a job in the not-too-distant future as gynecologist, obstetrician, and pediatrician to the chimps.

I have often rued the day that little chimp hit me behind the knee. If it hadn't been for him, I might not have spent the rest of my life brooding and pondering, an increasing sense of guilt eating away at my heart, questioning the morality of what I was doing, this seemingly noble use of nonhuman animals for the betterment of humankind.

Although I am a veterinarian, I also became a research scientist in my own right. My first research project at LEMSIP, in fact, involved a study of pelvic inflammatory disease in baboons fitted with various types of human intrauterine devices, the results of which were a major reason for the withdrawal of one of the contraceptive devices from the market. As the years went by, I also became increasingly involved in overseeing research projects that dealt with vaccine development and testing in hepatitis and, in more recent times, studies on HIV and AIDS.

Yet I considered myself an animal lover. How could that be? How could I so readily accept using animals in research, locking them behind bars in relatively tiny cages for years on end, perhaps for the rest of their lives? It wasn't that I didn't care about the animals: I could stand on my soapbox and shake my fist and angrily shout my head off with the best of them when it came to fighting blatant cruelty to animals. But that was as far as it went in my mind—blatant cruelty.

At that moment in 1977, however, such questions were far from my thoughts. Like most people in their mid-30s with a growing family to support, I was absorbed in my career, struggling to establish myself, trying to impress upon the world and everyone in it that I knew what I was doing and where I was going.

I started off as a young country vet in the southwest of Scotland, Robert Burns's country of "wee sleekit, cow'rin, tim'rous beastie[s]." I should have known even then that I was in for a rough ride as far as animals were concerned. I remember with bitterness struggling through many a cold winter's night attending to cows who were having difficulty calving, the elation of eventual success soon crushed by the farmer dragging the calf away to be reared in a pen all alone, never to see his mother, even for a moment, never to feel her rough tongue lick dry his sodden skin. The farmers didn't want the calves to nurse for fear that their suckling would deform the cows' teats and make it impossible to attach the suction cups of the milking machine to them.

Then there were the agonizing decisions I sometimes had to make that meant life or death for an animal. I remember all too well Farmer Ferguson and his call for me to examine his ten cows to see if they were pregnant. "Bought these *coows* as *quays* last year," he lamented, "direct off the boat from Ireland." (*Quay* is the Scots dialect word for a heifer, or first-year cow.) "But I canna seem t' get them in calf. If they're no' pregnant this time, then it's off to the slaughterhouse wi' 'em," he added with finality.

"Let's see," I said, stripping off my pullover and shirt, a blast of wintry air coming through the open half door of the byre and shocking the bare skin of my chest. I began to lather up my arm with the bar of soap that Mr. Ferguson had set aside for me, along with a bucket

of ice-cold water and a threadbare towel, in preparation to insert my
hand, all the way to the shoulder if necessary, into the welcome
warmth of each cow's rectum.

The cows, all black and white Frisians, stood in line down the
length of the byre, their bottoms facing me, their tails flicking, their
feet stamping. The first splatters of diarrhea were hitting the concrete floor, a sure sign of their agitation with my unwelcome presence. "They always know when the veet's here," Mr. Ferguson said
with a condescending smirk, his way of letting me know that even
the cows had my measure.

The first cow wasn't pregnant, her uterus no bigger than the size
of a young virgin heifer's; nor was the second or the third. And so I
went down the line, feeling more and more like judge, jury, and
executioner as I pronounced my stark words of certain death: "No,
I'm afraid she's not pregnant, either."

I came to the last cow in the line. She turned her great head and
stared back at me, her baleful brown eyes pleading with me to give
her a reprieve, I couldn't help feeling. But she was no more pregnant than the other nine. I couldn't take it anymore! Throwing
honesty out the window, I announced to Mr. Ferguson as he stood
rooted to the ground like a statue: "I don't know about this one, she
just *might* be pregnant. We should wait and see. I'll check her again
in two weeks' time."

None of the farmers intended to be cruel: I knew that well
enough. The farmers who took the calves away from their mothers
at birth would certainly make sure that the newborns were well
dried with towels. Then either they or their wives would hastily rig
up a cozy pen of straw bales in the barn and suspend a heat lamp
from the rafters overhead to keep the little creature warm. Even Mr.
Ferguson didn't mean to be heartless when he threatened to send
his cows off to slaughter if they weren't in calf. He depended on a
regular supply of milk to keep his farm going and support his family.
To guarantee that, he had to make sure his cows got pregnant and

had calves on a regular basis. But still, I found these conditions hard to accept.

I was being unreasonable, of course. Looking back on it now, I wonder what I had expected. Had I thought that being a country vet would be an idyllic life of gamboling calves and bleating lambs and cows lowing contentedly as they grazed the heather-clad mountainsides?

It had never been my intention to end up in research. When I was young, I used to shudder at the very thought of animals being used in experiments. For me, researchers were vivisectors in the realest sense, people hell-bent on a desire to torture fully conscious animals just for sadistic pleasure, not for any "higher" good that might come of it. All that would change for me, however, when I was accepted into a master of science degree program to study comparative mammalian reproduction and embryology at the University College of North Wales, in Bangor.

Reproductive physiology had been my weakest subject at vet school, but to my consternation I found that 80 percent or more of what I dealt with on a daily basis in large-animal practice depended directly or indirectly on a sound knowledge of the subject. A master's degree in this field could only make me a better vet, I thought.

I was among four students who were taught by twelve professors the wonders and mysteries of the reproductive physiology of just about all of God's species, from elephants to mice, with kangaroos, yaks, and many others thrown in—except, oddly enough, primates. For the first time, I realized the sheer joy of learning for learning's sake.

About halfway through the master's degree program, I discovered that I was developing a fascination for delving into the unknown—in other words, an interest in research. We had been given pregnant mouse uteri to study under the microscope. I began to notice an exquisitely beautiful cell containing large purple granules in the wall of the uterus close to where the placenta was attached. None of my professors had ever seen this cell before or had any idea what it was. In my naive enthusiasm, I thought I had made a major discovery. I drew up a list of experiments that I would perform to determine when the cells first appeared in pregnancy, what might happen to them after the birth of the pups and the delivery of the placenta, and what their function might be. At that moment, I didn't think about the fact that I would have to kill many mice to achieve this goal, something that would later cause me great anguish. I had not even taken into consideration that someone else, a person unknown to me, had already had to do this in order to prepare the tissues that my fellow students and I had been studying. My zealousness was crushed when one day I saw in a scientific journal a photograph taken through the microscope of "my" cell, the cell I had been studying day after day for weeks. It had first been described in the early 1930s and even had a name, the metrial gland cell. Reading on, I soon discovered that others had done all but one of the experiments I had planned. I was devastated. This was the first disappointment—what I regarded as a failure—I would suffer in science, but it was not the last.

Nonetheless, I had been bitten by the bug for research. I set about applying for a grant to study for a PhD at the Royal College of Veterinary Surgeons in London once my master's degree in Wales would be over, focusing on a common, often life-threatening condition in cattle known as retained placenta (where the placenta fails to separate from the uterus after calving). I was fortunate to be taken under the wing of an enthusiastic professor.

During one of my visits to London to attend to formalities so that I could start my studies at the beginning of the coming academic year, the professor pulled a crumpled piece of torn-off newspaper from his back pocket. It was an advertisement for a position at the Royal College of Surgeons of England to be a veterinarian for a colony of monkeys. "Look into it," he said—more an order than a suggestion. "You never know, it could be interesting." I later discovered that the professor was afraid my family and I, already with one child and a second on the way, might not be able to survive on the grant I had been awarded to study the cattle condition and that a position at the Royal College of Surgeons might offer me greater security than the Royal College of Veterinary Surgeons.

This abrupt switch from cows to monkeys was quite unplanned, a sort of turn at the drop of a hat. Why I even went for the interview, for a job in a dental department, a branch of medicine for which I hadn't the slightest interest, and to work with monkeys, animals that I knew practically nothing about, I will never be able to adequately explain. But go for the interview I did, and I found myself immediately captivated by the monkeys.

As I was led into the animal rooms dressed in the protective clothing the professor of the department had given me to wear, one after another the monkeys barked and threatened me with their throaty *grrr* sounds. They rattled the bars of their cages defiantly, a sure sign that they regarded my uninvited presence in their territory as an affront. I was enchanted by their silver-mustachioed little black faces, their Spock-like pointed ears, the quaint pixie coifs atop their heads, the delicate little human-like fingers with which they gripped the bars of the cages, and their long curling tails. From some cages, tiny round-headed babies with large, sad eyes peered out at me from under the mothers' breasts, nipples in mouths, calling plaintively and then squeaking in sudden terror when they caught me gazing directly back into their eyes (something I soon learned you should never do to monkeys, especially when they don't know you; they regard eye-to-eye contact as a threat). How I would ever be able to put a stethoscope on a monkey's chest to listen to his lungs or stick a thermometer into his rectum to take his temperature without getting my fingers bitten off, I couldn't begin to imagine.

To my surprise, I soon discovered that the successful candidate for the job would be expected not only to act as resident veterinarian to the primate colony, which comprised some 150 Java monkeys and 70 pairs of tiny South American marmosets, but also to take care of colonies of rabbits, rats, mice, and cats; 300 dogs; and a small herd of goats (the latter of which would cause me more head-aches than all the rest of the animals put together). One last require-ment was paramount: the successful candidate would be required to study the reproductive characteristics of the monkeys for a PhD thesis. *Interesting!* I thought.

Little was known about the reproductive physiology of the Java monkey (or crab-eating or cynomolgus macaque, as it is also called), which was beginning to become the primary primate species for medical research in Europe at that time. Fetal ultrasonography was in its infancy; radioimmunoassay of serum hormones, such as estro-gen and progesterone, was still a few years away; and techniques like laparoscopy were in the earliest stages of development.

In particular, the dental researchers wanted someone to develop methods for diagnosing ovulation in the female monkeys so that precisely dated pregnancies could be obtained. The candidate would then be expected to explore ways of determining when the monkeys were about to give birth, a dicey guessing game at best in those days, so that the pregnancy could be interrupted at the last moment by cesarean section and the babies delivered into sterile conditions. This was essential to the dental researchers, who wanted to study precisely how the mouth, which is normally sterile at birth, becomes populated with bacteria, especially the bacterial species that causes dental caries—the cavities that most of us acquire as children. From this knowledge, the scientists hoped to develop vac-cines against the dental caries organism and determine whether young children could be protected by vaccinating their mothers during pregnancy or by vaccinating the babies themselves shortly after birth.

There would be no killing of the monkeys, no causing them dis-comfort or pain. Even when the monkeys would develop carious lesions—a surprisingly difficult thing to accomplish, and only after they had been fed high-sugar diets for considerable periods—their teeth would be filled even before they had developed cavities using general anesthesia and the most up-to-date dental techniques. There would be more than enough to keep me intellectually challenged for the four and a half years it would take me to finish my PhD.

Strangely enough, in those days I found nothing disturbing about seeing the monkeys in their cages day after day, with little to do except eat, drink, sleep, and stare endlessly into space. Although a few of them maintained a sort of social life in small groups, most of the monkeys were caged singly so that their dietary intake could be carefully monitored and controlled. The psychological consequences to the animals of this social deprivation—the endless loneliness, the abnormal behaviors some of them developed, like rocking, hair pulling, and even self-mutilation in a few cases—didn't strike me then. The research itself was not taxing on the monkeys in a physical sense, and certainly no one set out to be cruel to them.

The young technicians who looked after the monkeys obviously cared greatly for them and developed deep bonds of attachment to them. Consequently, I saw nothing cruel in the monkeys' incarceration and almost total lack of ability to control or manipulate their environment. These concerns would not confront me head on for many years to come—not until I got to LEMSIP, in New York, in the late 1970s.

At that time, I did not recognize the more pervasive and insidious form of cruelty—that caused by *omission* rather than *commission*. As I became more involved with the animals, I began to see not only their individuality, but also their unique needs. At times, before the lab had developed what I regarded as a real nursery, I brought babies home with me at night or on weekends for a little extra love and care. In particular, it took three very special—and yet, when I stop to think about it, not so special—little animals to awaken me: one baby chimp and two baby rhesus monkeys, all orphaned at birth. My family and I, with the help of our dog, Angus, reared them for the first year of their lives.

It was through watching these little animals grow and face life's challenges that I began to realize just how much we rob animals in the research laboratory. Once the infants went back to the lab permanently, there would be no more climbing trees in the forest, no skeltering across frozen ponds in the dead of winter, no picking peaches fresh from the tree, no chance for self-expression.

This was the beginning of the long journey through my soul, the coming to terms with my relationship with animals, whether in the wild or in captivity, debating the need to use them in research versus the profound desire to set them free.

Nothing is black and white when it comes to this relationship. Might over right, we collide at all levels of our association, with animals almost invariably being the losers. It is perhaps only with dogs and cats, opportunistic rogues that they are, that we most often meet a happy compromise; and that, probably, because they had a big hand in laying down the rules from the beginning.

Whether in the research laboratory or in nature, animals demonstrate a comportment far beyond our understanding. That chimpanzees, our closest living relatives in the animal kingdom, can exhibit remarkable levels of social intercourse is, perhaps, not surprising, but that they can also spontaneously mimic complex human behavior is rather humbling. But what if a little fish in a pond is capable of demonstrating a sense of humor with a human being? Do we regard it as a little less noteworthy because he's only a fish? And what about a pearly-eyed thrasher who fights with courage and bravery to protect his home and offspring? Or imagine a 40-year-old male Indian elephant in the wild, master of his own destiny, who stubbornly refuses to surrender his dignity to his captors.

These are just some of the remarkable animals I have been privileged to know; these are their stories.

1

The Power of Dignity and Courage

The dog is man's companion, the elephant is his slave.

—Sir Samuel Baker (1821–1893)

They referred to him as "the Makhna," the tuskless one. "Rogue," they also called him, because he destroyed crops, trampling them flat with his five-ton weight and tearing them apart with his massive feet and grasping trunk. He was also branded a killer. According to one newspaper report, he had taken the lives of three people in the village of Devarsalai, in the neighboring state of Karnataka in South India. His last victim had been a young boy, it said. Another newspaper claimed that he had killed twenty-three people over the past four years.

How did they know it was he and not some other marauding elephant who had committed all these crimes against humanity? They claimed it was because one of his hind feet was smaller in

Loki plays submarines in the River Moyar.

diameter than the other, the telltale footprint left in the red loamy soil of the sorghum and ragi fields clear evidence of his guilt.

Forty years old, they guessed he was, because the upper edges of his huge ears were curled and flopped over. He stood nine and a half feet tall at the shoulder, not particularly large for a male Asian elephant, but still a foot and a half higher than the kitchen ceiling in an average American house. He towered above me in the tight eighteen-by-eighteen-foot quarters made of teak trunks, leaving me with an overwhelming feeling of inadequacy, if not outright insignificance. I tried to hide this feeling from everyone around me.

The workers at the elephant camp estimated that he weighed only three and a half tons now—a mere shadow of what his former, probably five-ton self must have been when he had been free and wild just five months earlier. Now he was a captive of the Forestry Department of the state of Tamil Nadu, locked in a web of petty politics, a jealously guarded symbol of national pride, and a focal point for international misunderstanding. As is often the case, animals are the ones to suffer when they get trapped in human politics, like children caught in the crossfire of an ugly divorce.

He was a huge, magnificent, and, as I would later come to find, sensitive creature. I knew him for only three short weeks during that first of two "house calls" I made to India to treat him, yet he would come to take a place in my heart that is now filled only with pain. This is his story—the Makhna's story—"that little elephant," as I used to call him.

One November evening in 1998, I got a telephone call from a Dr. Michael Fox in Washington, D.C. I knew of him as one of the true intellectual lights of the animal rights movement, but I had never had any contact with him. *What on earth does he want with me?* I wondered.

Michael is a veterinarian by training, having received his degree at the Royal College of Veterinary Surgeons and later a Doctorate of Philosophy and then a Doctorate of Science at the University of London. He became deeply involved in toxicological research using puppies in his early career until he developed a serious revulsion against what he was doing.

"Would you consider going to India to treat an elephant that has been badly wounded and needs help?" he asked with little fanfare in his accent-less English voice.

I informed him that I knew very little about elephants, having dealt with only one in my whole life, and that was to assist another veterinarian in trimming the elephant's toenails. Michael said he was aware of that, but he had been told that I was experienced in the treatment of severe chronic injuries in animals. His interest in contacting me went beyond that, however. He and his wife, Deanna, who had created an organization known as IPAN (India Project for Animals and Nature), ran an animal sanctuary and a charitable veterinary clinic in a tiny village in South India. They wanted a vet who believed in the concept of animal rights (even though Michael knew I had been in biomedical research, using chimpanzees and monkeys for many years); who was somewhat small in stature (I think he meant short and skinny), because most Indians are built that way; who was preferably not American or English, because some Indians had a thing about neocolonialism; and, most of all, who would jump to the challenge at a moment's notice (he knew I was semi-retired).

Above my protestations of ignorance, he said, "Come see us in Washington. We'll pay your airfare, of course, put you up for the weekend, wine and dine you, no strings attached. If you decide by Sunday afternoon that you don't want to get involved, for whatever reason, there'll be no hard feelings." I agreed to go that coming Friday afternoon.

Michael was waiting for me outside the main doors of the National Airport terminal in a beat-up old Volkswagen Beetle. I opened the door, climbed down awkwardly into the passenger seat, and came nose-to-nose, and eye-to-eye, with a snarling little black dog named Mickey who pompously straddled the gearshift. As I reached for the seat belt, I noticed that it was bound in silver duct tape at several points along its length. There were square patches of duct tape on the seat covers as well. "What's with all the sticky tape?" I asked Michael.

"Him!" he replied, nodding his head sideways toward Mickey with no further explanation.

With every curve we took to the left, Mickey was thrown against my left shoulder, causing him to immediately expose his front line of pearly whites to me as if it were my fault we had collided. He eyed me with distrust for the remainder of the drive to Michael's house, and throughout the whole weekend. And an intense weekend it was.

Michael and Deanna gave me a crash course in Hindu mythology and religious beliefs with respect to animals, much of which went straight over my head, followed by some background on IPAN. They had founded the organization in 1996 (although recently it has been taken over by Nigel Otter, then the field manager). It has a fascinating and unusual philosophy. Its mission, in IPAN's own words, is "to reduce and prevent cruelty towards animals, to promote the health of domestic and wild animals, to protect the environment and by so doing improve the livelihood of people depending on their well-being and balance." In practical terms, this includes providing local farmers and townspeople with free veterinary care, vaccination programs for the control of foot-and-mouth disease in cattle and other farm species, and rabies and distemper vaccinations for village dogs. All of these diseases, through physical contact, present substantial risks to wildlife, such as deer and bison, and the rare Indian wild dogs, or *dholes* as they are known. An outbreak of distemper had occurred among the wild dogs some years earlier with devastating consequences.

IPAN takes very seriously its education program for children, the importance of which, according to IPAN, "is invaluable in a country like India where, quite often, lack of knowledge leads to prejudice against animals."

My hosts then showed me horrific videos of electrocutions of dogs in town population-control programs, the botched throat-slitting slaughter of calves, and the annual cattle drive, which began in Gundalpet in the state of Karnataka, cut across the northern tip of Tamil Nadu (where the slaughter of cattle is illegal), and ended three days later in Yedakara in Kerala state (where slaughter is legal). The hapless animals were kept constantly on the move, the drivers thrusting sticks and hot pepper paste into their eyes. The clip-clop patter of cloven hooves on hard road surfaces at the beginning of the journey gradually gave way with the passing days to a sibilant sound as hooves wore down and completely sloughed off the feet of those still able to ambulate on bloody stumps of bone. The others were left to die or be killed where they lay. After tremendous pressure from Indian animal rights groups and the American organizations IPAN and PETA (People for the Ethical Treatment of Animals), the annual drive has been replaced by truck transportation of the cattle. Now the problem is overloading the trucks with cattle and finding suffocated and trampled dead bodies at the end of the journey!

The featured movie of the evening, however, was a video of the Makhna's capture in the village of Pullyambara, near Gudalur, and his march to the elephant camp at Mudumalai. State government officials of the Forestry Department had shot the video, and proud they seemed to be of their efforts.

There must have been thirty or more trackers, handlers, mahouts, cooks, department supervisors, and veterinarians assembled, as well as five helper bull elephants (known as kumkhi), each with long, curved, sharp-tipped tusks. Everything was circus-like, with people yelling and shouting to and at each other, trying to get themselves organized. Eventually silence descended and the marksmen moved off with their dart rifles to tranquilize the Makhna. Creeping up on him from all sides with as much stealth as they could summon, they managed to get several darts into him more or less simultaneously.

As the tranquilizer started to take hold, the Makhna stumbled aimlessly around in diminishing circles until finally he fell to his knees and then rolled over onto his side. Cheers erupted from the force. Once it was determined that the bull was completely immobilized, the handlers moved in fast to secure him in chains. First his front feet were chained together, and then his rear legs. Long lengths of chain were then toggled together in complicated arrangements, running from the leg chains up over the shoulders and around the elephant's chest and neck.

Then the five tusker elephants were brought into position. The two kumkhi positioned in front of the Makhna began to slowly pull on the chains attached to his front legs, while the single helper at the rear gently raised the Makhna's rump up and forward with his long tusks. The remaining two tuskers were positioned on either side of the Makhna. Their job appeared to be to raise him off the ground with the aid of their tusks onto an equal footing of all four legs. It was clear, however, that he had not yet fully regained consciousness and, wobbling badly from side to side, could not contribute his necessary input to the maneuver. As the kumkhi at the front continued to pull on the Makhna's chains, they had the effect of raising both of his forefeet off the ground, causing him to lose his footing and fall backward, impaling his bottom on the sharp tips of the tusks of the helper elephant behind. He recoiled from the obvious pain.

After prolonged effort, the Makhna was finally brought into a stable, upright position. There must have been a real sense of urgency to get him standing because it is very dangerous to leave elephants lying sedated on the ground for long periods; the massive weight of their abdominal organs pressing forward on the diaphragm can cause them to suffocate. Even so, it took one and a half days for the Makhna to regain consciousness to the point where he could begin the grueling twenty-eight-mile, five-and-a-half-day march through forest and along road to the elephant camp at Mudumalai.

By the end of the evening, overwhelmed though I was, I found myself saying yes to Deanna and Michael: "I'll help you, if I can." How could I refuse?

We spent the rest of the weekend discussing strategies, as well as what special sorts of equipment and medical supplies I might need to treat some of the more major injuries the Makhna might have. Two weeks later, with visas in hand and half a dozen large, stout cardboard boxes packed carefully with medical supplies and surgical equipment, Deanna and I set off for India.

After a grueling twenty-five-hour flight with stops in Amsterdam and Mumbai, Deanna and I arrived in Coimbatore. Nigel was waiting to take us north by jeep on the last five-hour leg of our journey, straight to the elephant camp. We would take a preliminary look before it got dark.

Very proud of her Scandinavian origins, Deanna had named the Makhna Loki, a god in Norse mythology. This induced the senior staff of the Forestry Department to name him Moorthy in honor of the retired director and venerated elephant veterinarian Dr. V. Krishnamurthy. I tried as much as possible to remain neutral and referred to him as "my little elephant," which at least used to get a laugh out of my Indian colleagues.

The wildlife warden, Mr. Halan, and the camp manager, Mr. Moni, met us at the entrance to the camp and took us directly to Loki. He was housed in what is termed a *kraal*: a twenty-foot-high and eighteen-foot-square structure made of sturdy teak logs. A large green tarpaulin to keep off rain and provide shade from the sun covered the open roof. The floor was a thick layer of sand. Being only twice as long as Loki in either length or width, the kraal was not large enough to allow him to lie down or, even more difficult, get back up. He had lived in this structure for five months, never once being able to lie down and take the weight off his feet.

I shall never forget that first moment I laid eyes on Loki. He was massive. Taking one short step forward, then one back, he flapped his vast lugs and snorted like a half-plugged vacuum cleaner hose. Was he warding off the buzzing flies or showing his displeasure at my uninvited presence?

I looked up into his wrinkled face. His eyes seemed distant and unseeing, as if he were off in another world. There was a great, empty telepathic void between his head and mine. It was as though someone had switched off a radio that had been playing loud rock music—and I found myself suddenly engulfed in a cotton-wool cloud of silence. *What am I doing here?* I asked myself. *What on earth made me fly 10,000 miles, through ten and a half time zones, to treat an elephant that I can't even talk to?* You can't work with an animal and get his cooperation unless you are able to communicate with him, or at least get to a stage where you can fool yourself into believing that you are communicating with him.

I was reminded of a situation related in Jeffrey Moussaieff Masson's and Susan McCarthy's book *When Elephants Weep: The Emotional Lives of Animals* (Delacorte Press, 1995). Masson describes in amusing prose what must have been a terrifying experience: an encounter with a herd of wild elephants, and one huge male in particular, in a South Indian game reserve. I wouldn't mind betting that it had been Mudumalai. The bull flapped his ears in what Masson thought was a greeting. "Blissfully ignorant," he proceeded to address the elephant in Sanskrit: "Bhoh, gagendra"—"Greetings, Lord of the Elephants." He remembered asking himself, "How could you have been so stupid as to approach a wild elephant?" as he turned, ran, tripped, and fell in the tall grass, the bull close on his heels.

"You can see the wounds on his feet here, here, and here," Mr. Moni began, pointing from one leg to another. "He also has a large abscess up under his left foreleg," he continued, but my mind was already overwhelmed, and I could not absorb his endless list of medical injuries. I would have to make some simple anatomical drawings of the elephant and mark down the precise location of each wound, otherwise I would never be able to keep track of them all.

I drew a series of crude outlines of Loki's body in my spiral notebook, the first as seen from his left side, then his rear, moving on to the right side of his body, and ending up facing his front.

As methodically as I could, with Mr. Moni's guidance, I began at Loki's upper left forelimb, marking down two pus-oozing abscesses on his shoulder and several thickened sizable lumps in the skin of his upper and lower leg.

Most shocking of all was a ragged band of skin missing around the circumference of his fetlock (the lowest joint in his forelimb). It was about an inch wide and as deep as the full thickness of his skin, as if the skin had been worn or torn. On the outer surface of this band, a bloody, partially jellified stump of heavily infected tissue, around four inches in diameter, protruded three inches or so from the wound. To my horror, I realized that this was a completely severed tendon. *How could the elephant walk with a severed tendon hanging out of his foot?* I wondered. *How could such a thing have happened to him?* Then I noticed similar groove-like rings of missing skin on two other legs, only his left hind foot being free of such injury, but none of these had severed tendons jutting out of them.

Mr. Moni explained that as Loki had been marched day after day, the large-linked, loose-fitting metal chains around his lower legs had continually bounced up and down against the ground, the links wearing to razor-sharp edges that cut deep into the skin above the elephant's feet. Apparently, nobody in the great mass of attendants and helpers had noticed this happening or, more likely, was equipped to do anything about it. I could only imagine the misery the elephant must have felt having suffered these wounds for the past five months.

It must have taken me close to an hour to complete my initial examination of Loki's body and pinpoint all his lesions on the drawings. The sun was close to the horizon now, and the light was fading fast; twilight rapidly descends into darkness in the tropics. For the moment it wasn't clear in my mind how I would proceed to begin treating the elephant's wounds in the morning. Jet lag was setting in and I needed some food, a cool Kingfisher beer, and a good night's sleep.

I got up at 6 o'clock that first morning. My bedroom was one of three converted horse stalls in a row that opened onto a low-walled cobbled patio with a gate at either end. The room had all the essentials for comfort—a bookcase, one armchair, and a hard upright chair. The camp bed had been comfortable enough, and, despite the all-night braying of donkeys, I felt well rested.

As I opened the upper half of the divided door, I gazed out across a vast expanse of gently rolling, wild-grass hills. As far as the horizon, there was not a hint of other human habitation in sight.

Close by, long wisps of leaden rain clouds silently licked the ravines of the towering, mystic Blue Mountains, the Nilgiris, as if in search of their deeply hidden secrets. There was a tremendous beauty and tranquility about the scene.

Hill View Farm, the IPAN sanctuary, is a charming collection of little red brick and terra cotta tiled buildings. It is located on the edge of the 260-square-mile Mudumalai Wildlife Sanctuary, a few miles from the tiny village of Mavanahalla. The sanctuary in turn is part of the 2,000 square miles of what is termed the United Nations' Nilgiris Biosphere Reserve, which straddles the states of Kerala, Tamil Nadu, and Karnataka. It is said to have the largest population of wild elephants in India, as well as tigers, leopards, gaur (Indian bison), sambar deer, and the rare dholes, or Asian wild dogs (*Cuon alpinus*).

As I opened the lower half of the door to make my way to the main house for breakfast, I noted that I would have to step carefully to avoid the abundant goat pellets and cow pats. I said good morning to Bingo the dog, who was still asleep in his wooden fruit box condo outside my bedroom door. I had to push past the cow, who stood stoically chewing her cud. The goats rushed toward me to nudge my trouser pockets, presumably to see if I had any treats hidden within.

Breakfast comprised thick slices of white bread cooked, not toasted, on a large cast-iron skillet and a mug of thick, heavily sweetened coffee. An audience of sixteen dogs and one small goat stood or sat patiently on the floor of the kitchen, eyeing the table. The goat obviously considered himself one of the dogs until he got pushed around too much by one of them, when he remembered he had a pair of horn buds that he could use to butt the offender. Janet, the pony, leaning in over the open half door, was within easy reach of the table and snorted into my ear, her way of letting me know that she wanted a piece of my toast and jam.

In between mouthfuls of toast, Nigel and I began to discuss how we would set about treating the elephant. Nigel would be a godsend for me. Not only could he speak English, Hindi, and Tamil, but he was also fluent in two of the local tribal languages, Bettakurumba and Irula, and would be my only means of communicating with the mahouts. He was also highly trained in medical procedures, and I had an innate sense that I would be able to trust his judgment. I would also find over time that animals, no matter what the species, seemed to have a natural trust in him. For all his height, he was not intimidating even to the tiniest lost puppy. Most of all, I was confident that he would not allow me to get myself into a dangerous situation with Loki or any of the other elephants.

Before we went to the elephant camp, I had to sort all the supplies and medical equipment I had brought from America and whatever IPAN already had in stock at the sanctuary into separate cardboard boxes. While I set about that task, Nigel could go off in the jeep, as he apparently had done every morning for the past two or three months, and buy whatever browse he could for Loki from the local tribal farmers. "We should try and make it to the camp by no later than 8 o'clock," he stressed.

When we arrived at the camp, the first order of the day was to give Loki the pile of browse that Nigel had gathered. I watched in utter fascination as Loki slowly went through the pile with the tip of his trunk. Elephants have a highly sensitive, finger-like prehensile process on the upper side of the tip of their trunk, which they use to carefully sift through food to pick out the pieces they want and throw away what they don't want, down to the level of a single weed stem or flower. They don't even need to look down at the browse as they perform this intricate maneuver. As Stephan Alter rather eloquently describes in his book *Elephas Maximus: A Portrait of the Indian Elephant,* "No other creature has an appendage as versatile as an elephant's trunk, which is sensitive enough to sniff the faintest scent, capacious enough to suck up several bucketfuls of water, sensuous enough to engage in foreplay, and strong enough to kill a man with a single blow."

I would have eight men to assist me: four from the elephant camp and four from IPAN, whom I could divide into pairs. The two mahouts would work together, of course, since their skill lay in commanding Loki when to move and how to stand. Mr. Moni and his assistant, a wise, gentle elderly man by the name of Mr. Kannan, would act as my chief medical assistants. I instructed the two youngest boys, Shivakumar and Dasha, both IPAN trainees, how to aseptically handle syringes and hypodermic needles, and they set about the arduous job of making up the eighty vials of antibiotic we would need for Loki's first day of treatment. This task took them a good hour and raised several blisters on the palms of their hands. Nagaraj, a young man who was well trained medically and a longtime IPAN worker, would assist Nigel in a more independent fashion. My goal was to rotate each pair, all but the mahouts, every one or two days so that they would all learn how to perform and understand the various medical procedures and situations.

We set up a makeshift table from a long board of wood resting on large rocks, and I carefully laid out the medical supplies and equipment I had brought in the cardboard boxes so that in an emergency we could get to whatever we needed quickly. We were ready to begin.

First, I wanted to examine the abscess under Loki's left armpit, the one that Mr. Moni had brought to my attention the evening before. This wound bothered me greatly; I had thought about it all night, wondering how I might be able to treat it in such a difficult and inaccessible part of the body without exposing myself to undue risk of injury. I would have to be very careful indeed.

"How did he ever get an injury in a place like that?" I asked Mr. Moni.

"We're not sure," he said. "Maybe one of the helper elephants accidentally gored him as they were all trying to lift him up from the ground during his recovery from anesthesia."

I recalled having seen on the video of the capture that weekend in Washington, D.C., how Loki had fallen backward onto the tips of the tusks of some of the helper elephants. Maybe one of the tusks had slipped in under his arm.

Not wanting to take Loki by surprise and frighten him, I slowly rubbed the palm of my right hand from side to side over his flank, like the wagging of a car's windshield wiper, as I would to approach an unfamiliar horse that I might need to examine. Speaking softly, I pattered on, "Don't be frightened, that little elephant. Don't be frightened; I would never want to hurt that little boy." Little by little I moved my right hand toward his elbow and slid my left arm up and over the horizontally placed teak-log safety bar. I would have to be very careful in my next move because his front foot could easily trample me if he took a step backward. Slowly I stooped, supporting the weight of my body by hooking my left arm over the safety bar, and let my body swing in below his massive chest. It was a strange feeling to have my ear tight against Loki's warm, rough skin. With my right hand, I reached up under his armpit, keeping my eye on his foot below, ready to withdraw in a fraction of a second if need be. My fingers soon found the large, puss-filled hole in the hollow of his armpit.

Gently I squeezed the edges of the wound together. To my surprise, pus oozed from a hole in the skin three feet or so farther down the inside of Loki's leg. *That's strange,* I thought. Again I squeezed the upper wound. Sure enough, pus oozed out the lower wound. The two wounds were connected!

The anatomy of an elephant's leg is quite different from ours, of course, but imagine you had a ruptured abscess under your armpit that communicated through a long tunnel running beneath your skin, and perhaps even between your muscles and tendons, to an oozing abscess situated just above the inside of your wrist. This is what Loki had, except, in his case, the tract was three feet or more in length. I would have to probe the wound very carefully.

The only way I would be able to treat this lesion would be to thread some sort of catheter into the upper wound, under his armpit, and gently work it down the length of the fistulous tract in his upper leg to the lower wound. Thank goodness I had brought with me a fifty-foot-long coil of transparent rubber hose. It was half an inch in diameter, soft, yet stiff enough that it wouldn't collapse or kink—ideal for threading into Loki's wound. Once this pipe was in place, I would have to thread a narrower, plastic stomach tube, a quarter of an inch or so in diameter and close to three feet long, down the inside of the larger tube in order to flush the wound with bags of sterile intravenous saline. I thought of my father, dead many a year, and his oft-pronounced axiom, "You can fix anything with a paper clip, a rubber band, or a wad of chewing gum." *Maybe not this time, Dad,* I couldn't help thinking.

I hoisted myself out from under Loki's body and explained my plan to Mr. Moni and Mr. Kannan. "Once I get the pipe in place in the elephant's wound, Mr. Kannan, you will have to have several 60-milliliter syringes ready to pass to Mr. Moni. You, Mr. Moni, will have to attach one syringe after another to the stomach tube, as fast as you can. Then, Mr. Kannan, your job again will be to have the next syringe full of solution ready for Mr. Moni to attach once he disconnects the syringe he has just finished. We'll need lots and lots of syringes full to be effective, so you have to refill them as fast as you can. My job will be to try and work the larger tube up and down inside the tract in the elephant's leg to loosen the pus."

When all was ready, I resumed my position under Loki's elbow. Threading the tube into Loki's wound was quite difficult at first, and required a great deal of gentle thrusting up and down until finally I was able to slide it about halfway down inside his leg. Mr. Moni began to flush the saline on my command.

Loki was remarkably tolerant of it all. Only once or twice did I have to stop and have a little heart-to-heart chat with him. Looking up into his eyes and wagging my finger at him, as you might lecture an errant little boy, I implored, "That little elephant has to stand still. He can't keep moving about. Does he understand?

He's got to stand still." (For some reason, I usually speak to animals and very young children in the third person.) I was beginning to get the impression that Loki might understand me after all. Then I would go back to try once again to thread the long catheter down the inside of his leg. I continued, one syringe full after another, until the solution that drained out the lower end of the tract had no visible pus in it. We had used quite a few 500-milliliter bags of saline in the process.

While Mr. Moni, Mr. Kannan, and I worked on Loki's elbow region, Nigel pared, as much as he could, Loki's hind feet. His feet were in very bad condition. Several of the toenails were split down their lengths, and the skin of the choriom around the top of each nail, what we call our quick, was badly frayed and ragged. There were also a number of puss-oozing fistulas between some of the nails that required opening with a sterile scalpel and searching with cotton-tipped applicators to encourage pus drainage. The most worrying aspect of these types of lesions is their healing from the outside in, rather than the inside out, trapping infection deep in the tissues. We would have to keep this from happening to Loki at all costs.

It is estimated that 50 percent of zoo and theme park elephants in the United States suffer severe, incurable chronic foot problems, constituting the most common reason for euthanasia. The cause is almost invariably that elephants are confined twenty-four hours a day mainly to nonyielding hard surfaces, such as concrete, rather than well-established grasslands, and are given insufficient exercise. In many zoos, elephants are chained to their sleeping stalls for the night or during prolonged periods of inclement weather and are unable to lie down. To make matters worse, because they are not free to move about, by morning they find their feet deep in urine-soaked excreta, further adding to the infections of their injuries.

Of course, Loki's wounds were more of an acute nature. Intensive treatment applied from the very beginning might well have had a rapid healing effect, but five months had elapsed since they had been inflicted, and many of his wounds were showing a degree of permanence.

Now that my little team of three had finished irrigating the elbow wound, Nigel and Nagaraj could get in and treat the wounds on Loki's front feet, especially the herniated tendon stump.

The most unpleasant treatment for Loki, however, was for his infected left eye. How do you make a nine-and-a-half-foot-tall elephant lower his head so you can do something to him that he won't like? I had to finger-walk the deep wrinkles of his face, gently pulling downward with my fingertips, one by one. His eyelids started to flutter uncontrollably. "That little elephant has to be very brave," I tried to soothe him. Little by little, he lowered his head to the level where I could reach his eyelids with my fingers. With my index and middle finger, I stretched the lids apart and, with my other hand, squeezed the ointment into his eye. "He is so brave, that little boy," I said in an encouraging tone as I massaged his lids. "He's so brave."

Loki's reaction reminded me of an incident I had had a few years earlier at the lab with an elderly male chimp named Herbie. One morning, I walked into his room and found him furiously rubbing his eye with the back of his hand. "What's up, Herbie?" I called out to him. He stopped for a moment to show me his eye. It was swollen and red, and a watery secretion ran down his face. Most likely he had inadvertently stuck a finger in his eye. "Let me see that little eye," I said. He shuffled over to me and clamped his teeth over one of the horizontal bars of his cage, like a tested old soldier biting down on a bullet or piece of rope while his leg is amputated. His eyelids fluttered, just as Loki's did now, but Herbie allowed me to stretch them apart so that I could examine his eye. Apart from a little capillary dilatation, there was no sign of injury or the presence of any foreign body. "That Herbie wait a moment [ignore my improper English]. Won't be long," I said as I turned to leave the room.

I returned a few minutes later with a tube of ophthalmic ointment. "Let me see that little eye again, Herbie." Again he waddled over, took hold of the bar in his teeth, and stretched his face up to me. "He be very brave," I said as I pulled his lids apart and squeezed some ointment into his eye. "That little boy mustn't rub his eye," I warned, as Herbie raised the back of his hand to do just that. He stopped. "Here he is," I whispered to him as I took one of the red-and-white striped peppermints I always carried in my pocket, unwrapped it, and passed it to his teeth. Herbie let me treat him twice a day for ten days, hating every moment of it, except for the peppermint candy.

The final treatment of the morning for Loki was an antibiotic injection. Nigel volunteered for the task, which required his climbing up the inside of the wall of the kraal and then stepping over onto Loki's back. This was a dangerous maneuver: Nigel would have to be careful not to slip off the side of Loki's back or have Loki reach up with his trunk and thrust Nigel against the bars of the kraal, which could easily kill him. Nigel had two 60-milliliter syringes with six-inch-long, large-bore spinal needles attached, each filled with antibiotic. He walked along Loki's back, arms spread sideways for balance, and carefully sat down, straddling Loki's spine. With the greatest of care he selected the most muscular site and inserted the needle deep into the underlying muscles with a slow, firm, gentle thrust. Loki showed not the slightest reaction of pain.

The various treatments had taken us three and a half hours to complete. We cleared up all the equipment and supplies and stayed a while to pet Loki, rubbing his trunk up and down, talking to him and telling him how good he had been. Nigel helped the mahouts give him the remainder of his breakfast. I felt that we all had done a good job.

* * * * *

The next day went very much the same as the first, but by the end
of the treatment I realized that my plan would not work over the
long haul. Overcoming Loki's infections would require weeks, if not
months, of daily antibacterial treatment. The antibiotic injections we
were giving him would be a good start and would give us a week or
so of coverage, but that was the most we could expect. Plus, the antibiotic was inordinately expensive, and neither IPAN, which had paid
for it so far, nor the elephant camp would be able to cover the long-
term cost. We would soon run out of bags of sterile saline as well.

I got Deanna, Mr. Moni, and Nigel together to discuss my concerns. "What we need is an abundant supply of cheap sterile saline
solution so that we can flush the wounds and wash the infection out
of the tissues every single day. We need to get hold of rock salt, make
an appropriate solution, and boil it so that all the bacteria are
killed."

"I'll see to getting what you need," Mr. Moni assured me.

Before sunrise the next morning, the mahouts had secured a
cast-iron caldron that they placed on an open rock-rimmed fire they
had built close by Loki's kraal and filled it with water. By the time
we arrived at the camp, the water was already on the boil, bubbling
away furiously. It remained only for me to determine how much
rock salt we would need to add to the water to make a hypertonic
solution strong enough to kill the bacteria in the water, yet not so
concentrated that it would pickle poor Loki's tissues and send him
stampeding around the kraal in agony. We boiled smaller containers of rock salt solution and added measured amounts to a larger
container of boiling water to get the desired final concentration as
determined by taste test.

Arriving finally at what tasted to me like the desired concentration, I tested a little by irrigating one of the smaller fistulas in Loki's
shoulder. He evinced no sign of pain.

* * * * *

After six consecutive days of treatment, Mr. Moni asked that we not come the next day to give the camp staff a chance to catch up on some of their other chores.

I wasn't entirely happy about this because I knew that the pus would build up rapidly in Loki's tissues, even in a period of only forty-eight hours, and set us back a day or more in getting on top of the infection again. I had to admit, however, that the mahouts' work schedule must have been seriously interrupted, as were Nigel's commitments in the running of IPAN.

Although we had no intention of performing any treatments on Loki, Nigel said that he and I should at least deliver some browse for him, and then we could continue with the calls we were scheduled to make to the farms in the area, or the spays and neuters we had to attend to at the sanctuary clinic in Mavanahalla. We arrived at the elephant camp at around 8 o'clock, pulling up in front of the kraal.

As I opened the door of the jeep, I heard strange sounds coming from inside the kraal—*flick-flick, flick-flick*—and the clipped voices of the two mahouts shouting what seemed to be commands, presumably to Loki. "What's going on?" I asked Nigel, as I turned to clamber down from the passenger seat. "They've started training the elephant," he replied, a dark expression looming across his face.

I made my way around to the other side of the kraal, where I could better see what was going on. The mahouts had already installed the horizontal protective guardrail inside the kraal, tying it securely at either end to the upright supports with hefty ropes. They were now inside the reduced six-foot-deep enclosure, warming up. No one else was around. So this was the reason they had wanted a break today, I realized: to allow them the opportunity to begin the "breaking-in" process away from the prying eyes of strangers.

Armed with long, supple bamboo stems, they already seemed to have established a rhythm, one tapping the backsides of Loki's forelegs, or occasionally the exquisitely sensitive underside of his trunk, the other following with a flailing of the hind legs. Now and then, the younger mahout, who had taken up the forward position, would strike the elephant's left flank or shoulder, sending thick spatterings of cream-colored pus that oozed out of one or another of the abscesses in his upper leg or shoulder area flying across the kraal to land on the horizontal teak beams. Loki let out long, low moans like the forlorn sounds of a tugboat's foghorn, rising in anguish to a crescendo, and trailing off with a grumbling rumble, like the gurgling effluent of a sewer pipe vent.

I took the camera I had strapped around my neck and tried to concentrate on taking pictures. Something drove me to do so, although I never stopped to consider what I would do with the pictures. *Is this how professional photographers feel when they witness wartime atrocities?* I mused. *Is this how their consciences deal with the situation?*

Over and over, with a mind-numbing rhythm, the mahouts shouted with sharp, resonating nasality, *"Hulla! Hulla-hullahhh!"* They were ordering the elephant, in their special elephant language, to lift his right foreleg at the same time they expected him to lift his left hind leg. Then, with the next strokes of their wands, they commanded him to lift diagonally opposing legs. But he couldn't do this, as much as he tried, without risking a fall to the ground. The fetlock of his right foreleg was ankylosed, the bones of the joint fused together because of the injury he had received from the chains five months earlier. He couldn't bear his full weight on his right hind leg in order to raise his left hind leg because it was swollen from a deep infection of the tendons and ligaments. *"Parra, parra, parra!"* ("Lift the trunk!"), the mahouts yelled over and over as the elephant tried desperately to maintain his balance by holding onto one of the horizontal side bars of the kraal with his trunk. *"Goolah, goolah, goolah— goolaaay!"* they bellowed in unison—expecting the elephant to crouch low on all four legs while bringing his bottom down to almost touch the ground. *"Bite, bite—bitoo!"* ("Sleep, sleep, sleep!")

his tormenters screamed. This was the ultimate, what they had been aiming at for the last twenty minutes. If the two mahouts could bring him literally to his knees, they would have figuratively succeeded in bringing him into submission. The elephant was now pressed against the horizontal restraining bar, his massive body crumpled like a rag doll's, his sagging rump almost touching the by-now urine-soaked sand floor, his face a contorted confusion of wrinkled anguish, his eyes scrunched pitifully closed and flickering. He was about to surrender, to offer up his soul to his captors. But somehow he managed to hold on! It was the mahouts who were beaten, too tired to continue, their breathing reduced to ragged gasps. The younger of the two was the first to climb out of the kraal, mopping his sweat-drenched forehead with the tail of his headband. The other continued alone for a few minutes more, but even he lost his resolve and called it a day.

Unknown to me at the time, Nigel had secreted a tiny audiocassette recorder in his trouser pocket and had recorded much of the training session we had witnessed. We would later calculate that the elephant had been struck a total of 587 times over a twenty-minute period, a very conservative estimate on my part. In the last eleven minutes alone, he had been struck 387 times. He had moaned, cried, and screamed forty-nine times, each wail lasting three to five seconds, some much longer.

The silence that followed was eerie. Only the mournful caws of circling pied crows jarred my consciousness back to reality. I couldn't help thinking of the melancholy that one feels at the funeral of a loved one, when the twittering of the birds as they flit from bush to bush, the swaying of the daffodils in the cold spring breeze, and the carefree giggles of children playing in a distant schoolyard remind you that this sad and very personal event had little consequence in the grand scheme of things. *Life would carry on,* I had to remind myself. *What had I just witnessed?* I wondered. *What barbarity had I really seen? Was it a meaningless cultural portrait? Was my judgment clouded by an unrealistic Western point of view, or had this been a cruelty that anyone in this world—anyone with a sense of justice and compassion—would recognize as appalling? Do we conclude, for example, that ill treatment of women or the support of slavery, is acceptable in one part of the world but not in another because of cultural differences in social mores? I think not. Why would we accept that the treatment of animals would fall into a different category?*

My mind was in turmoil. *What should I do?* During the beating I had felt like climbing through the bars of the kraal, snatching one of the canes, and flogging the mahouts with it. But that sort of crude bravado achieves nothing. All I knew was that I had to leave. An intense anger began to well up inside me, directed mostly at Nigel, not at the mahouts. He counted himself as an animal lover, yet he had done nothing to stop this cruelty. He seemed to have wantonly ignored my gaze, as if he could not bring himself to recognize my anguish.

I set off along the narrow, twisting road through the forest toward Masinagudi, the closest little town, about seven and a half miles away. At worst it would take me only another two hours or so to reach Mavanahalla, about ten miles farther on, and with a bit of luck I might even get a lift from one of the infrequent lorries that passed along the way. What would I do, though, if I met a herd of wild pigs? The curled tusks of the boars looked menacing indeed, and if they were anywhere near as nasty as their American cousins, the javelinas, who are quite a bit smaller, I could find myself in big trouble. And what if I came face to face with some Indian bison bulls, the endangered gaur? Their semicurved horns formed massive buttresses, as strong and deadly as any cattle grid on a steam locomotive of America's Wild West days. Then I remembered the herd of wild elephants Nigel and I had seen on the drive to the elephant camp that very morning. There had been a dozen or so adult females with a couple of babies. Maybe my idea of walking all the way to Masinagudi was not really so great.

My concern turned to outright fear. I picked up my step and tried to be as invisible and silent as possible.

I had gone little more than a mile when the blue IPAN ambulance jeep drew up beside me. A somber-looking Nigel leaned out the window and ordered me to get in.

"I don't understand you, Nigel," I yelled at him, as I climbed up into the front seat of the jeep. "Why didn't you say something to stop that?"

Without a word, he reached into his trouser pocket, pulled out the little recorder, and pressed the play button. I could clearly hear the thwacking of the sticks and Loki's pathetic cries. We drove in silence to Masinagudi. Perhaps a second spot of breakfast might clear our minds.

It was midmorning by now. Nigel had some pressing business to take care of after breakfast. I decided to stay on my own in the IPAN jeep and wait for him: I needed some time to think.

Masinagudi is a special little place. Its population of around 15,000 is fairly equally divided among Hindus, Muslims, and Christians. There is even a small Roman Catholic cathedral on the edge of town, and the mosque is halfway along the main street. To this day, and despite recent terrorist attacks in Mumbai and occasional interreligious tension in many parts of India, there has never been unrest in Masinagudi.

The main street is about a quarter of a mile long. Most of the time, it's a pretty busy place. It is certainly more than a match for any Friday night rush hour along Fifth Avenue or Oxford Street. Two cars driving in opposite directions can pass each other, no problem, so long as no one is parked on the side of the road. But that's usually not the case. A jeep, or a single-decker bus spewing its sardine-packed passengers, is almost invariably to be found parked on one side of the street, and a bullock cart on the other. Little room remains between them. You have to stop, toot your horn, and wait to see which of the two will give way first. If it's a sacred cow that has parked herself, you might as well not bother, because she is going to stay put no matter what.

In the evening, as the sun goes down and long shadows are cast across the street, life becomes especially busy as last-minute shoppers buy fruits and vegetables for the evening meal or stop to have chai, a rich sweet tea, in one of the cafes. The bullock carts stop to pick up garbage or deliver river water—for there is no running water in Masinagudi. Old women rush out from side streets and alleyways to pick up fresh cow plops from the street with dustpan and brush, or bare hands if nothing else is available, disappearing back to wherever they came from with their valuable prize. Businessmen, dressed in smart trousers, shiny black shoes, white shirts, and tasteful designer ties, just off the bus from Ooty, step sprightly along the garbage-strewn street, an attaché case in one hand, a rolled umbrella in the other. Loud, scratchy Indian music blares from speakers hidden among the arrays of produce and merchandise stacked on the shelves and display tables of the little open-fronted stores. Massive posters adorn the side walls of double-storied buildings, advertising the current movie showing in town, depicting a bare-chested, handsome young rake and his diminutive moll dressed in micro-length leather skirt and half-thigh boots, staring up longingly into his burning, obsidian eyes.

I couldn't help thinking that if I could only understand 10 percent of what I had seen in Masinagudi over the last week or so, I might understand what I had witnessed with Loki's beating. Indians are very kind people on the whole and are very friendly toward foreigners. They also revere the elephant, the incarnate form of the Hindu god, Ganesa. Yet the two mahouts had been unmerciful. How could this be? What did they, or the administration of the elephant camp, expect to achieve? Why could they not see that beating the elephant when he had so many deep-seated wounds would achieve nothing except to cause him pain and make him hate them? Loki could not bend his lower leg joints to achieve the squatting and kneeling that the mahouts required; doing so was physically beyond his capability. Yet they beat him.

Loki had a certain rare value, and this may have been one of the main reasons for trying to "break" him as soon as possible. He was a makhna, a tuskless male. As such, he would be less likely to injure females if he mated with them or to injure the mahouts who oversaw the process. It is common practice in elephant camps throughout India to stake captive females in the forest by chains when they are in estrus and hope that wild males will approach and breed with them during the night, a potentially dangerous procedure for the helpless female. Loki could also be trained to provide semen for artificial insemination programs as another way to boost the captive breeding of the endangered species. A makhna is also somewhat less dangerous than a tusker for providing elephant rides to tourists.

In his fascinating book *Elephas Maximus* that Stephan Alter published some six years later in 2004, he commented extensively on Loki's beating and the bad feelings it engendered between the elephant camp and IPAN. "IPAN advocated a gentler and less restrictive approach to the makhna's care," he wrote, "while the forest department still considered him dangerous and treated him as such." Of course, it was not that IPAN thought Loki was anything less than dangerous, but they wanted Loki to be placed in a kraal that could offer him the opportunity for gentle, if limited, exercise of his limbs and was large enough to allow him to lie down, to give his feet a chance to heal. "A sma' request," as Robert Burns would have said.

Alter concluded, "Traditional methods used by mahouts to subdue and train an elephant are likely to offend some observers but it must be recognized that cruelty is not the motive." Saying that cruelty was not the motive does not mean that cruelty had not been committed.

I had to concede, however, that taking a 40-year-old wild male elephant into captivity poses far greater dangers than rearing an infant or preadolescent calf who might have been abandoned because his mother had died. One hears and reads terrible stories in Indian newspapers of the killing of mothers and the fates of their calves. A story that had captured everyone's attention while I was in India tending the Makhna the first time concerned a mother who had swallowed a breadfruit that a farmer had baited with a home-made bomb. The bomb exploded midway down the elephant's gullet, blowing out much of her throat. It took about six weeks for her to die; her calf stood with her all that time. A bull elephant turned up and took the lamenting calf away, presumably to join his own herd.

When we returned to the farm and related the beating to Deanna, she exploded. She would announce to the world what had happened. She came with Nigel and me the following day and ranted, using some choice words, none of which the mahouts would have understood. There was another person present, however, although out of sight, who did understand enough English and reported the gist of what Deanna had said to some of the officials of the elephant camp. Suddenly I had a mini-international crisis on my hands.

Much to my surprise, I was allowed to continue with Loki's daily treatments, but on Christmas Day, two days after I left India to return to the United States, senior officials of the Forestry Department closed the camp gates to any further participation of IPAN personnel in the treatment of the Makhna. Loki disappeared into a mist of secrecy, along with everything I had tried to achieve.

Three years later, in late November 2001, a most unexpected series of events began to unfold. Deanna Krantz phoned me from Washington, D.C., to inform me that the High Court of Madras, State of Tamil Nadu, was ordering me to return to India to treat the Makhna. I seem to remember bursting out laughing.

"What are you talking about?" I asked. Deanna explained that an advocate, a Mr. G. Rajendran, had lodged a writ petition in the

High Court accusing the State Department of Forestry of Tamil Nadu of cruelty to the Makhna. This advocate had already made a name for himself by winning a big case involving cruelty to horses. Apparently he had found a reference on the Internet to an open plea ("A plea for freedom") that I had written about Loki's plight soon after I had returned to America in December 1998. From reading this plea, he discovered that I had taken photographs and that Nigel had made an audio recording of the elephant's beating.

Mr. Rajendran obtained copies of these materials and presented them to a patently stunned and silent High Court. According to Mr. Rajendran, the court, in essence, made me the legal guardian of Loki, and no one could do anything to him without my written permission.

I returned alone to India early the following January 2002. *What a strange state of affairs*, I mused. *What possible hope could there be of my getting anyone's cooperation at the elephant camp? Everyone would hate and distrust me, nothing more than a troublemaking foreigner.*

There was one silver lining to the very gray cloud: two volunteer veterinarians had started work at the sanctuary just a few days earlier. Dr. Aleksija Neimanis was from Canada and Dr. Johan Lindsjo hailed from Sweden. They had been thrilled to learn that they would be part of a medical team that would treat an elephant. I was pleased that they would be staying for three months or more, which would provide extended coverage for Loki that I would never have expected possible.

So, back to packing stout cardboard boxes with medical supplies and equipment, I prepared to return to India. Michael gave me two special ropes that he had had made specifically for Loki to take the place of metal chains to secure his legs.

Nigel and Mr. Rajendran met me at the airport in Coimbatore, and we proceeded directly to the elephant camp, this time to the plush conference center in Theppakkadu. A waiter showed us into the main dining room. A spread-out group of perhaps a dozen formally suited men, obviously high officials, stood resolutely still, their backs to us, as they studied a small group of wild elephants who were passing by the picture windows that offered a panoramic view of the edge of the forest. Not a single person turned to greet us, even though they had surely heard and seen us enter. Some minutes later, Mr. Moni entered the room. He immediately saw me and came over to warmly shake my hand. He then introduced us to the rest of the company.

The following morning, Nigel, Mr. Rajendran, the two visiting veterinarians, and I went in the two blue IPAN ambulance jeeps directly to the warden's office to announce our arrival. It was a cold reception. The warden informed me that under no circumstances could any of my companions be allowed to enter. I would have to inform the department officially in writing of the names of any and all people I wished to have present to assist me in treating the elephant. For the present, I would have to go alone to visit Loki.

Mr. Moni soon appeared and agreed to take me to see Loki, while Nigel and the advocate waited in the jeep outside the camp's front gate. Aleksija and Johan departed separately: they had farm calls to make.

Loki, no longer confined to the kraal, walked freely over the open areas of the elephant camp, dragging a twenty-foot-long chain along the ground that was attached to one of his hind legs. The older of the two mahouts followed closely behind.

I can't say whether Loki remembered me, but he certainly showed no fear or hostility toward me as I slowly approached him. He was heavier than when I had last seen him, two years earlier. In fact, he might have been a little overweight. I immediately saw that he no longer had the tendon stump hanging out of his left forefoot. The wound had completely healed over, but when I pressed down on it firmly, I could feel a distinct soft mushiness in the tissues deep beneath the skin surface. The surface of the skin over the dome-shaped swelling was a feathery whirl that sloughed at the slightest rubbing. He still had a deep-seated infection in his foot, that was for sure: I would have to try and examine him more closely once I got permission to have Nigel with me. There was a discharging abscess on his right cheek, below what is termed the parotid gland. It oozed pus when I gently pressed down on it. There were also a half dozen fresh diagonally running wounds high up on the inner surface of his right hind leg. I wondered whether chains had caused them.

I realized that I would not be able to treat Loki without Nigel's help. Although it was wonderful to see Loki free and no longer confined to the kraal, it made it dangerous to handle him at such close, unprotected quarters. Furthermore, without Nigel's assistance, I was unable to communicate with the mahouts.

I wrote a letter to the department, requesting permission to allow entrance for certain named individuals whom I would need to help me treat the Makhna. Each morning, Nigel would drive me to the camp and wait outside in the hope that the permission had come through, but it took several days to get a response: valuable time lost.

I took the opportunity to try and develop a relationship with Loki. I began to realize that he had a distinct sense of humor and obviously enjoyed playing tricks on his mahout. One day we were passing an area where young saplings had been planted a few days before, part of a reforestation effort. *Is that a twinkle I see in Loki's eye?* I wondered. Sure enough, he took a sudden diversion from the path we were on, wrapped his trunk around one of the young trees, and effortlessly pulled it out of the ground. Waving it in circles over his back, he shook it until all the earth had fallen from its roots, and then let it drop to the ground. For once, I felt really sorry for the mahout, because I knew he would get into trouble for allowing Loki to do this.

On another occasion, the same mahout had taken Loki down to the river. The River Moyar divided at that point, and the mahout had waded up one of the branches, leaving Loki behind. Having taken off all his clothes and thrown them over some rocks, the mahout started to take a stand-up bath. I stayed on the riverbank by a bush whose leaves had burst into autumnal reds and purples; Loki was splashing around in the other branch of the river just a few yards upstream. All seemed normal until I caught the same twinkle in Loki's eye that I had seen just before he uprooted the tree. *He's going to pull the red bush up*, I said to myself. But no; as he slowly lumbered toward the bush, all calm and innocent-like, he suddenly broke into a high-speed trot up the middle of the river in the opposite direction to the mahout. Seeing what was happening, the mahout panicked and, not stopping to put his clothes back on, dashed up the river stark naked. Loki had had his fun; he came to a stop and started to play with the water, sucking it up in his trunk and spraying it over his back, waiting for the mahout to catch up to him, once more all calm and innocent-like.

Early each evening, Nigel and I would follow Loki and his mahout down to the small branch of the river that flowed by the little village where the camp workers lived. This was where the younger children of the village played together while the older girls brought all the aluminum plates and cooking utensils stacked on their heads to be cleaned after the evening meal.

This was also where the elephants were brought each night for their bath and rubdown. On command, Loki would step into the river and roll over onto his side to allow his mahout to crawl all over his flank, chest, and neck to scrub his skin with soap and a stiff-bristled brush. It was easy to tell that Loki enjoyed the bath, luxuriating in the attention being paid to him and the coolness of the water. He didn't seem to care if his head or face became submerged: after all, he had his trunk to breathe through. When both his sides had been scrubbed, he got up and walked freely deep into the river until his massive body gradually disappeared beneath the surface of the water, as if he were playing submarines. For long minutes at a time, there would be no telling where he was in the river, not a ripple or wave to be seen, until his trunk would surface, like a submarine's periscope, and shoot a fountain of spray high into the air. When it was all over, he would climb the steep, muddy embankment, with the mahout in the lead, and make his way to the mahout's small mud-walled, tin-roofed hut, to where he would be chained by the ankle for the night to a stake buried deeply in the ground.

That last morning, on the day I was due to begin my journey back to the United States, I went to see Loki one last time. I had only a few minutes before I would have to leave.

It was the Pongul Festival, an important day in Tamil Nadu, and all the villages and towns were decorated in green, white, and orange bunting and small Indian flags.

Loki was way off on the rolling land between the outcroppings of forest. He was already in a steady lope toward me. I was pleased to see that he had no drag chain on his legs, but he had a soft, thin yellow rope around his neck with a brass bell on it, which jingled with his every movement. He came to a stop, and I walked up to him and kissed his trunk. "Good-bye, that little elephant," I said, as I looked up into his face. I felt a tear begin to trickle down my cheek. Not wanting anyone to see, I turned and walked away. I looked back one last time. Loki's body swayed from side to side as he padded away. I couldn't help thinking with a smile, *Loki will probably never know that his bottom is wrinkled.* I had meant to tell him so many times.

The day after I returned home, the forestry officials of Tamil Nadu obtained a restraining order through the Federal High Court in New Delhi, overturning the Madras High Court's ruling. IPAN workers were forbidden further entry to the elephant camp to treat Loki's wounds.

The last I heard, Loki had been taken to a camp deeper in the forest, away from the public eye, but he is still described as the sweetest and most gentle of all the elephants in Mudumalai.

2

A Life in Captivity

One of the joys of freedom is surely the ability to control one's own destiny.

—Jeffrey Moussaieff Masson and Susan McCarthy,
When Elephants Weep

The small group stirs, but only for a moment. It's the noontime siesta and the sun is high in the sky, the heat beginning to become oppressive. Even the tsetse flies and the mosquitoes know to take a rest, hiding from the sun in the dense shade of the forest.

The baby feels the sun on his back and reaches out to take one of the berry-laden branches his mother lazily turns in her hand as she munches on an odd fruit here and there. Annoyed by his being so bold, she pulls his hand back, readjusting his position on her breast. He's 2 years old now, and, like all youngsters at his stage in life, he thinks he's special and deserving of his elders' unlimited patience and forbearance. Why shouldn't he think this way? The other members of the band—his older sister, his aunts, and even the top males of the group, who are often aloof to all the others—give him deference and a wide margin of tolerance. There is one other mother in the group. She, too, has an infant at her breast, this one a female about a year and a half old.

The band of a dozen or so chimpanzees is part of a much larger troop, perhaps eighty all told, that fragments and then regroups in constant social motion, like raindrops coalescing and then breaking up as they trickle down the smooth face of a rock in a thunderstorm. Yet there is a deep, rich family history here: everyone knows his or her relationship, not just with parents but with aunts and uncles, nieces and nephews, cousins, half brothers and sisters, top-ranking males, and stately old dowager females.

Most of the animals get on well with each other, nothing more than the occasional squabble or bickering to disturb the peace. Perhaps the only troublesome individuals are the older juvenile males—three of them—around 12 to 14 years of age. They are full of piss and vinegar as their hormones are starting to rise, and they exude an abundance of brawn and daring but little political skill or social grace. At the end of the siesta, they are likely to show off again, as they did this morning at the first light of dawn, waking the rest of the group in the treetop nests that everyone builds anew each night. They'll shout and swing their arms, hair erect on glossy black bodies, their male sexuality exposed proudly for all who wish to see (which no one seemingly does)—typical male buffoons who will scream in terror come the first serious challenge to their tottering self-proclaimed position of importance.

These chimps have lived in this forest, tucked away in a remote corner along the eastern border of Sierra Leone, in West Africa, for generations, maybe even hundreds of years. Information crucial to the survival of the troop is passed down from one generation to the next, like where the best fruit trees are located, how to find medicinal plants when intestinal parasite loads get too high, where other bands of chimps live and how best to avoid confronting them, and how to recognize the boundaries of territory. The chimps may even know how to fish for termites by inserting long twigs or coarse grass stems into the holes of red-earth termite mounds, scooping them off in their lips without getting bitten, or how to split large baobab fruits by smashing them on the ground, or how to crush open nuts placed on stone anvils by using hand-sized rocks as hammers.

The two elderly females in their early forties sit huddled at the edge of the group, grooming each other with finger and thumb, chewing now and then at each other's sparse, rust-tinged hair to remove a fleck of bark or an imaginary flea. The rest of the group falls back into fitful sleep; one yawns noisily, another passes gas.

Suddenly, a sharp sound pierces the tranquility: the snapping of a twig. The leader male immediately vaults to a sitting position, his ears alert, his hair raised, his eyes straining to penetrate the dense foliage. He lets out a soft alarm hoot, a hollow, tentative sound that echoes eerily through the thick, humid forest air. A more distant sound is heard, and the whole group springs to its feet. Panic fills their eyes; something terribly wrong is afoot. Half a dozen long-tailed coucals fly up in panic from a stand of bushes, their clacking calls sending the chimps into a fit of ear-piercing screams. Everyone is plunged into pandemonium and confusion, the chimps unable to determine what is happening or where the danger they sense might be coming from.

They turn to make an escape from the clearing, but too late; a ragtag band of men bursts from the trees, shouting. Two deafening reports of pellet-loaded shotguns, blunderbuss relics from the early twentieth century—as likely to backfire and kill the hunter as to fire forward and strike the victim—explode, and the two mothers, their babies clinging to their breasts in rigid terror, fall to the ground, dead. In moments, the other chimps have fled and the men have surrounded the two dead bodies. Two of the men let fly hefty old rope nets that enshroud the still bodies, while others rush in to grab the infants snared beneath the coarse tangle, wrenching loose their viselike grips on their mothers' chests, pinioning their skinny, sinewy arms behind their backs, shouting instructions, and screaming warnings to one another with mind-paralyzing intensity. Babies though they might be, these two little chimps could give painful bites with their sharp front milk teeth. The infants are hoisted in the air, still engulfed in the nets, and roughly pushed, headfirst, into thick, dusty gunnysacks that two other men are carrying.

The men drop the tied-up sacks on the ground, which immediately begin to carom about with their writhing, screaming contents, and start to skin the dead chimps and cut up the meat into anatomical sections. Animal protein is hard to come by for most forest-dwelling people in this part of Africa, and chimpanzee flesh will be a welcome addition to the village's menu.

And so begins the nightmare for the babies. It may be days, weeks, or even months before they find themselves in semi-tranquility again, forever uprooted from their families, forced to live until the day they die in a strange, unnatural world created by man, as tragic and ruthless a despoliation as any slave may have suffered.

The babies will fetch a high price in this part of Africa, the equivalent of at least a few U.S. dollars, when the white boss man calls next week or next month, or whenever he gets around to it. He calls himself a trapper, even though the village hunters do most of the trapping for him. He's been working these forests for years, ever since he fled a ravaged Europe at the end of the Second World War. When the hunters from the various villages have obtained enough live specimens—antelope, duikers, snakes, monkeys, and, with any luck, one or two more baby chimps—he'll have the animals carried or trucked to Freetown, the capital city on the coast, where he'll hold them temporarily until he can arrange to have them shipped to the zoos and research facilities in Europe, Japan, and the United States that have commissioned him.

In the meantime, the hunters will take the babies back to their villages and tie them to a post or tree trunk with a thin rope or wire wrapped around their waists. If the babies tug too hard or are left tied up for too long, the nooses will tighten and eat through their skin into their abdomens, and they will die a slow, painful death from peritonitis. They'll be fed rice and cassava, and maybe even some bananas if the villagers can get a hold of them, and they'll be given dirty water to drink from a bowl. But it will be days before the babies stop trying to bite anyone who comes near them, and they'll spend every night crying themselves to sleep, until they are finally able to forget their lost mothers.

At least these two infants survived the initial horrors of capture; many others are killed along with their mothers and other adults in the shooting orgy, or die sometime later from gunshot wounds they received. It has been estimated that for every young chimp who made it safely to his foreign land of destination, nine others died from injury, disease, malnutrition, or starvation. How many chimps were taken from the wild from the 1950s to the mid-1970s, before the passage of the CITES (Convention on International Trade in Endangered Species of Wild Fauna and Flora) agreements in 1975, and how many were killed or died along the way will never be known with any accuracy. The total must have been in the many hundreds, and possibly even thousands.

This rape of the wild would have far-reaching effects. In the early part of the twentieth century, chimpanzees were abundant in a broad belt of tropical rain forest and savannah woodlands extending from the west coast of Africa, through the center of the continent, to central East Africa. The pressures of trapping and hunting for zoological purposes, medical research, acquisition for the pet trade and circuses, rampant destruction of habitat, and, in more modern times, the even more devastating harvest for commercial bush meat have reduced the population from what undoubtedly would have been two million or more in the early part of the twentieth century to little more than a recently estimated 200,000 animals. Chimpanzees are now found in substantial numbers in only a handful of the former twenty or more countries in which they once thrived, like Cameroon, Congo, Gabon, and Uganda.

With chimpanzees now classified as an endangered species in the wild, it is illegal to hunt, capture, or export them. There is little solace to be had in this legal protection, however; the carnage continues unchecked.

Bush meat has always been a source of dietary protein for local villagers and forest-dwelling people in western and central Africa. However, hunting for bush meat has reached truly catastrophic proportions. The opening up of the forests to mining operations, oil exploration, and the continuation of illegal logging activities is destroying the natural habitat of the wildlife. The increased availability of more efficient firearms, the spread of civil war and international strife, and the pressure of hunting for bush meat to feed camp workers and soldiers, who often have no other source of protein, intensify the killing of endangered species, such as the chimpanzee and bonobo. This in turn puts pressure on the many chimpanzee sanctuaries that have sprung up across western and central Africa in the fight to save the growing numbers of babies and infants orphaned by the killing of their mothers.

Some experts gloomily predict the extinction of the chimpanzee and the other species of apes—the bonobo, gorilla, and orangutan, and even the gibbon and siamang could be close behind—by 2020. By what many animal protectionists view as a purposefully created loophole in the law, the chimpanzee's tenuous status is considered only *threatened* in captivity, leaving countries like the United States free to continue to use them in research and for any other pursuit that society deems lawful.

* * * * *

The capture of chimpanzees for use in research began in earnest in the late 1950s and early '60s with the development of the United States' aerospace program at the Holloman Air Force Base in Alamogordo, New Mexico. It was the largest captive chimpanzee facility in the world at that time. Just to read the titles of the scientific papers that resulted from this work is enough to make your blood curdle: "Effects of positive G on chimpanzees immersed in water," "Physiologic and pathologic effects in chimpanzees during prolonged exposure to 40 transverse G," and "Rapid decompression of chimpanzees"—brace yourself!—"to near vacuum." This is not to mention the studies on car-crash head trauma and whiplash and whole-body X-ray irradiation with bone marrow replacement. The pinnacle of this research was the 1961 and 1962 journeys into space by Ham and Enos, the two young chimps who paved the way for the historic flights of astronauts Alan Shepard and John Glenn.

But the real surge in capturing wild chimpanzees for use in biomedical research didn't begin until the mid-1960s to early '70s with the urgency to get to the bottom of a human disease that seemed to be transmitted through blood transfusions. Serum sickness, or hepatitis B, as it would later be called in order to distinguish it from the already characterized hepatitis A, is caused by a virus. It is one of the world's major diseases, on a par with malaria and far more prevalent and infectious, then and now, than the scary AIDS pandemic that engulfs the planet at the dawn of this new millennium. It is estimated that some two billion people in the world are infected with hepatitis B, 400 million of whom become lifelong carriers of the virus. This chronic state of disease is the most common cause of death, from liver cancer, in people under the age of 40, especially in emerging countries.

Yet it took only 200 chimpanzees and ten years of research from the time scientists first isolated the virus causing hepatitis B from human blood to the time an effective vaccine against it was put on the market—a truly remarkable feat that could not have been achieved without the chimpanzee.

Flushed with their success in breaking the back of hepatitis B, scientists were confident by the mid-1970s that they would soon get to the bottom of yet another blood-borne virus that they suspected was a major contaminant of national blood supplies and the cause of hepatitis worldwide. They were able to verify through specific serum tests that this virus was not hepatitis A or hepatitis B, so they called it non-A, non-B hepatitis virus. The chimpanzee would prove to be the unique model for the study of yet another major human disease.

Unfortunately, the scientists' expectations were not to be realized so soon. While the hepatitis A virus can be seen in human feces under the electron microscope, and the hepatitis B virus is similarly readily visible in the blood of infected patients, the virus of non-A, non-B hepatitis stubbornly evades visual detection. Its concentration in human blood is just too low. As Dr. Mike Houghton of the Chiron Corporation, one of the world's leading experts in hepatitis C, once told me, "Looking for the virus in human blood was like trying to find a needle in a hundred haystacks."

Then in 1989, a breakthrough occurred. After almost fifteen years of intense searching, the virus was finally isolated from the blood of two chimpanzees named Don and Rodney. They had been challenged with contaminated human factor 8, which is used in the treatment of hemophilia. "Suddenly," Houghton said, "the search for non-A, non-B virus was like finding *1,000 needles in a single haystack.*" Chimp Don's blood proved to contain more than 100,000 virus particles per milliliter, and Rodney's one million virus particles per milliliter—veritable pea soups. As a final test of infectivity, a one-million-fold dilution of Rodney's blood was able to transmit infection when injected intravenously into two other chimpanzees. The virus was partially cloned from Don's and Rodney's blood, a major effort in itself, and within three years a reliable test for hepatitis C was available. Scientists at last had a clear shot at developing a vaccine—or so they thought.

Houghton estimated that it took around 200 chimps to enable scientists to isolate and identify the hepatitis C virus, that one achievement alone saving millions of human lives worldwide. National blood supplies could now be tested for hepatitis C before using them for transfusions, and infected people could take measures to avoid spreading the disease.

Of course, one could argue that given time, scientists would have been able to isolate the hepatitis C virus through other, yet-to-be-discovered methods, without the need to resort to using chimpanzees. There can be no denying, however, that succeeding through known technological means had already taken fourteen years and a great deal of money (not to mention a good bit of brilliance on the part of Houghton, Don Bradley, the lead researcher at the Centers for Disease Control and Prevention, and their colleagues). Scientists would have to make an enormous shift of mind to knowingly give up lines of research that historically have been shown to work at least sometimes, rather than risk the years that exploring new approaches might, and almost certainly would, take.

Although there is a glimmer of light at the end of the tunnel, the search for a vaccine against the enigmatic hepatitis C virus continues.

Just as with the hepatitis A, B, and C viruses, chimpanzees can be infected with HIV but do not go on to develop symptoms of AIDS.

In the early attempts to develop vaccines, many facilities were less than frugal in their use of chimpanzees, not yet aware of the failures everyone would come to face left, right, and center. It was not that the different candidate vaccines were failing to induce antibody production in the chimps, which, based on the scientists' experience of infectious agents, was almost a foregone conclusion. It was that the terminal molecules of the vaccine-induced antibodies were not able to physically reach the attachment sites on the surface of the virus, which would result in their neutralization.

Chimpanzees are being used less in AIDS research today than in former years more because of expense and unavailability of adequate numbers than because of their biological unsuitability. (Human beings are cheaper to study than chimps!) There are now only 1,000 or so chimpanzees in research colonies in the United States. They range in age from quite young to very old, with varied histories of research use. Even if every single one of these chimpanzees were to be used in vaccine development, there would not be enough chimps to enable scientists to overcome the failures that would certainly occur. Thus it is more economical to carry out mass vaccination testing of human populations at high risk of contracting HIV, such as in Africa; and only then, when preliminary findings prove encouraging as was reported in October 2009 in a study carried out in Thailand, would chimps be used for the purposeful exposure to the virus.

Scientists haven't failed to develop an effective vaccine against HIV after twenty-five years of intense research because the chimpanzee has been a poor model for human AIDS, as many animal rights advocates claim. It is because the virus is so well crafted and so difficult to predict, owing to its rapid ability to mutate, that scientists have yet to find a way of dependably overcoming the virus's defense mechanisms. It's as if the virus has a mind of its own and is able to sense the defense strategy of its host and figure out how to thwart it. Ironically, human beings have proved to be no better models than chimpanzees in the development of an AIDS vaccine, in spite of the somewhat encouraging news out of Thailand.

Yet for all the disappointments, failures, and impasses, science could not have progressed even as far as it has without the help of the chimpanzee.

* * * * *

An often sweeping accusation made by animal rights advocates is that using animals in medical experimentation is not only cruel, but leads to erroneous, even dangerously misleading results. Some, such as Jane Goodall, even go so far as to proclaim, "No good ever came of using animals in research."

The tragedy of thalidomide in the late 1950s to early '60s is a classic example, a stark reminder of the risks of not using appropriate species of animals as human models. The drug was prescribed as an antiemetic for the treatment of pregnancy-related morning sickness in women, and was tested in dogs, rabbits, mice, and many other laboratory species with no ill effects observed. Yet if scientists had tested the drug in just one rhesus monkey in early pregnancy, they would have discovered its tragic effects on limb development in the fetus.

We may argue that we need to use animals in research, but we must never stop asking ourselves whether we have the right to take them from the lives they are meant to lead and cast them into the cold, sterile environment of the laboratory cage.

Peter Singer's book *Animal Liberation,* published in 1975, drew people's attention to the concept that animals might have rights. The concept was not new. Henry S. Salt wrote of it in 1894 in his book *Animals' Rights: Considered in Relation to Social Progress:* "I saw deep in the eyes of the animals the human soul look out upon me. . . . Come nigh, little bird, with your half-stretched quivering wings—within you I behold choirs of angels, and the Lord himself in vista." One has only to read some of Robert Burns's poems such as "To a Mouse" and "The Twa Dogs" to sense that a deep reverence and respect for animal life existed for some people at least as early as the second half of the eighteenth century.

The use of chimpanzees, but not other animals, in biomedical research is now outlawed by a small but growing number of countries, such as Britain, Spain, and New Zealand. It is worth noting, however, that these countries have never used chimpanzees in research. Yet it is unlikely that they would, out of principle, fail to take advantage of any medical breakthroughs resulting from such research carried out in other countries, like the United States and Japan.

Over a welcome cold beer after a long, exhausting day of listening to scientific papers at the national and international conferences I attend, I often ask fellow investigators, "Have you ever stopped to wonder what the consequences might be to advancements in human health if a law were passed that forbade the use of all animals in biomedical research, under any circumstances, come next Monday?" Or, better still, a slightly easier question: "Where would we be today if dogs had not been used in early work on diabetes, or monkeys in the development of vaccines against poliomyelitis, or chimpanzees in the study of hepatitis B? Denied access to the use of live animals, what alternatives would scientists have explored?" I reserve such questions for scientists who I think might have the patience to stop and ponder when animals are mentioned—a rare breed indeed. Yet over the years, I have found myself believing that I have met a few who would be prepared to seriously consider the philosophical conundrum. (Getting them to commit their thoughts to paper and publication, however, is another matter altogether.)

The most common argument against stopping the use of animals in biomedical research is the time it would take for scientists to develop alternatives and new lines of research that would obviate such need. Since the days of Louis Pasteur, Robert Koch, and the other great scientists of the mid- to late nineteenth century, the use of animals has been an essential part of the study of human disease and how to combat it. As with any avenue of human endeavor, mistakes will be made in such an approach, but no one can argue that most of the major breakthroughs in medicine could not have been made without the use of animals. In the study of hepatitis B and C and HIV/AIDS alone, the chimpanzee has proved to be the unique—the one and only—model, simply because these viruses do not propagate within the body of any other species of laboratory animal. If you were to inject HIV into a dog, for example, all the virus would be dead by the next day. Hybrid viruses, in the form of part-HIV and part-SIV (simian or monkey immunodeficiency virus), have been engineered in the laboratory and used in certain types of research relating to AIDS, but these are still not HIV.

Predicting how many years it might take to establish alternatives to the use of animals in research would be impossible. Who is going to tell dying patients, "Sorry, but we can't make any breakthroughs to help save your life because we still haven't come up with an alternative to animals? If it were only twenty years down the road, I'm sure we would have made some progress by then."

Science and scientific thinking advance in irregular steps, not in the smooth, progressive manner that laypeople might imagine. Real breakthroughs come only now and again, quite often serendipitously. Pasteur, the genius of serendipity himself, concluded, "In the science of observation, chance favors only the prepared mind." In between these breakthroughs, progress is usually sluggish and frustratingly nonproductive.

In his book *The Limits of Medicine,* Edward S. Golub writes, "A common misconception about science is that . . . once one is confronted with [the facts], understanding follows. Nothing can be further from the truth: The facts that come from scientific experiments are always understood within the context of the assumptions made when designing the experiment."

Imagine yourself standing on a beach of smooth, rounded pebbles. The majority of them are a pale pink in color; others are pale green and brown. The pink stones represent all that you and all the other scientists, present and past, understand. The pale green and brown stones are various areas in science that you don't understand fully, but you are working on them and know that sooner or later, they will unveil their secrets. Then you turn over a couple of the pale green and brown pebbles and are shocked to find that all the pebbles underneath are dark green and blue, and red and yellow. You are suddenly struck by paralysis: what are these, and what do they represent? Suddenly, all your collective knowledge hardly seems of value. It is almost as though you have to start over again from the beginning.

This is what happened when scientists came face to face with HIV for the first time in the early 1980s. Naturally assuming that it would be more or less like any other virus they had known, they did not expect to find that immediately after entering the bloodstream of its new host, the virus would go straight to the nucleus of the cell, pop into one of the cell's chromosomes when it next divided, become part of its genetic makeup, and then tell the cell to start making viral DNA to the exact design it dictated for the rest of the person's life.

This is very much the case in, for example, the genomic revolution that began at the end of the twentieth century and will continue for decades to come. Genes may turn out not to be quite what we thought they were, the be-all and end-all of biological inheritance, but only the slaves to other molecular complexes that we are only just beginning to discover but don't necessarily understand yet.

What exactly does it mean to share 98.6 percent of our DNA with chimpanzees, or 90 percent with rats and mice? Or, even more striking, 26 percent with the lowly dandelion that invades our lawns? And why can't we jump to using tissue cultures to replace living animals? After all, some scientists already do just that. Why can't we go further in developing computer models? We have to bear in mind that we probably know less than one iota about the intricate relationships among tissues and organs of the living body, something we would need to know fully if we ever hoped to abandon the use of live animal models.

And when all is said and done, who is going to take the awesome responsibility for halting the use of animals in research this coming Monday?

In my work as the chief veterinarian at the Laboratory for Experimental Medicine and Surgery in Primates (LEMSIP), I came face to face with the dilemma of using animals in research every day.

No matter which way I looked at it, however, I came to realize that the greatest cruelty we were committing upon animals in the research laboratory was depriving them of a normal childhood. If we couldn't do better than that, what hope did the animals have for a better future?

These concerns would not be fully brought home to me, however, until my family and I became entangled with three little hellion primates—Spike Mulligan, a baby chimp, and two little rhesus monkey reprobates named Finnegan and Erin.

For me, Spike represented the epitome of the animal in research. I delivered him by emergency cesarean section when his mother, Bella, became seriously ill with kidney failure. It was touch and go trying to save mother and unborn baby. Spike was in critical condition when I delivered him onto the surgery table, unable to breathe, his heart barely beating. He made it only after I gave him mouth-to-nose resuscitation. Bella died four days later, her kidneys shriveled to the size and shape of walnuts (compared to their normal four inches or so in length and smooth, unwrinkled surface). Spike was now an orphan.

Spike could not have come into this world at a worse time. Every young chimp who had been born at LEMSIP during the previous five years, all government-owned, had already been shipped to another laboratory in Texas, one that had been awarded the renewal of a five-year hepatitis B vaccine contract. Spike was entirely on his own, no mother to hold him, no infants to grow up with and learn what it means to be a chimp.

I brought him home from the lab with me every night, and he'd play with Angus, our white-haired, short-legged, barrel-chested,

Young Spike Mulligan is mesmerized by the television.

mongrel dog. Angus had literally wandered into our lives while we were having a picnic on the shores of Lake Mendota in Madison, Wisconsin. His and Spike's nonstop roughhousing drove everyone to distraction. Our children, Pádraig (then 13 years old), Nathalie (11), and Christopher (10), were happy to serve as nursemaids and playmates, carrying him around in an infant sling tied around their chests. Spike became a member of the family.

Spike wasn't the first chimp my wife, Marie-Paule, had reared. Dilly and Gabby had preceded him, and many others would follow in the years to come until we managed to establish what I regarded as a real nursery at LEMSIP and find the people dedicated enough to run it.

I began to be concerned about Spike's long-term future, however. Without members of his own species to play with and learn the intricacies of chimpanzee social politics, Spike would not become a real chimp but would end up a misfit, stranded somewhere between being human and a poor representation of his own species. Even under ideal conditions, adolescence is a rocky road for any young male chimp to follow. Spike needed the companionship of his own kind, and quick!

Help came in the form of an offer from Paul and Jo Fritz, who ran the Primate Foundation of Arizona in the desert around Tempe.

The Primate Foundation was the closest thing to a chimpanzee sanctuary that existed in North America in 1980. Paul had worked as a keeper at the Phoenix Zoo for years, and Jo had been an administrative secretary. (Paul had also worked in the Berlin Zoo when he was a young lad in the 1940s, and took the wolves he cared for out on leashes and hid them and himself in a ditch as Russian troops marched in.)

The Primate Foundation started with two chimps who, dumped by a zoo because they were no longer wanted, faced the prospect of euthanasia or being sold into biomedical research if a home could not be found for them. The Fritzes began their sanctuary on a chicken farm with these two chimps only to find soon thereafter that tens, and maybe even scores, of chimps across the country faced a similar plight. Leasing the skeleton of a derelict powerhouse on Indian land near Tempe, the Fritzes built a semiunderground facility to house the chimps.

Raising money to support the growing number of abandoned chimps was not easy, however. The Fritzes turned to LEMSIP for help. LEMSIP paid the foundation a lease fee for each chimp, who was then used for one year in hepatitis B safety testing. This was a difficult tightrope to walk when you claimed to be a sanctuary, and the Fritzes received a lot of unfair criticism for associating with a biomedical laboratory.

I sent Spike to Arizona to socialize for eighteen months with two young chimps his age: a little female, Tulik, and a male, Akimo. They became an incredible trio. Spike's future and current social needs were secure, at least for the moment.

As part of the arrangement with the Fritzes, Spike returned to LEMSIP, along with Tulik and Aki, where all three underwent a two-phase hepatitis B vaccine safety test together. The first phase was a six-month prestudy isolation period, a strict scientific requirement to determine whether any of the three young chimps had already contracted hepatitis in Arizona. (At that time, there was no specific test for the virus. Scientists had to rely on determining infection solely from the pattern of liver enzymes in the bloodstream and the microscopic appearance of the liver tissue obtained through what is termed punch or needle biopsy.) In the second phase, they were injected with the vaccine under test and caged separately in the same room. This phase also lasted six months, during which the trio were subjected to the same schedule of blood sampling and liver biopsy. Biopsy required obtaining a one-sixteenth-inch core of liver tissue, about one and a half inches long, by punching a large-bore needle, like that used for spinal injections in human beings, between the lower ribs into the liver through the upper abdomen (not the chest cavity). In chimpanzees, liver biopsy is performed under general anesthesia, not local anesthesia, as it is in human patients, who sometimes find the procedure quite painful. The purpose of safety testing the vaccine was to make sure that it did not accidentally contain live hepatitis virus, which would cause infection rather than protect the test subject. Any foul-up in the testing procedure could cost the drug company millions of dollars in lost revenues on future vaccine batches. Because it was not what is called an efficacy test, the chimps would not be challenged with live virus. The greatest discomfort Spike and his friends might have to suffer was being caged alone, which sometimes, though not in this case, proves stressful to animals.

At the end of the year of study, Spike found himself once again alone and without the companionship of his own kind. Tulik and Aki's days in research were over, and they returned to Arizona; Spike's had only just begun. He missed them very much.

I tried as often as I could, barring inclement weather, to take Spike for walks in the forest around lunchtime and share my brown bag with him. In spite of his fast growth and increasing strength, he remained remarkably obedient. Spike had close relationships with Ray, the supervisor of the husbandry crew; Mike, one of my breeding technicians; and Roxanne, who had known him since he was a *wee fella* in the nursery. They would sometimes come along.

Spike and I used to have lunch together on a large, flat rock deep in the woods that surrounded the lab. This was the only time of the day, except in the evening when most of my colleagues had gone home for the night, that I could get some peace, away from the constant pages for me over the loudspeaker.

"Mama's" lunch consisted of a ham or tuna fish sandwich, a piece of cheese, a banana, and orange juice, which we shared out of a paper cup. Spike insisted on trying the sandwich every day, spitting it out the instant he put it in his mouth, with an expression as if he had been poisoned. His favorite item, however, was Mama's rich fruitcake, which again we shared between us, a mouthful each at a time.

It was in these woods that Spike gathered the confidence to climb trees and explore on his own, without the need to cling to me as if the world might come to an end. I never needed to fear his getting lost; he would come back the instant I called him.

One particular lunchtime will always stand out in my memory, however, because of three unusual events that occurred, one after another. It was summertime. Spike was around 6½ years old then: The years had gone by. He was quite big and very strong but still in many ways a baby, not too sure of himself.

With one arm around my shoulders for moral support, Spike reached out to touch the first caterpillar he had ever seen as it climbed in its undulating fashion up the trunk of the tree that grew right next to the rock we sat on. He recoiled in horror at the strange feel of its spiky bristles.

Then, again with his arm tight around my shoulders, Spike had his first encounter with a snake, a little garter snake, which caused him to break into deep alarm hoots that reverberated eerily through the stillness of the forest.

But most unexpected and inexplicable of all was Spike's mimicry of my killing a large black ant that had been wounded. Spike must have stepped on the ant as he was about to jump off the rock to go and play by himself. The ant's abdomen was partially squashed into the rock. Seeing him wriggling desperately to try and free himself, I knew I had to put the ant out of his misery as quickly as possible. I picked up a small fragment of a leaf and laid it over the ant's body, and with the tip of a short twig, I crushed him with a sharp jab. I removed the leaf to make sure I had done a proper job of my mercy killing.

I had paid no attention to Spike's whereabouts at the time, vaguely thinking, I am sure, that he was far away by then, climbing some tree or rooting around the forest floor in search of something or other. But he must have been observing me all the time from a distance. A few minutes later he reappeared, springing onto the rock to sit next to me, like Superman landing from a skyscraper dive. He looked deeply into my face and made a whimpering sound. He then proceeded to lay a minute white flower—a chickweed blossom, less than a quarter-inch across, which he had brought back with him— over the squashed body of the ant. Positioning the tip of a long, wiggly stick he carried in one hand over the ant's remains—quite a difficult feat for chimps, who have short, non-opposable thumbs— Spike grasped the stick further up in his other hand, grimaced at me, and then gave a short, sharp jab, just as I had done.

I have known only three other animals who showed an ability to mimic human behavior, not by training, but spontaneously. All three were chimpanzees.

Rufe was a very tall, elegant, and stately chimp in his late thirties. One day, he broke out of his cage and stepped out into the room that housed eight or nine other adult chimps. On hearing the emergency warning over the PA system, several of the caregivers and I ran to the room as fast as we could to assess the situation. We couldn't believe our eyes as we peered through the small shockproof Plexiglas window in the door. Rufe had taken the mop and rolling bucket and was in the process of washing the floor. He got bored after a while, probably realizing that it was not as much fun as he thought it would be. Dropping the mop, he made his way to a small set of shelves on the wall and recovered the metal clipboard that contained the daily health log of each chimp in the room. With the board over his right arm, like an artist with his palette, Rufe moved from one cage to the next, staring intently through the bars at the chimp inside, flipping each card over with the middle finger of his left hand (chimps tend to be left-handed) as he went, just as Mike, the caregiver, would have done.

As everyone knows, chimps are pretty smart, sometimes embarrassingly so when you find yourself pitting your wits against theirs.

In the early 1980s, Jerry, the chief supervisor of technicians at LEMSIP at the time, and I began exploring ideas of how to link two to five cages together so that we could keep the chimps in various sized social groups. We got Pete, the lab's welder, involved in the project to come up with a way of fabricating a makeshift tunnel of steel bars that we could fit between two cages, held in place by adjustable toggle hooks and four hefty bolts loaded with spacer washers and heavy-duty nuts.

We chose Donna-Rae as our test subject, a wonderful old female chimp who had ridden a motorbike in a circus and had played guitar when she was young. You could really talk to Donna and get her to do just about anything you wanted.

On the day of our test, Jerry, Pete, and I were as excited as little kids who had made their first skateboard. We transferred Donna through the front door of one of the cages from her home cage and then opened the sliding door to allow her access to the neighboring cage. She immediately began to run back and forth through the tunnel, obviously enjoying the larger space that the two cages provided. Pete determined what would be needed to develop slide tracks, how to mount the tunnel in the final model, and all the other little engineering intricacies that would need to be manufactured.

The time came to return Donna to her home cage so that Pete could begin work on the prototype. Jerry took hold of the ratchet wrench to undo the four huge bolts securing the tunnel to the cage containing Donna. "Big problem!" as the saying goes. Jerry had placed the bolts the wrong way. While he had had no difficulty securing them when he first attached the tunnel, with no chimp in either cage, he now found that he could not reach between the bars to undo the bolts.

Donna looked on in deep fascination, scratching her nose with a crooked finger, as was her habit, as if she were trying to think of a solution.

"Donna!" Jerry called out. "Would you undo those nuts for me, like a good girl?" he said, as he passed the spanner to her. To our amazement, without a moment's hesitation, Donna took the wrench and began to undo the nuts on each bolt, one after another, with a determined, unhesitating counterclockwise motion, while Jerry held the head of each bolt with another wrench. She collected the nuts and washers as they fell off each bolt into the palm of her hand, and passed them over to Jerry. Amazement was hardly the word to describe our reaction.

The most spectacular and scariest example of mimicking behavior that I ever saw in a chimpanzee was in a sanctuary in the Gambia, West Africa. I was performing health examinations on the chimps maintained on a group of islands in the River Gambia National Park. One afternoon, Bruno, one of the Senegalese park rangers who looked after the chimps, had gone with his colleagues to dart the chimps on one particular island, leaving his boat moored by a long, stout rope to a tree overhanging the river.

I was stationed on the opposite bank of the river with all my medical supplies and equipment laid out on tables, awaiting the next group of anesthetized chimps to be brought to me for health examinations.

I happened to be looking through my binoculars, birdwatching, when I saw the black silhouette of a large male chimp emerge from the dense forest and make his way down to the bobbing little boat. He climbed in and began to repeatedly pull the cord of the outboard motor in an attempt to start the engine, as he had no doubt seen the rangers do time and again. Fortunately, Bruno had not left the key in the ignition. No doubt frustrated by his failure to start the boat, the chimp turned his attention to the mooring rope, pulling on the short end of the horse-hitch knot. The rope let go, and the swift current instantly took hold of the little boat and began to carry it downstream toward Banjul, the capital, some 200 miles away.

My repeated yelling did nothing to attract anyone's attention or deter the chimp from his mission. The biggest danger was the chimp falling into the water; he would certainly drown if he did.

Some minutes later, René, one of the other rangers, appeared, saw the chimp sailing down the river, sitting back in the stern of the boat like a Cambridge don out on a Sunday afternoon's punt, minus only a flute of champagne and boater hat, and sounded the alarm. He and Bruno made it to the other boat that was tied up farther along the island's embankment and set off very cautiously to grab and secure the long rope that was trailing behind the boat in the water without panicking the chimp.

All these occurrences were amusing, but none of them had the depth and possible symbolism of Spike's behavior with the ant. I often wonder what it had all been about. There is no doubt in my mind that he was imitating me, but why? Why did he feel a need to imitate such a complex process, first searching for the little flower, which doesn't grow deep in the forest but only around its edge; then acquiring the stick and the extreme difficulty of positioning the tip of it over the ant's squashed body; and finally the grimace he gave me as he jabbed? Had Spike felt a need to impress me? He had gripped my shoulders tightly when he confronted the caterpillar and the snake: Was this his way of showing me we were buddies and shared in everything? Was I an adult male chimp to him, and did he need to emulate me, to gain my respect and love, as he probably would have done had he lived in a wild troop of chimpanzees? I can hardly believe he would have had the notion that the ant was suffering pain. If only one could rig an experiment to analyze such behavioral reactions. But some things must be left to the imagination. All I knew for sure was that Spike was a very special little guy.

I sometimes wonder, what if a bunch of wild- and captive-born chimpanzees from varied captive backgrounds were to get together when they were old and mature and wise to reflect on their lives—a sort of larger version of Robert Burns's poem about Luath and Caesar in "The Twa Dogs"? What might they have to say to one another?

The first one might begin, "Oh, I ended up in a circus, made to perform these stupid tricks. All my front teeth were knocked out so I wouldn't be able to bite people in the audience. Then my owner sold me off to a research laboratory when times got tough."

The second might chime in to say, "I started out as a pet to this young woman. She used to give me bubble baths every day and paint my fingernails purple. Then her boyfriend, who wanted to marry her, told her to 'get rid of that damn monkey and sell it to a research laboratory.'"

The third chimpanzee might relate how he had been sent to a zoo to take part in tea parties with little children (which was so at the London Zoo during the late 1940s and early '50s), until he became too big and strong and got sold off to another zoo as a breeder. But he didn't know what to do, so they exchanged him for a rare bear from another zoo, who eventually sold him to a research laboratory after changing his name.

A fourth chimp might tell of how he had been taken to a laboratory where he joined the aerospace program. "I nearly got shot off into space," he related, "but Ham and Enos were chosen instead of me. I lost count of how many laboratories I was sent to after that."

"I had eight babies," said the fifth chimp, "but they took every one away from me immediately after they were born." "Why did they do that?" another chimp asked in amazement. "So I would have more babies quicker, sooner, if I didn't rear any of them myself."

"I was born in America," said the sixth chimp. "They started to teach me how to speak Human by making signs with my hands and fingers. Almost every day, different people were teaching me. Sometimes they would take me home with them for the night. It was very confusing. Then, when I got older, they sold us all off to a research laboratory; I'm not really sure why."

"I was born in America also," said the seventh chimpanzee. "I was reared by my mama and my dada, but they took me away from them when I was about eighteen months old, and I got put in a nursery to be reared with other chimps my age. I was used for research, too, but I stayed in the lab until I was sent to a retirement place when I got older."

They drooped their heads and cried. Chimps are not supposed to cry, but they did cry, inwardly.

3

Survival of the Fittest

It is not the strongest of the species that survives, nor the most intelligent that survives. It is the one that is the most adaptable to change.

—Charles Darwin (1809–1882)

After completing my PhD, I was given a postdoctoral fellowship from the Medical Research Council, a government organization in the United Kingdom, to continue my studies on ovulation in monkeys in the United States at the Oregon Regional Primate Research Center near Beaverton. It was one of seven federally funded regional primate centers that existed at the time. The fellowship provided a modest stipend, which would cover my family and me for a year or so, after which we would return to Britain.

With three suitcases, three children ages 3 to 6, each with a favorite toy or teddy bear held lovingly in arms, and sixteen dollars in our family pocket, my wife and I landed in Oregon.

The director of the Primate Center assigned me laboratory-bench space and encouraged me to get to know all the scientists at the center and what their work entailed. I felt that I had begun a great adventure, and I was determined to make the best of it.

I was given office space as well, a long, narrow, windowless room, which I shared with a large, shy, gentle man named Ernie Ediger. Ernie was the chief technician of the rhesus monkey breeding colony, and he would teach me a great deal not only about the reproduction and behavior of rhesus monkeys and all the other species of primates at the center, but also about birds and wildlife, and how to appreciate the beauty of nature in general. When I look back on it, I realize that he had been my mentor.

I soon learned that when Ernie had something important to say, he would press his glasses up the bridge of his nose with his middle finger and give a short, shallow cough to clear his throat. Then it was just a matter of waiting for him to get the words out. "You'll probably think I'm crazy, Doc," he announced in his Kansas drawl, "but I've found a way of telling when rhesus monkeys are going to ovulate."

I sat up immediately with a rush of interest. "Tell me about it," I said.

Ernie reached down into the lowest drawer of his desk and took out a tight roll of EKG trace paper held together by a rubber band. "Here, you take hold of this," he said, as he handed me one end of the roll. He stood up and slowly walked to the other end of the office, carefully unrolling the paper in the air as he went.

Two lines drawn in ballpoint pen wiggled their way along two-thirds of the length of the two-inch-wide roll, one in red and the one below in blue. As far as I could see, the graph covered a period of almost eight months, starting on the first of January, with not a day's observation missing.

"What is this?" I asked.

"It's a graph showing the daily changes in color intensity of the perineum [the scientific word for the bottom, or what is also known as the sexskin in nonhuman primates] of an individual female rhesus monkey," he said. I was aware that the perineum of the rhesus macaque goes through distinct color changes during the menstrual cycle, from various shades of red to purplish tones (unlike the closely related Java monkey that I had worked with in England, which shows no external signs of ovulation), but I was under the impression that there was only a poor correlation between these changes and the occurrence of ovulation. The biological purpose of the phenomenon was more as a long-distance visual signal to let the males in the troop know that the female was ready for mating. Yet I could clearly see from Ernie's graph that the red line reached a sharp spike for one day only in the middle of each cycle, a clear indication of a hormonal relationship.

"I don't understand what the blue line is, Ernie."

"That's the big problem," he replied. "You might think the sex-skin is just various shades of red, but it is actually a mixture of reds and blues on top of the underlying natural tone of skin color. I haven't been able to find a scientific way to express this; that's why nobody takes any notice of what I have to say."

"But how do you know there is blue in the red? How do you measure that?" I asked.

"I don't know, that's why I haven't been able to find a way of explaining it to anyone."

The expression on my face must have given away my skepticism. I had to grip my cheeks to stifle a laugh. Poor Ernie, I could see the frustration mounting in him. He must have felt like someone trying to describe the beauty of a red rose to a blind man.

"Tell you what," he said. "Let's go see the monkeys together tomorrow morning and I'll show you what I mean." Ernie then gave me a brief lecture on the dos and don'ts of behaving around monkeys: "Don't talk to them, and don't look them directly in the eye; otherwise they'll get stressed out. Once you get to know them and they get used to you, you can do anything you like, but not 'til then."

Ernie was waiting for me when I arrived the next morning, a long coiled electrical cable and a reflector lamp in one hand and a clipboard and notepad in the other. He plugged the cable into the nearest electrical outlet outside the door to the animal room, and we entered without speaking.

I stood back as Ernie switched on the light and shone it on the monkey in the first of the upper tier of cages. He began to delicately smack his lips, making soft muttering sounds. With the greatest of care, he then gently rotated the index finger of his right hand in the air, and the monkey responded by turning around and presenting her bottom to him with her tail raised. I realized that Ernie and the monkey were talking to each other in a sort of facial sign language.

Ernie then went through the same ritual for maybe a dozen other monkeys, recording the results of his observations on the clipboard notepad at the end of each session.

I was impressed. The monkeys responded to Ernie in a calm, relaxed way. He had obviously built a trust with them, and I could clearly see what he was trying to verify. I was doubly impressed when, during his observation of one female, another technician entered the room and called out loudly to someone, not realizing that Ernie was performing his observation rounds. None of the monkeys liked this man. To my amazement, the one who was under observation let out a mournful cry of distress, and her nipples began to alternately glow and dim in obvious agitation, like red warning lights on a piece of electronic equipment.

I joined Ernie on his observation rounds each morning after that and became increasingly convinced that he had discovered something that could be very useful to science. The problem would be to come up with a way to duplicate the method, to reduce its subjectivity, and to devise a system that could be reliably used by others. These are basic tenets of science.

We set about planning an experiment, selecting twelve females with the most regular menstrual cycles. Over the three- or four-day period when we most expected ovulation to occur in each female, we drew small blood samples every six hours around the clock to measure the level of estrogen and progesterone, the two main sex hormones. The study, which lasted three months or so, was exhausting, requiring our return to the center twice a night, at around midnight and 6 o'clock in the morning, for many nights in a row to obtain the blood samples. The hormone results, determined later, clearly indicated that the peak and then sharp decline in the blood level of estrogen exactly mirrored the peak and fall in intensity of the sexskin color.

Try as we might, however, we were unable to develop a reliable system for expressing the color changes. Ernie and I spent many a frustrating hour at the Portland Public Library poring over a copy of the Munsell Book of Color, the only universally recognized scientific system of color analysis that we could find. Of the 1,605 tabs shown in the book, not a single one came close to matching the color tones of the rhesus monkeys' sexskin. Ernie would never get the recognition that I felt he so richly deserved; our results went unpublished.

Some nights, when the workload was extra-heavy, Ernie and I would stay on at the center until it was time for the next round of blood draws from the monkeys. It wasn't worth the effort of driving home, only to have to turn around and come right back once I got there. Ernie and I would use the time to explore the woods for owls, or the open grass areas for skunks, raccoons, opossums (animals that were new to my experience), and foxes, which could usually be found hunting for the peafowl that lived on the grounds. There is no doubt that these middle-of-the-night forays were the beginnings of my interest in birds and wildlife in general, and in my later recording of my findings and observations in a diary.

I had never regarded myself as an ornithologist, and I would hardly call myself a birdwatcher in the usual serious-amateur sense. There was a time when I thought people who spent their lunch hours walking fields or woodlands to study the birdlife were a bit carried away with themselves.

Now I was faced with seeing practically none of the bird species that I had known all my life and being unable to identify any of those species that I was now seeing. Even the chickadees were not exactly like the great tits I knew back home, and there was something subtly different about even the crows. As for the robins, they weren't the least bit like the fiery little birds I knew, flitting from branch to branch in the honeysuckle hedgerows.

One day I complained to Ernie that someone should do something about oiling the belt in what I presumed was the air conditioning unit housed on the apex of the roof over our office. The repetitive double squeak, day after day, was beginning to get on my nerves. "That's not the air conditioner squeaking," he chuckled. "That's the call of the red-winged blackbirds up in that tree." That sort of summed up my level of knowledge of American birds.

Instead of returning to Britain when my fellowship expired, I took a position at the Wisconsin Regional Primate Research Center in Madison. Dr. Robert Goy, a psychologist, had been the director for about two years. In many ways, he was a person far ahead of his time. In particular, he wanted someone who would take charge and lay down the rules for how surgery could be performed on the monkeys in research projects, someone who would assume the authority to stop a surgery if humane procedures were not strictly adhered to. This was long before any federal regulations had been developed for the humane care of animals and before strict oversight of research projects became a mandate of the United States Department of Agriculture in early 1993.

The man in charge of the rhesus monkey breeding colony in Madison was Steve Eisele. A good deal younger than Ernie, Steve was also shy and every bit as gentle and sensitive toward the monkeys, who obviously adored him. Like Ernie, he had also developed a system for predicting ovulation from the color changes in the monkeys' sexskin, but, alas, it was no less arcane.

Steve and Ernie had very different approaches when it came to interacting with the monkeys. Ernie was the quiet, unobtrusive type, Steve more outgoing and chatty, yet both were equally committed to the animals and trusted by them.

Except for Mrs. Stone, an elderly female rhesus monkey who had simultaneously adopted and raised six abandoned infants, and the Five Star General, the most prolific breeder in the colony, none of the monkeys in either the Oregon or the Wisconsin primate centers had a name. This has always been one of the many bones of contention between animal rights advocates and scientists.

Madison, with its three lakes and its numerous woodland areas to walk, was a great place to live. As a family, each winter we would go skating on the lakes. The first autumn frost would take us to the Wisconsin River to watch the migration of the thousands of Canada geese, their V-shaped formations, leader in front, spread vast across the sky, the whir of their wings, the yak of their calls, to head south down the Mississippi Flyway.

Wisconsin certainly made a nature lover out of me.

After four happy years in Wisconsin, we moved to New York in the late '70s. It was a big adjustment for all of us, but for the first time we had a piece of land that we could call our own. We call it "our land" not out of any pretension—after all, it's only an acre in size—but simply because I can't think of a better word to use. It's not a garden and it's not a yard; it's just a little piece of land that we've had the good fortune and pleasure to be able to share with nature. Its location on a quiet dead-end street, far from any major highway, surrounded by woods and open grassy areas, gives it a certain appearance of remoteness. The lichen-covered dry stone walls date back to the iron-mining days, a hundred years ago and more. A small stream runs through the land and connects to a pond that we share with our closest neighbors, Arnold and Brenda.

There are two species of fish in the pond—bluegills and large-mouth bass, as well as snails, frogs, toads, salamanders, turtles, snakes, and Mrs. Muskrat, as my wife, Marie-Paule, refers to her. Great blue herons, green herons, and kingfishers come by to catch the fish, and crows line up to feast on a gourmet menu of snails. Foxes and otters used to help themselves to Arnold's ducks until he accepted that it just wasn't worth keeping them any longer. A herd of white-tailed deer makes its twice-daily round of its grazing range, not hesitating to chew off our rhododendrons, azaleas, and hydrangeas as they pass by. Bears trundle through quite frequently during the summer and fall, wrecking everyone's birdfeeders and strewing garbage all over the place. All this within fifty miles of Manhattan.

I started to keep a diary of the wildlife goings-on on our land, and in the region in general, in February 1980, mainly to record the migrations of the various species and their breeding patterns each year. Although still not an ornithologist or even a birdwatcher, I at least aspired to the level of being a bird spotter, especially in recording the first or new appearance of each species. But I began to realize that much more interesting than logging the various species was being witness to the goings-on of some of the individual birds and other wildlife. I began to see the land around me, whether it was the forest, a city street in New York, or even a garbage dump, as my own private laboratory where I could get lost in thought, observing the birds and other animal life, whether wild or domesticated.

I am so glad I have kept the diary, which spans a period of three decades now. Every now and then, I sit with a beer and read a random selection of entries. Many describe events that I would have long since forgotten had I not written them down, or have no memory of at all.

Dutifully I record the date of the return of the slate-colored juncos, harbingers of the dreaded winter to come, from their northern summer climes, and their disappearance north the following spring. One of the most welcome birds in spring, the brilliantly yellow-colored male Baltimore oriole, repeats his short mating call over and over ad nauseam, starting from the beginning again should he make the slightest musical mistake. The house wren's short gurgling, bubbling, repetitious outbursts are errorless at least. After all these years, however, I find that I still have to relearn how to identify the warblers each spring, and by the time autumn rolls around, I have to relearn them all over again because their plumage has changed so much.

In my diary there is a short story about three crows perched in a row atop a tree by the pond. One grooms the other two, pecking them every now and then to make them keep their necks stretched up in the air so he can groom their throat feathers, a behavior I had never seen before in crows. On another occasion, I counted nine species of birds in one black birch tree, excitedly chasing insects among the autumn leaves.

Some of the diary's entries are truly amusing, like Mrs. Muskrat having a squabble with a green heron by the pond, and a recording I made in the village of a pair of red-eyed vireos fiercely fighting with a starling at one end of a branch while a robin, quite unconcerned by the commotion, was feeding her infant at the other end of the branch.

Most hilarious of all is a recording of two bullfrogs sitting in the same small puddle, loudly croaking to each other all day long. What could they possibly have been talking about?

One incident is vividly impressed upon my mind. It was a very hot June afternoon, and against all good gardening practice I began to water the parched potted plants that I had shamefully neglected on the balcony. Two daddy longlegs made a desperate dash up the outside of one pot and over the rim to avidly drink the water that had pooled around the plant. Moments later, two tiny chipping sparrows swooped in over the railing and began to drink the water from the same pot, either not noticing my presence just two or three feet away, or too thirsty to be concerned by it. Flabbergasted, I turned to step through the sliding glass door, back into the house, only to find Rags, one of our three dogs, sitting behind me, pawing the air, waiting her turn to get a drink, but hers would be directly from the sprinkler head of the watering can. It must have been very hot indeed that June afternoon.

Yet I have to recognize that not all stories in nature are humorous or touching: very occasionally some are outright horrific. The most shocking I ever witnessed was the rape of a female Mallard duck. My diary entry reads:

> May 5, 1987: On Indian Lake. Three Mallard drakes trying to mate with one female. Great struggle. Female continually held under water with males constantly jumping on top. Feathers all over water. After several minutes, female came to surface, tried to fly away but too weak [even at a distance, I could see that her neck was bald of feathers]. Process continued. Tried to intercede by whistling, yelling, throwing stones on water—too far away [to be effective]. Finally all four flew close together to further bank, but female appeared weak. Could not locate them again.

Another story in my diary spanned a three-year period. It was sheer fluke, of course, that I was able to make the observations over such a length of time. Undoubtedly, I missed a great deal more than I saw.

It was early May. At long last, spring had come to the forested Ramapo Mountains of southern New York. The delicate white flowers of the shad trees had already bloomed, and the leaves of the maples and ash were unfolding. As I looked out the kitchen window, I saw Mrs. Muskrat paddling along on the surface of the pond like a little tugboat. She was on her way home to her underwater den beneath the roots of the big maple tree that stands by the bank of the stream. She had a bouquet of chewed-off red tulips in her mouth. Marie-Paule and I had waited all winter to see them bloom. Oh well, I sighed; at least her babies will enjoy eating them.

Then my eye caught two large birds swooping down through the air at high speed in great wavelike flights. They landed with a silent clunk high on one of the dead limbs of the huge old elm tree, like a couple of picture magnets plunked onto the door of a refrigerator.

"Move over, everybody," they seemed to announce with their loud, raucous laugh. "We are the flickers; we're back!"

Most species of woodpeckers stay up in the trees, but flickers spend much of their time on the ground. They like to prod the earth with their beaks and then insert their long, sticky tongues into the holes in search of ants, their favorite food. There were a lot of ants in our weedy lawn!

Flickers are elegant birds, with large black spots all over their creamy yellow breasts and bellies. A striking red half-collar adorns the back of the neck, and a large black crescent forms a bib beneath the throat. Dazzling golden feathers line the undersides of their wings, which you don't see until they burst into flight. They remind me of exotic birds you might see and hear in the rain forests of West Africa as you awake at dawn in your tin-roofed mud hut.

I recognized the male by his prominent black mustache. He immediately began to peck great chunks out of the dead wood with his sturdy beak. The female watched intently as he worked. Tarzan and Jane, I began to think of this pair.

Are they going to build a nest? I wondered. *That would be great.*

To my disappointment, after just two days, they seemed to lose interest in their creation and disappeared.

The next day I noticed a pair of starlings paying a great deal of attention to the hole, repeatedly climbing in and out to inspect the inside, as if they were checking it out for size. What were they up to?

It is unusual to find starlings in forested areas. In fact, this was the first time I had seen any around our house in the fifteen years or so that we had been living here. They are more birds of towns or open fields and swamps. Just like flickers, though, they love to eat ants.

You would hardly call starlings elegant. Only flashes of irides-cent green and purple break the drabness of their mottled plumage of browns and black as they turn this way and that, catching the sunlight's glint. The feathers at the back of the head and around the

Flickers are elegant birds.

throat stick out like uncombed fuzz, giving them a scruffy appearance, as if they had just gotten out of bed. They remind me of the Cockney Pearly Kings and Queens of the East End of London, with their tiny pearl buttons sewn over their silvery-gray coats, ready to sell London Bridge to the next gullible American tourist, as the story goes. There is something brazen and bold about starlings.

Most people dislike starlings, seeing them as mean, noisy, and very messy, especially around stately buildings and parked cars. I must admit that I've always had a soft spot for them, seeing them, like myself, as immigrants from the old country. Over a hundred years ago, an eccentric man named Eugene Scheifflin had the notion to transplant to North America all the European species of birds that Shakespeare mentions in his plays. In 1890, he brought sixty starlings from England and released them in Central Park in New York City. The following year, he released another forty. Now there are countless millions of them living throughout North America. Alfy and Ethel, I decided to call our pair of starlings—or *Owfee* and *Effwl,* as the London Cockneys would pronounce the names.

I was a bit surprised to find that by the following day, like Tarzan and Jane before them, they too had lost interest in the nest hole. Perhaps the hole wasn't quite big enough to suit their tastes.

Starlings don't make what you might call a real nest. If forced by circumstance, the male squeezes in under the eaves of old houses, where it is nice and cool in summer, and throws together a few strands of dried grass and straw. There wouldn't be anything soft and cozy for the babies after they hatched if it wasn't for the female, who lines the nest with moss and feathers.

It just so happens that starlings prefer flicker nest holes. Perhaps a flicker awakens in the starling a genetic memory of its European equivalent, the green woodpecker, which, except for its striking lime-green color, is identical in size, shape, and general behavior. Throw in their mutual preference for ants as food, and you have yourself a party.

Starlings are small but full of spit and fury.

To my amazement, Tarzan and Jane reappeared a couple of mornings later. *Well, I'll be damned!* I said to myself. Tarzan immediately set about pecking and chipping away at the inside of the hole to enlarge it, littering the ground around the trunk of the tree with an untidy mess of wood chunks. By noon, he had finished, and Jane retreated inside to lay her eggs (as I later determined).

Who should show up later that very afternoon? Alfy and Ethel! *Uh-oh!* I thought. Flickers are nearly twice the size of starlings but are no match for their spit and fury. Ethel disappeared inside the nest hole only to emerge moments later with a white flicker egg in her mouth. To my horror, she let it fall to the ground, forty feet below, before the panic-stricken Jane could stop her. "There you go, Ducky!" Ethel seemed to scoff. In a flash, she was back inside the nest, reappearing an instant later with a second egg in her beak. Despite Jane's desperate attempts to stop her, Ethel threw it to the ground.

While the two females continued to fight like a couple of fishwives, the males were also having a go at it. Their claws were locked together in what seemed like mortal combat, and Alfy pecked viciously at Tarzan's throat. They tumbled and fell from branch to branch until they hit the ground in a tight ball, flicker feathers floating down around them like softly falling autumn leaves. Exhausted, Tarzan managed to break free of Alfy's grasp and struggled valiantly back up the tree to assist Jane. But in an instant Alfy was on him again, and they fell once more to the ground in a flurry of plucked feathers.

By this time, Ethel was throwing the fourth and last of Jane's eggs out of the nest. That was it; the battle was over! Conceding defeat, Jane and Tarzan flew off. I never saw them again that summer.

I couldn't help feeling a deep sorrow over what had happened and a certain resentment toward the pillaging starlings. But I knew that was wrong of me. This was part of nature: survival of the fittest, as Charles Darwin would have said. Yet life can be hard on starlings. In captivity, they may live as long as sixteen years, but faced with the rigors of the wild, over half of them die before they reach even a year and a half of age. Alfy and Ethel turned out to be exemplary parents that summer, seeing to the needs of their ever-demanding brood of seven squawking chicks.

The following spring, they returned. All they had to do was tidy up the nest hole a bit, and Ethel could lay her eggs and incubate them straightaway. Our neighbors reported having seen Tarzan and Jane turn up once, but, no doubt realizing that Alfy and Ethel had already taken over the nest again, they saw no point in arguing ownership. The starlings went on to rear their second family.

But the third summer, Alfy and Ethel had already begun preparations for their next brood when, quite unexpectedly, Tarzan and Jane appeared. This time, they began to peck out a new hole for themselves about four feet beneath Alfy and Ethel's stolen nest. Within a day, Tarzan and Jane had completed it without interference from Alfy and Ethel in the "upstairs apartment." Peace and harmony finally reigned between the two couples.

October was rough that year, a sign of the hard winter to come. One night the winds raged, the rain lashed, and the thunder roared. A bolt of lightning must have struck the old tree during the night. By dawn's gray light I could see it lying on its side like a majestic bull elephant downed on a desolate African plain. A jagged brown scorch mark ran down the side of its split trunk.

In all the years since, no flickers have built another nest on our land, although they descend on the patchy lawn, sometimes in numbers, to scour for ants. Not a single starling has appeared again, though. I often wonder what was so special about that old elm tree.

4

Humor in Animals

The animal has all the emotions of humans, such as joy, grief,
fear, anger, love, hatred, strong desire, envy, and so on. The great
difference between human and animal rests solely on the intellect's
degrees of perfection.

—Arthur Schopenhauer (1788–1860)

If someone had asked me a few years ago, "Have you ever seen an instance of humor in apes?" I think I would have immediately answered, "Yes, of course." Then I might have stopped to reconsider my response for a moment. "Well," I might have added, "I've seen humor in chimps and orangutans, but I don't think I've ever seen it in gorillas." That would have been unfair of me, though, because I can't communicate with them. I can stand in front of a gorilla all day long, and nothing would pass between her head and mine. How, then, would I know if she were finding something funny or amusing? It's the same with sooty mangabeys, which are sooty-colored, long, skinny monkeys from Africa—just an empty void. I recall that I felt the same emptiness when I first met Loki, the elephant.

Then I might have gone a step further with the person who had posed the question: "Do you mean have I ever witnessed a moment of humor in an ape, or do I think apes have a sense of humor?" Is there a difference between these two questions? I think there might be. A sense of humor involves a certain degree of planning, even if only short-term, whereas a moment of humor might be in response to being tickled.

One of the fondest memories I have of sharing an animal's humor involved Samantha, or "Samanth," as I often called her, a truly sweet girl in her late thirties, a little skinny but full of fun. I was attending a LEMSIP staff meeting when a question came up regarding the precise design and dimensions of one style of cage that we used. No one could recall the details exactly.

Rather than rely on guesswork, I volunteered to go and get the necessary measurements and design details in one of the chimp rooms. I would be gone for no more than a few minutes, I assured everyone. I dropped by the workshop, picked up a tape measure, and made my way to the adult chimp colony.

Each chimp room had a double system of doors at either end: the outer doors, which led immediately into a small anteroom, and an inner set of doors, which gave access to the actual animal room. To prevent animals from escaping into the anteroom and beyond, these latter doors were secured by a heavy plastic bar, which was held in place by heavy-duty iron brackets.

Taking the security bar off the inner door, I entered the main room, picked the first communicating tunnel I came to, and reached in deep between the two cages to take the measurements I needed. I would have to be careful that someone didn't enter the anteroom and, seeing the security bar raised off the door, replace it, locking me in. No sooner had that thought crossed my mind than one of the technicians entered the anteroom and, not seeing me inside the main room through the small observation window in the door because I was hidden deep between two cages, replaced the bar, turned on his heel, and walked out. I hollered as loudly as I could, but the technician would not have been able to hear me above the din of the chimps responding to my shouting. I was locked in.

This was before the days of cell phones, and we already knew that two-way radios didn't work because of the interference from all the heavy steel work in the walls and ceilings of the chimp rooms. I rushed to the door and shouted repeatedly, hoping that someone outside would still be in range to hear me. Then I whistled as loudly as I could, but all to no avail. I stood looking at the chimps in the room and couldn't help thinking, I'm supposed to be more intelligent than you, yet I know you'd figure a way out of here in thirty seconds. *Think!* I kept saying to myself. *Think!*

If I could climb up on the iron rails that suspended the cages from the ceiling, I might be able to swing myself so that I could kick the doors and force the hinges or overpower the latches, but I was no Tarzan. My 130 pounds wouldn't even scrape the paint off the doors.

I carefully examined every square inch of the ceiling and every wall and corner, looking for some item or structure that I might be able to work to my advantage. The chimps were obviously mystified by my behavior, many of them looking up themselves to see what I was staring at on the ceiling or in the crannies of the walls.

The only thing I could find was a single three-foot-square ventilation hatch that opened between the end wall of the room by Samantha's cage into the anteroom next door. If I could find some way to undo the eight to ten hefty screws that held the hatch in place, I might be able to remove it and crawl through into the anteroom. "Would that Samantha like to help me?" I stooped to ask her. She huffed a series of coarse, raspy pants, her version of laughs, and nodded her head repeatedly, her way of saying, "Let's have some fun."

Of course, I didn't have a screwdriver, but I did happen to have a quarter in my pocket. Needless to say, I couldn't get enough purchase with it to undo the screw heads. What could I find that I could use as a screwdriver? "See the Samanth in a moment," I said, pinching her lips together.

I walked slowly around the room again, looking carefully about me for something I could use as a screwdriver. Then I noticed that the feeder and water container mounted on each cage had wide metal flanges that allowed the container to be slid into channels welded to the cage walls in the front. If I could get one of them off, I might be able to use the flange as an overly large screwdriver.

This task wouldn't be easy, and it might take me a while to accomplish. *Was it worth the effort?* I wondered. I looked at my watch; it was just before 11 o'clock. The caregivers had long ago finished cleaning the rooms, and they might be another half an hour before they began feeding the midday meal or handing out enrichment materials. *No*, I thought. *I can't just sit here and do nothing.*

The flanges on the feeders and water boxes were held in place by a number of heavy-duty bolts. I had nothing that I could use as a wrench. I went around each cage, checking to see if any of the containers were loose enough that I could slip it out of the retaining channel by rocking or jiggling it from side to side, but the bolts were securely screwed into place—except for the last one I tried. I couldn't believe my luck. The person who had replaced this particular water container had forgotten to tighten down the bolts. With a little difficulty, I managed to unscrew the bolts with my fingers. Now, would I be able to hold the aluminum water container and turn the flange in the groove on the screw heads in the ventilation hatch?

With the water container in hand, I returned to the hatch. Samantha was waiting for me; party time!

It took me a little while to figure out how best to hold the water container, which was about eighteen inches long by nine inches wide by six inches deep, so that I could turn it like a screwdriver.

Samantha sat watching what I was doing, hands folded across her knees, bouncing up and down every now and again, repeatedly trying to distract me so that I would stop and play with her. With quite a bit of difficulty, as every step in this process seemed to be taking, I finally undid the last screw and removed the vent panel from the air duct. There wasn't much room between the side of

Samantha's cage and the end wall of the room—three feet at most. I laid the panel on the floor, leaning it against the wall.

To my frustration, I found that the duct through the wall into the anteroom was much smaller than the ventilation hatch, only about eighteen inches square. To complicate matters further, I realized that I would not be able to reach the screw heads holding the vent panel in place on the outer surface of the wall in the anteroom; I would have to use the water container as a hammer and break the screw threads. The guys in the maintenance department would be pleased about that, I was sure.

In order to squeeze through such a narrow shaft, I would have to align my body in as near a horizontal plane as possible, with my arms stretched out in front of me, hands clasped, introducing my shoulders into the shaft at a diagonal (for once realizing that weighing only 130 pounds might have its advantages after all). To achieve this, I placed my feet on the bars of Samantha's cage and locked the edges of my heels on the lowest horizontal bar. I tried to raise my body up on my hands, about eighteen inches off the floor. It was truly difficult.

With many of the chimps, I would not have dared to risk exposing my legs to being scratched or even bitten, but I knew I could trust Samantha. She found the whole exercise to be great fun, obviously put on entirely for her benefit. Laughing her head off, she huffed and puffed nonstop as if she might go into cardiac arrest or respiratory collapse. Tickling me behind the knees and around the ankles with her bony fingers, she ran both her hands up and down the insides of my trouser legs nonstop.

After a good ten minutes of uncomfortable struggle, with Samantha continuing to tickle me, I finally got myself through the duct into the anteroom. It had taken me forty minutes to work out my escape. Not bad, for a human being. I lifted the security bar off the door, re-entered the room, kissed Samantha on the fingers, and told her what a good girl she had been.

Then I hurried back to the conference room, wondering how I was going to explain my long absence, only to be greeted by everyone breaking for lunch. So much for my colleagues! It seemed that not one of them had wondered what had happened to me or why I had been gone so long. On top of everything, I realized that I had forgotten to take the measurements. Ah, well! At least Samantha had had a good time.

Because of their genetic similarities to humans, we might readily accept humor to be an emotional trait of the great apes. Even some of the Old World monkeys—like the sixteen species of macaques, which are much further away from us on the evolutionary tree than the chimp and the other great apes—seem to enjoy taking advantage of others, whether fellow macaques or people.

One of my favorite games with the rhesus and Java macaques at the lab was to allow them to believe that they had stolen candies out of my pocket as I made my inspection rounds. This game was doubly fun for them because not only did they obtain an illicit treat, but they also had the satisfaction of outsmarting a human being. It even involved a certain short-term planning, the observing monkeys not giving the game away.

I would stand close to their cages as I passed down the length of the room, turning my back so that they could reach gently into my pocket and steal the candies, little white peppermints with red stripes that I would have taken from restaurant counters. The other monkeys in the room would look on silently, ready to rattle their cages and burst into barks, growls, and screeches of satisfaction: "You got him, you got him!"

Unlike Java macaques, rhesus monkeys are exquisite little thieves, as any tourist to an Indian temple can testify. I often used to think that Finnegan (an infant rhesus monkey my family and I had reared) and I could have made a fortune together back in the bazaars of Old Delhi, he stealing people's jewelry and hiding it in his cheek pouches, I selling it if I could get it off him later.

When I recently came to consider the question of humor in animals, I turned to Masson and McCarthy's book *When Elephants Weep*, my usual port of call when I want a quick assessment of a particular subject to do with animal emotions. To my disappointment, I discovered that their index references only one page for "Humor, sense of." References to other emotions and personality traits, ranging from aggression, empathy, and gratitude to altruism, compassion, and sadness, listed from six or seven to fifteen or more pages per topic. Their own review of the anthropological literature of the nineteenth and twentieth centuries led them to conclude, "Uniqueness is claimed for the human sense of humor, the ability to understand virtue, the ability to make and use tools." My search wasn't starting off too well, but I was not going to give up.

In his recent book *The Pattern Recognition Theory of Humour*, British science writer Alastair Clarke explains, "Humour occurs when the brain recognizes a pattern that surprises it, and that recognition of this sort is rewarded with the experience of the humorous response, an element of which is broadcast as laughter. It is not the content of the stimulus but the patterns underlying it that provide the potential for sources of humour." He goes on to explain, "Peek-a-boo can elicit a humorous response in [human] infants as young as four months, and is, effectively, a simple process of surprise repetition, forming a clear, basic pattern. . . . Understanding the basic function and mechanism of humour as it begins in infants will benefit the ongoing research into the presence of humour in primates and other mammals." *Humor in primates and other mammals?* I thought. *Encouraging!*

Perhaps the most clear-cut example of humor in a nonhuman animal that I have ever come across involved a monkey. His name was Bernard, and he was a very gentle, wise, old rhesus monkey in his early thirties. He had been the alpha male of the breeding colony for many years, the only male who had never once hurt another animal, female, male, or infant.

One evening at the end of a busy day at the lab, I was in my office trying to catch up on some paperwork. A tentative knock came at the door. It was a young technician, Mark, who had only recently been hired. He was filling in for an hour or two for the regular nighttime caregiver, who had come down with some type of illness, until a more experienced person could be called back to the lab to take over. He seemed very agitated. "Sorry to bother you, Doc, but one of the rhesus monkeys seems to be in trouble. I don't understand it; I saw all the monkeys in the room only half an hour ago, and they were fine. Then I went back to get something I'd left in the room, and one of the monkeys is dead. I can't believe it. He was perfectly fine."

"Could it be Bernard, by any chance, in room 106?" I asked.

"Yes," he replied, somewhat surprised. "How did you know that?"

"We have trouble with him every now and then. Let's go see him together."

We made our way to the room. Opening the outer door, I entered the small anteroom, with Mark close behind me. Through the large window in the inner door I could see Bernard's cage, which was about a third of the way down the room on the right-hand side of the central aisle. Bernard was sitting up, but as he saw me begin to open the door, he threw himself onto the floor of the cage. By the time we reached his cage, Bernard was lying on his back, his arms and legs sticking up in the air, his eyelids seemingly closed. To all intents and purposes, he was dead: except I saw his eyeball rotate just a little and his pupil look out at me through the slit between his not-quite-closed eyelid.

"Looks pretty bad," I said to Mark, as I tried to stifle a laugh. "Squat down and reach up under the floor of his cage and tickle his bottom to see whether he's conscious or not. Be careful, though. Never assume an animal is dead just because he's lying still on the floor of the cage, and never put your fingers through the bars of the cage in case the animal's not dead and ends up biting or scratching you. And whatever you do, don't let your face get close to the cage wires."

Obviously not feeling too comfortable about what I had asked him to do, Mark went down on his haunches, reached up cautiously under the cage floor, and gently prodded Bernard's bottom. All the monkeys in the immediate vicinity were silent, staring intently to see what was going to happen. Bernard exploded, jumping to his feet in an instant, rattling the bars of the cage with his hands, and issuing vocal threats, as did all the other monkeys. Mark almost collapsed onto the floor in fright.

"Don't feel bad about it," I shouted over the uproar of the monkeys. "He does this—pretends to be dead—to every new person. He did it to me when I first came here, and that was years ago. It means so much to him. He gets a real kick out of making a fool of you."

Bernard had done the same thing to Elizabeth Muchmore, the resident physician at the lab in charge of infectious disease programs, who delighted in telling visiting scientists that she had started out in 1965 as LEMSIP's MD (Monkey Doctor) before it had a veterinarian.

Mark turned out to be one of our best technicians, always sensitive to the needs of the animals and deeply concerned about their plight in captivity.

To me, what was so amazing about Bernard's antics was that he recognized people as new, but once he had initiated them, he never repeated his performance on them again. Was his purpose to lure people into believing he really was dead so that he could grab their finger if they jabbed him, or was it just to give them a fright when he jumped up? He seemed to recognize that he could play his trick only once on each person.

How much we deprive these wonderful animals by our way of keeping them in captivity.

We tend to think that only *Homo sapiens* can really laugh or have a sense of humor or feel compassion or empathy for another. Our unique ability to make and use tools used to be considered one of the hallmarks of our being human; that was until Jane Goodall came along in 1960 and blasted that theory to Timbuktu. She discovered that chimps (David Greybeard and Goliath) at Gombe, Tanzania, used long twigs from which they had stripped the leaves to extract termites from deep inside their mounds. Since then, other scientists have discovered that chimpanzees may use other cultural types of tools, such as rocks, which they keep in little piles on the ground in defined places to smash fruits and nuts, or wads of stripped leaves, which they use to soak up water from holes in trees. In the Ivory Coast in West Africa, prehistoric evidence has even shown that chimps may have been using rock tools as far back as 4,300 years ago.

Ah, but they are chimps, some might respond. They are our closest living relatives, and we diverged from each other on the evolutionary tree only four to six million years ago; you would expect them to share some of our primitive discoveries.

Who would imagine, then, that Java monkeys in Thailand have been filmed using human hair that they pick up off the streets or pluck from the scalps of unsuspecting tourists as dental floss, and then teach their infants how to do the same? But they are monkeys, closer to us in terms of evolution than most animals.

Then what about New Caledonian crows (*Corvus moneduloides*)? They are just birds, only one or two classes further up the evolutionary ladder than the amphibians and reptiles. Yet research over the last ten years has shown that they actually create and craft twigs and metal wires to extract grubs from crevices and deep holes in branches and tree trunks, to the point of creating hooks of different sizes and curvatures with a finesse and speed that would put chimps, orangutans, and monkeys to shame (surpassed in skill only by human beings).

So, could fish have a sense of humor? I can hardly imagine a crocodile finding anything amusing, but I can imagine a big, fat toad having a chuckle. A fish? Who knows?

* * * * *

It was a pleasantly warm day in mid-May, one of those days that makes you feel good to be alive. The leaves of the maples and ash trees still had that delicate clean-scrubbed look of spring, and the cherry blossoms were out in full by the stream. Magnolia warblers in profusion, with a few yellow warblers mixed in, flitted from tree to tree, their delicate, short *ssttss-ssttss* sounds carrying on the light breeze. A catbird was already mewing, angry that I had invaded her territory, and way off in the distance I could hear the repetitive, monotonous call of a Baltimore oriole.

I stepped onto the little wooden humpbacked bridge that spans the stream and leaned my elbows on the railing. Gazing aimlessly down into the water, I suddenly realized that there was a large-mouth bass beneath the bridge, a foot or so in length. Motionless except for the rhythmic opening and closing of his mouth, the non-stop wavering of his pectoral fins, and the figure-eight fanning of his tail, he seemed to be in suspended animation.

He must have realized that I had seen him because he immediately went into reverse gear and disappeared from view beneath the deck of the bridge. With the greatest care, so as not to make any noise or vibration that might frighten him, I turned on the balls of my feet, leaned over the parapet on the other side of the bridge, and looked down into the water. There he was again, just his nose sticking out this time. I repeated this maneuver back and forth maybe half a dozen times, and each time he shot back under the bridge only to reappear on the other side.

Was he testing me, just as I was testing him, to see if I would play his game? He was playing hide-and-seek with me, there was no doubt in my mind about that.

Realizing that my presence seemed not to cause him any distress, I announced loudly, "I'm going for a walk. If that little fish wants to come with me, he can." To my amazement, as I took my first step off the bridge onto the embankment, he shot forward in the water, overtook me by three or four feet, and then kept a steady pace ahead of me as I walked toward the pond. If I turned to retrace my steps, he would turn; if I stopped, he would stop, but always a few feet ahead of me. We were playing follow-the-leader, with him as the leader and me as the follower.

I continued to play with him for what must have been the better part of an hour, during which time I carried out a series of simple behavioral experiments. If I stood facing the opposite bank at the widest part of the stream, he would face me directly, about ten feet away. If I squatted on my haunches, he would come to within five feet or so of me. If I immersed my finger in the water, he would approach to within two feet, and if I wiggled my finger in the water, he would shoot forward to almost touch my fingertip. Who would imagine that a fish could be capable of transspecies communication at a level like this?

Excited though I was about my new friend, I was hesitant to announce to anyone, including my wife, Marie-Paule, that I had been talking to a fish for the past hour. People might think I had finally gone insane. Anyway, I was sure there was a ready and logical explanation for the fish's behavior.

When I got back home, I phoned Arnold, our neighbor on the other side of the pond. "Arnold, do you ever feed the fish in the pond?"

"No," he said.

"Do you think Brenda might sometimes?"

"No. Why?" he replied in a mystified tone.

"I was just thinking, it might not be a good idea if we did. It could easily put the fish at risk of being eaten by the herons and kingfishers."

There was a certain reason for my falsely professed concern. I had often seen fishermen lined up along the banks of the canals in Holland, spaced fifty feet or so apart, with great blue herons standing sentinel-like between them, ready to grab the first fish that appeared—not the least bit concerned by the proximity of the fishermen. A kingfisher was as likely to make a high-speed vertical dive from the top of a nearby tree or overhanging branch, beating both the heron and the fisherman to the catch. I felt pretty sure, however, that a fish the size of my "little fish" was too big for a heron or king-fisher to catch. Arnold's assurance that neither he nor Brenda had habituated the fish in the pond to being hand-fed suggested that the fish's response to me was spontaneous in nature.

I still had not told Marie-Paule about my piscine behavioral study, when, a few days later, she asked me whether I would like to read a fiction story she had written for young children and give her my opinion. "You will think I've gone crazy," she said. "It's called *The April Fish*. It's about an elderly bachelor who starts to talk to a fish that he sees in a pet shop window that he passes every evening."

I wasn't sure how to take her remark that I might think she was crazy for writing such a story. Did it mean she would definitely think I had gone over the edge by actually talking to a fish? I liked the story immensely and found myself admitting to Marie-Paule that I had had this encounter with a fish in the pond. I emphasized to her that he was the one who had started it, not me. I'd swear she gave me a slightly sideways look.

I keep referring to the fish as "him," but there is no easy way to tell the sex of a largemouth bass. Both sexes have the same promi-nent black line along each side of the body and a divided dorsal fin. An adult female is said to be bigger than a male, but I think our pond, being only about a fifth of an acre in size, is probably too small to allow the fish to attain the full physical characteristics of the species. In the more than thirty years we have lived here, never has more than one fish attained a distinctly larger size than any other. Only once could I positively identify the same largest fish from one year to the next, in this case over three consecutive years, because he was missing his left eye.

The other fish showed a distinct deference to my "little fish," including two fish that formed an inseparable pair and were only slightly smaller than he. In fact, the largest fish would become quite aggressive if the two smaller ones came between him and me, and he would chase them off. I don't think these fish were interested in the least in interacting with me, and they behaved quite skittishly if I moved too briskly or they found themselves too close to me.

It was his behavior more than anything that convinced me he was male. As spring progressed, he began to spend more time in a serpentine bend in the stream, where the water was deepest. It was at this spot every spring that the largest fish in the pond would make a nesting place by fanning his tail and fins above the mud bed of the stream in obvious preparation for the females to come and lay their eggs. Presumably, the male would then deposit his sperm over the eggs (although I never witnessed this), and the fry would hatch later. The minute fry, numbering in the scores if not the hundreds— hardly bigger than three hyphens on a page—would have to take refuge amid a patch of water plants that grew close by in the stream, or the other fish would eat them up in an instant.

My routine rendezvous with the fish started each morning after breakfast. I would call out to our dog, "Ragsie, let's go see the fish," and she would rush down the stairs of the veranda with me in excitement. I think her enthusiasm was more in anticipation of seeing the frogs, especially the bullfrogs, than the fish, which she seemed to find quite boring.

I would stand on the bank of the stream or by the pond and shout out repeatedly, "Has anyone seen that little fish? Where is he?"—always the same phrases—until he showed up. "There he is, that little fish," I would say as he sailed right up to me. But I could tell that Rags was never able to see the fish. The frogs, on the other hand, offered her all sorts of excitement as they screamed and threw themselves into the water upon her arrival.

After ten or fifteen minutes of walking and talking, I'd announce, "Bye, that little fish. See him tomorrow."

I continued to talk to him (with Rags joining in) every day throughout the summer and into the autumn, when all the fish retreat to the deeper water of the pond to take up their winter residence.

Come late March the following year, the winter ice on the pond had finally melted. I began to look carefully each day for the reappearance of the "little" fish. The days went by, but I never saw him again, although I did see what I presumed were the same pair of somewhat smaller fish who still followed each other closely. He had been only a little fish, yet I felt that something truly unique and special had gone forever.

On our last vacation to Jamaica, in 2008, Marie-Paule and I discovered a fantastic little island off the northwest coast with spectacular snorkeling possibilities. The corals were in good condition, which is hard to find these days, and the fish were plentiful. After a little while of snorkeling with Marie-Paule, I decided to go off on my own and explore the other side of the island.

What a difference! As far as I could see, the waters off the western side of the island were an endless wasteland, like a derelict city after a war of the worlds. Blobs of sea grass waved to and fro in the gray, featureless desert. One blob was different from the others, however. It had one piece of dead brain coral, its own frond of live purple fan coral, a large sea urchin as sentinel, and one lonely little fish. He reminded me of Antoine de Saint-Exupéry's Little Prince, who had one flower and three volcanoes to look after on his tiny planet.

As I slowly approached his Lilliputian kingdom, the little fish shot out to attack me in a rapid series of sorties, returning to hide behind the sea urchin each time. *What a cheeky little squirt*, I thought. I continued to slowly circle the lump of brain coral, wiggling my fingers at him very gently every now and then.

As best as I could tell, he was a dusky damselfish, just one of the many species in the damselfish family. He was rather an ordinary-looking, dull, dirty-brown or grayish little chap, with a hint of purple at certain angles, depending on whether the clouds were covering the sun, or the sand was disturbed in the water. He was no more than four inches long. My *Guide to Corals and Fishes of Florida, the*

Bahamas and the Caribbean describes these fish as "small but pugnacious" and says that they "will nip at large fish or even divers when their territory is threatened," which seemed to describe this little loner to a T.

After a while, the little fish gave up his attacks and began to approach me gently, as if he wanted to nibble my fingertips. *Why would one little fish want to stay out on his own in a spot like this?* I wondered. He had practically no protection, no deep crevices in an endless shelf of coral to hide in. His little piece of brain coral was barely bigger than a football. And I could hardly imagine a sea urchin providing much company.

Marie-Paule and I visited the island every morning for the rest of our vacation, and I would go off on my own to see the little fish. He would see me coming from some distance away and swim out to greet me. I couldn't help thinking of the fish I had known in the pond at home.

I'm not sure that the behavior of the little Jamaican fish constituted a sense of humor, but it did show a recognition of friendship, which is perhaps a starting point for humor. The hide-and-seek play of the bass at home was certainly suggestive of a sense of humor.

Marie-Paule and I revisited the area for our vacation in the early winter of 2009. I was unable to locate the piece of brain coral, or even the landmarks that I had used before to determine its position. There were plenty of pieces of dead coral scattered about, but none had a purple fan coral for decoration or a sea urchin on guard, and there were no dusky damselfish to be seen. The local fishermen told me that there had been a hurricane, which had picked everything up in the air "and slammed it down again, hard, Mon; hard!" It had spoiled a lot of the fishing for a while, they said.

I wondered what might have become of the little fish.

5

Personality in Animals

If you have anything really valuable to contribute to the world it will come through the expression of your own personality, that single spark of divinity that sets you off and makes you different from every other living creature.

—Bruce Barton (1886–1967)

There was a time, not so long ago, when no one in his or her right mind would have applied the word *personality* to nonhuman animals—especially not a scientist. Since the early 1990s, though, things have changed, and all sorts of respectable scientists are beginning to use the term to describe species ranging from octopuses to water strider insects.

The majority of scientists, however, still shy away from accepting that animals might have personalities, just as they disapprove of naming animals in research colonies, for fear that they will be accused by other scientists of being anthropomorphic—one of the greatest sins a scientist can commit. "After all," they would say, "isn't one of the definitions of personality the quality of existing as a person?"

The late Vincent Dethier, a professor of zoology and psychology who studied insects at the University of Pennsylvania, wrote in a paper titled "Microscopic Brains" published in the March 13, 1964, issue of *Science:* "The farther removed an animal is from ourselves, the less sympathetic we are in ascribing to it those components of behavior that we know in ourselves. There is some fuzzy point of transition in the phylogenetic scale where our empathizing acquires an unsavory aura. Yet there is little justification for this schism. If we subscribe to an idea of a lineal evolution of behavior, there is no reason for failing to search for adumbrations of higher behavior in invertebrates."

In a fascinating in-depth and amusing article entitled "The Animal Self," published in the January 22, 2006, edition of the *New York Times,* Charles Siebert reported on a 1993 landmark study by Seattle Aquarium animal behaviorist Roland Anderson and Canadian psychologist Jennifer Mather. The study looked at animal personality in, of all species, red octopuses. Not only was Anderson and Mather's paper the first description of personality in invertebrates (backboneless animals), but it was the first time that the term *personality* had been applied to a nonhuman animal in a major scientific journal.

Using three categories from one of the standard human personality assessment tests—shyness, aggressiveness, and passiveness—the researchers carried out the study on forty-four red octopuses. One of the main stimuli they used to study the octopuses' reactions was to throw crabs into their tanks. "The aggressive ones would pounce on the crab," Anderson told Siebert during his visit to the aquarium. "The passive ones would wait for the crab to come past and then grab it. The shy animal would wait till overnight when no one was looking, and we'd find this little pile of crab shell in the morning." The study opened up a brand-new field of science known simply as Animal Personality.

Since that study, the field has blossomed to cover a wide range of species, from nonhuman primates to hyenas, birds, stickleback fish, and even water striders and fruit flies, the latter being the most commonly used species of animal in research.

In response to the growing awareness of personality in animals, Professor Jaak Panksepp, a psychologist and neuroscientist at Bowling Green State University, who was the first to discover that rats laugh when they are tickled, pointed out, "Every drug used to treat emotional and psychiatric disorders in humans was first developed and found effective in animals. This kind of research would obviously have no value if animals were incapable of experiencing these emotional states."

"Scientists," Siebert notes, "are beginning to get at the essence of that one aspect of the self we have long thought to be exclusively and quintessentially ours: the individual personality." He concludes his article, "Perched now, like entranced children, along the banks of their respective simulated streams, scientists are staring for hours at the least human of creatures—everything from bullying fruit flies to ravenous, oversexed water striders and fishing spiders to perilously fearless hordes of armored stickleback fish—and are beginning to see in them not just their distinct patterns of behavior but also something deeply and distinctly recognizable. Something, well, not altogether inhuman."

You don't have to be a rocket scientist to know that dogs and cats have personalities, even though they are not persons. But probably few people think that way about the birds and other wildlife that surround us in our gardens, parks, and even alleyways and garbage dumps. Yet discovering personalities in these creatures is just a matter of looking and listening carefully.

For quite a few years, two pairs of purple finches have resided in nests among the ivy that grows on the concrete wall of our garage, one nest on either side of the vent pipe from the clothes dryer situated at the far end of the kitchen on the floor above. In deepest winter, slate-colored juncos take over the nests, at least on the coldest nights. That creates a bit of a problem, actually, if we forget that the birds might be there and inadvertently open the side door to the garage. The purple finches wouldn't be put out by this type of sudden disturbance, but the juncos are very nervous around human beings, and they take off into the darkness in panic. Then I feel I have to leave the light on in the rear vestibule of the house that shines through the windowpanes in the door in case the juncos can't find their way back to the nest in the dark. That requires that I don't forget to go back twenty or thirty minutes later to turn the light off. What a pain!

For the past three years, we have played host to the same two pairs of purple finches; this I can tell from the henpecked male and the cold-hearted female of one pair.

Purple finches are usually very happy little birds as they fly out of their nest to perch on the tip of a favorite tree branch, even if only for a few minutes' break from incubating their eggs or feeding their young. They burst into instantaneous song, getting so carried away with themselves that they almost fall off the branch. Mrs. Grouch doesn't, however. Every time her lovelorn male comes anywhere near her, she turns and pecks at him. If he persists in his amorous advances, she flies off. I feel sorry for him.

I was not confident that the purple finches would return this past spring, in 2009. The winter was marked by frequent snowfalls and almost constant low temperatures, trapping the grass and shriveled autumn leaves beneath a thick layer of ice. Denied one of their major sources of food, our resident herd of seven deer that included twins born the previous spring had to avail themselves of whatever nourishment they could find. On one particularly cold night, they really went to town on the ivy, stripping many of the long, creeping branches off the wall and eating almost all the leaves. The two finch nests became dislodged from deep within the ivy and hung down sideways, no longer hidden by the ivy leaves. Surprisingly, the juncos continued to use both nests on and off throughout the winter, although I can't imagine how they were able to sit or lie in them.

When spring came, two pairs of purple finches made half-hearted attempts to repair the nests but quickly gave up. Mrs. Grouch was not one of them. I have since pruned the ivy and strengthened it. Hopefully the purple finches will return next year.

Every time I used to see Mrs. Grouch, I was reminded of a most amusing incident that involved Herbie and Mona, two chimpanzees in the breeding colony at LEMSIP.

Every year we would invite a class of students from the anthropology department of New York University in Manhattan to visit the lab. We started with a short lecture about the various primate species at LEMSIP and the types of research in which they were used; then, suitably dressed in protective clothing, we began a tour of the animals. First we visited the marmosets and tamarins, tiny primates from South America. Then we moved on to the various Old World species of macaques and baboons, and finally we called on the adult chimps and, most popular of all with the students, made a hands-on visit to the chimpanzee nursery and socialization unit.

The vast majority of the students who visited the lab over the years were deeply opposed to using animals, especially nonhuman primates, in research and made no apologies for their views. Yet every year we would end up recruiting two or three additions to our volunteer program following such visits. Some of these students volunteered at the lab until they finished their degrees or went on to pursue higher degrees. Five spent a summer each in training at the lab to learn basic veterinary medical skills, like taking blood samples, testing for parasites, and providing technical and surgical assistance to veterinarians working in sanctuaries or in the field in Africa and Southeast Asia.

Before taking the students on the tour, I gave them a short orientation lecture on how to behave around chimpanzees: "No sudden noises, no pointing fingers or waving hands, no laughing out loud until the chimps get used to you. Above all, for your safety, do not under any circumstances come close to the cages or try to touch the animals, no matter how much they seek your attention, or they may try to grab you. It is best to squat or sit on your haunches or sit cross-legged on the floor in front of them. If an animal spits on you, ignore it: Don't scream, or all the chimps in the room will know they have your measure." I finished by saying that after we had spent some time talking to the animals, we had everything set up in the room to watch a video, *The Lion King*. "Don't talk to them or make it obvious that you are observing them, or you will distract them."

The Lion King was the favorite of all the species, from the smallest five-and-a-half-ounce marmosets, who usually were disinterested in television, to the largest adult male chimps, weighing 150 pounds or more, outdoing in popularity any *National Geographic* nature documentary and even Jane Goodall specials.

I sat down on the floor in front of Herbie and Mona's cage. After a while, I sensed that Herbie was beginning to get agitated: He desperately wanted to watch the video, but Mona was sitting in his way, so he could not see the television screen. Seeing the scene that was beginning to unfold to my side, I tried as unobtrusively as possible to catch the students' attention by pointing a finger into cupped hand toward Herbie. By now he was grasping Mona gently about her waist with both hands and trying to nudge her to one side, just twelve inches or so, but that didn't work. In frustration, Herbie began to rhythmically bang his heel on the floor of the cage. This is Chimpanzee for "I want sex." Mona paid no attention to his exhortations and carried on watching the movie. Herbie tried to coax her by grasping her waist while continuing to stamp his heel, but that made no difference, either. In frustration, deprived of telly *and* love, Herbie gave up, walked over to sit himself down in the farthest corner of the cage, and masturbated. The students gripped their cheeks or pulled on their chins, desperately trying not to laugh out loud. I am sure they will remember that little sitcom for the rest of their lives.

One of the many delights of animals, and small children when you think about it, is their naturalness and refreshing spontaneity. Of course, with an animal like a chimpanzee, especially one as special as Herbie, you would expect a degree of depth and sophistication in his emotions, always a bit more than what you see on the surface. Given the choice at that moment, would he have preferred to watch the movie, or did he really feel that a little romantic fling with Mona would be so much better?

By sheer chance over the years, I have recorded a number of observations in my birdwatcher's diary that still make me wonder or laugh as I recall the incidents. I happened to see a male blue jay one time performing a mating ritual before a female on the oak tree in front of our house. I had never seen such behavior in blue jays before, never thought of them as the type of bird that would exhibit such intricate behavior. He fanned his tail and bounced up and down before the female, over and over again, while he uttered soft, barely audible squeaks. She must have been impressed, because she let him mount her. Then the universe exploded. From a branch way above, a male robin dive-bombed the pair, knocking the male blue jay completely off the female. *What was that all about?* I wondered. Had the robin just taken advantage of a rare opportunity to physically attack a blue jay, knowing he would get away with it? Did he feel that other birds couldn't participate in such behavior in his territory? Or was he just feeling ornery that day?

You would hardly describe orneriness as being an individualistic personality trait of pearly-eyed thrashers: grumpiness and bad temper are the distinctive hallmarks of all the species that make up the genera and families to which pearly-eyed thrashers belong. They are genetically programmed to be irritable and uncooperative. The characteristic cross-eyed glare of the pupils and the dazzling white of the irises of their eyes, along with their grumpy tone of voice, like the hostile mewing of a feral cat, let you know that you are not high on their list of ones to be trusted.

Marie-Paule and I had our first run-in with the species when we rented a little house in Virgin Gorda in the British Virgin Islands, during the same visit when we came across Ragsie.

Every evening, Marie-Paule cooked by an outdoor grill on the patio. We soon discovered that the tiny house with its small plot of land was part of a pearly-eyed thrasher's larger territory, and he made it very plain that he expected us to pay a toll for using his property. He had the audacity to try and bully Marie-Paule into frequently giving him small pieces of whatever meat she was cooking. As soon as she turned her back, he would make a lightning-fast attack and peck her on the tip of her elbow. As you can imagine, this was very painful, and Marie-Paule implored me to control the bird.

"Listen, you!" I would threaten him with a pointed wag of my finger. "I'll wring his scrawny little neck if he doesn't stop." He would immediately respond by running half the length of the table toward me and cawing, as if to say, "Oh, yeah? You and who else?" Invariably, I would not be able to keep myself from laughing, which made him all the angrier. He brought back memories of years gone by, when we had the infant rhesus monkeys, Finnegan and Erin, at home with us. When we would first arrive home after our day at the lab, Finnegan would feel he had to remind my younger son Christopher that *he*, not Finnegan, was the lowest member on the family totem pole. For ten minutes, Finn would chase Christopher around the kitchen, threatening him with open mouth and vicious sounding *grr* growls. The situation would only be made worse if one of us laughed. Just like the pearly-eyed thrasher, Finnegan would become incensed, although he never once actually attacked Christopher.

Our most notable encounter with pearly-eyed thrashers, however, was on Vieques, a small island off the northeast coast of Puerto Rico. We were staying for eight days in a remote spot in the hills

Our courageous pearly-eyed thrasher surveys the scene from a tree branch.

overlooking El Yunque National Forest far off on the mainland to the west and the U.S. Virgin Islands to the east.

The house had a somewhat Japanese style to it: a spacious kitchen combined with a dining and sitting room. Completely separate was a bedroom-bathroom combination. A single, continuous, richly tiled roof tied all the living spaces together, including the broad breezeway, which separated the sleeping and day quarters. The concrete walls, abundantly studded with French windows, reflected the soft hues of the setting sun.

On the first morning in the villa, I couldn't help noticing the constant comings and goings of a pair of pearly-eyed thrashers to their nest located somewhere up inside the eaves of the roof over the walkway. The parents alternated, more or less equally, in feeding their young. The favorite foods of the nestlings appeared to be mangoes, the black cherry–colored berries of fishtail palms, and the odd insect. Like our thrasher friend from Virgin Gorda, this pair never missed an opportunity to protest our presence.

A little larger than an American robin or mockingbird, the pearly-eyed thrasher has a dark brown head and upper body with an off-white throat and lower body. The male can be differentiated from the female with difficulty by the greater contrast between the brown and off-white feathers and the shockingly white feathers of the underside of the tail. The female is shier and less aggressive. The most striking feature of both sexes is the eyes, especially the contrast between the black pupil and the surrounding, glaringly white iris that tends to give the bird a permanently bad-tempered expression (which goes along with its general demeanor).

In the predawn light of our second morning in the villa, I was awakened by a loud thud, as if a body had struck one of the glass panes of the bedroom's French windows. I knew what had caused that sound, I was sure. "Damn," I said to myself as I rushed out of the bedroom in my pajamas. Sure enough, there on the tiled veranda lay the lifeless body of one of the thrasher parents: the female, I judged from the dull coloration of the feathers. Her head hung limp on a broken neck, her body still warm. What a disaster! How would the babies survive the loss of their mother? Would the male continue to feed them? Even if he did try to carry on supporting them, would he be able to provide them enough food all on his own?

I placed her body on the earth, hidden by one of the flowering plants. I would bury her after breakfast—a thoughtless plan that I would later deeply regret. I should have buried her immediately and not left her lying there.

I had not stopped to consider whether the male might have seen me handling his mate when I first found her. I had no idea whether birds in general, and pearly-eyed thrashers in particular, had notions of death. The babies were doomed, I was sure, and there was little or nothing I could do about it. Yet to do nothing seemed callous.

I needed to find out whether the father was actually feeding his young or, just by rote, visiting the nest. I discovered that he used a complicated flight pattern to approach the nest. Instead of turning directly left into the walkway as he returned from the fruit trees, he would fly on past at high speed to a dense patch of trees beyond the house. He would then turn and double back on his flight path, just below the level of the eaves of the overhanging roof, and only then make the sharp right-hand turn into the breezeway. I realized that this was a clever ruse on his part to confuse any pursuing bandit bent on attacking the nest or his babies.

Time and again, I tried to find a hidden position where I could observe where he went and what he did once he entered the breezeway, but everything happened so fast that he would disappear from sight, an elusive will-o'-the-wisp. I never once saw him depart the area: he must have used a different route altogether.

I decided I had no option but to take one of the ladders stored in the garage and climb up and examine the area beneath the eaves of the roof. That would risk my coming face to face with the male if he returned while I was on the ladder. That might be all it would take to frighten him off from looking after his brood. I would have to be careful and fast.

I got the ladder and hid it by leaning it up against one of the palm trees close to where I assumed the nest might be located. I estimated that I had at least five minutes to complete the task once he left the nest. As soon as he did, I quickly positioned the ladder against the wall and climbed up.

There it was, in the eaves of the roof over the walkway, hidden in a space behind an angle brace and a rafter. The parents had picked an ideal spot. The nest was a meager, haphazard arrangement of dried fan palm flower stems. It was out of sight to all but the most prying eyes, and even then, its precise location would not be disclosed unless the three scraggy chicks within stretched their scrawny necks into the air and gave themselves away. I made a sucking sound with my lips—my attempt at mimicking a bird sound—and all three babies responded, necks stretched up, mouths gaping like little cement mixers. Dad was doing his job; what a trooper. The nest was even clean.

To my delight, I found that one of the French windows situated in the corner of the sitting room overlooked the nest. With any luck, it would afford me a constant view of the nest from inside the room. I went inside to investigate.

Standing tiptoe on a wooden chair, I could just about see into the nest without disturbing the babies. The male would be different: If he appeared suddenly from behind the rafter, we would come face to face, and he would freak out.

The chicks were fairly well grown and required a great deal of feeding. How Dad managed to keep going was amazing to me, sortie after sortie to find insects and fruit from dawn to dusk. He must have been exhausted.

In the late afternoon of our last full day on the island, all hell broke loose, with constant shrieking and cawing. The commotion came from the front of the house, on the edge of the roof over the breezeway. Scanning through the windows, I saw a flurry of bird wings. Our male was under attack from three other male pearly-eyed thrashers.

Grabbing my binoculars, I rushed out the back door of the sitting room, making my way to the end of the house so that I could hide behind some bushes to see what was going on. I did not dare intervene or make my presence known. The intruders, one or two at a time or all three at once, swooped down in constant frontal and rear attacks. Spinning on the spot or thrusting forth, our resident male tenaciously kept them at bay, rebutting their every move, never once conceding his spot on the roof or making any attempt to retreat to his nest. It would have been all over for his family had he done either: He would have given away the secret of the nest's location.

It was almost dark when the attackers suddenly gave up and flew off. They had been at it for a good hour and a half. I had no doubts that they would be back at dawn. There was no way our male could keep up the defense on his own.

Come dawn, however, all was peaceful—just the normal morning chorus of birdsongs. The male went off again on his food rounds as if nothing untoward had happened the evening before.

Marie-Paule and I were due to leave for the airport at around noontime. Two new guests were scheduled to arrive a few hours after our departure. I quickly drew some notices explaining to all and sundry the story of the male and his brood of three chicks, and asked their help in trying to make sure that nothing terrible happened to them. I stuck one notice on the refrigerator door and another by the chair next to the French window overlooking the nest.

Bags packed, I made one last trip to the chair overlooking the nest. The young were waking up. I had forgotten to check when the male had last visited. Taking me by surprise, he suddenly appeared, hopping over the rafter into the nest. We came face to face, no more than eighteen inches apart, only a pane of glass separating us. For a brief second, we stared into each other's eyes, and perhaps into each other's souls. What a remarkable little guy he had been: he had reared his young after the loss of his mate, he had slaved to feed his young day after day, he had kept the secret of the nest's location, and he had protected his family from three ferocious marauders single-handedly. I would never forget this little hero.

The owner of the villa—Dr. Ben, as we referred to him—informed us later that the visitors who came after us had witnessed the safe fledging of the brood. Since then, four broods have been successfully reared in the same secret location, whether by the same male or not, I wouldn't like to say.

6

A Story of Love

Piglet sidled up to Pooh from behind. "Pooh!" he whispered. "Yes, Piglet?" "Nothing," said Piglet, taking Pooh's paw. "I just wanted to be sure of you."

—A. A. Milne (1882–1956)

Of all the animals I ever worked with in the research laboratory, the two infant rhesus monkeys Finnegan and Erin were to have the most profound effect on me, next to Spike Mulligan, the chimp. Theirs is a story of love. It is also a story about the struggle to succeed.

For the first five days after she gave birth to him, Finnegan's mother, Dime, gave all appearances of being a good mother. However, on the sixth day she turned on him, biting and scratching him severely around the head, for reasons I was never able to determine with any certainty.

Terry, the young technician in charge of the lab's rhesus monkey breeding colony, found Finnegan abandoned on the floor of the cage when he walked into the monkey room early that morning. Using a small hand towel, he worked the nearly lifeless little infant through the bars of the cage across the floor until he could open the

Finnegan leaves his incubator on his own for the first time—
a big step in the world.

sliding door, reach in quickly, and grab hold of him. Terry had to
be supremely careful to avoid being attacked by the other monkeys
in the adjoining larger cage; infant kidnapping is a major crime in
the rhesus monkey world. Only when he was clear of danger did he
call me over the loudspeaker to come to room 109, "stat!"

I realized immediately that Finnegan was ice-cold and barely conscious, but Terry had already wrapped him in the towel and pushed him down inside his surgical scrub shirt to warm him. He offered Finnegan glucose solution by mouth through a small one-milliliter syringe so as not to risk choking him.

What are we going to do with him? I wondered. His mother had almost killed him. He would need to be fed at least every two hours around the clock and given a lot of cuddles and love. This was in the days before we had developed what I liked to call a real nursery at the lab. I would have no alternative but to take him home with me.

Along with an incubator, I gathered all the paraphernalia I would need to feed him and keep him clean. I told my wife, Marie-Paule, that it would be for only one night or so, because I was sure I could find another female in the colony to rear him. Marie-Paule had heard this story before, but at least with rejected newborn chimps, they more or less stay put wherever you place them. Finnegan, now that he had gained some energy under Terry's care, was already able to run and jump and get into mischief. Stuffed down inside my shirt, however, he fell into a deep sleep, his little lips mumbling softly.

Over the next two or three days, Terry and I worked together, first trying to find out why Finnegan's mother had rejected him and then trying to coax her into taking him back. This required her to be mildly sedated. Dime had only small amounts of milk in each breast, although it seemed to be of a normal consistency. I would have expected her to have abundant milk considering that Finn had probably not suckled her recently. Her nipples were not bruised, cut, or inflamed in any way, suggesting that the infant had not injured her through his suckling. He had no teeth at this stage any-way. The most likely cause of her turning on her infant was stress. Dime was a young, first-time mother with a nervous disposition. Perhaps a hormonal imbalance had caused her milk supply to decline, and the baby's constant demands to be fed were more than

Erin munches on a piece of straw on her first day at the Fejervary Zoo.

she could handle. Infant rejection by first-time mothers is quite common in captive colonies.

After completing Dime's physical examination under tranquilization, we turned our attention to trying to get the baby to hold her chest and take her nipples in his mouth. He suckled well, though he seemed a little uncomfortable with us holding her arms around his body. As Dime began to recover from the sedative's effects, however, she started to push Finnegan away quite violently. When she fully regained consciousness, she lashed out at him, sending him flying across the floor of the cage. Poor little Finn looked like a landlocked crab, desperately reaching out to his mother. We had no choice but to remove him from the cage and place him in an incubator. A repeat of our efforts over the following couple of days gave no better results.

LEMSIP's rhesus monkey breeding colony was quite small, offering us few options to try to resolve Finnegan's dilemma. In comparison, the colony at the Wisconsin Primate Center, where I had worked before coming to New York, included around 250 monkeys, giving colony manager Steve Eisele almost endless opportunities to find suitable foster mothers. In one last, desperate effort, Terry and I tried to foster Finnegan to the only other female in the colony, Loretta, who already had a baby, a 1-month-old female named Erin. My hope was that Loretta would have enough milk to support two infants. Alas, this plan didn't work out, either. Although she wasn't mean to Finn, Loretta made no effort to pick him up, and her own baby was quite confused by the whole exercise.

Consequently, just as with Spike, the infant chimp, I ended up taking Finnegan home from the lab every night to be cared for by Marie-Paule, our three children, and Angus, our adopted dog. Angus provided the perfect blend of tenderness and rough-and-tumble play for young animals to develop the self-confidence they would need to face the challenges they would encounter later in life.

It was a wonderfully revealing experience to watch Finnegan develop—the antics he got up to, his special relationships with each one of us, including Angus. Finn quickly adapted to the daily ritual of driving to and from work.

He dreaded saying goodbye to Marie-Paule and going back to the lab each morning. Once there, he had to be confined to his incubator for much of the time, although Terry and two recently hired caregivers—Roxanne, who would become a major force in our developing a nursery, and young Jim—went out of their way to give Finn the extra attention he so desperately needed. They carried him around on their shoulders or pushed him down inside their scrub tops, nestled in his ski hat, while they cleaned the small nursery room or attended to paperwork.

The drive to the lab was six miles as the crow flies but ten miles along the narrow, pothole-riddled road that wound its way through the forest. For most of the journey, Finnegan would sit on my shoulder, his arms wrapped tightly around my neck as he kept his eye on the traffic ahead. Then he would break away and explore the nooks and crannies of the inside of the car. These little disappearances

Finnegan saddles up with Angus for a ride in the forest.

used to worry me because I often could not tell what he was up to. Finnegan constantly fiddled with the turn signal lever or turned the overhead light on and off. On one occasion, he got his finger stuck in the cassette player and screamed his little head off until I was able to reach down and hold his hand loosely while I came to a gentle halt by the side of the road. On another occasion—his first real macho display of open-mouthed *grrr* threats, erect hair, and kinked tail—Finnegan threatened through the hatchback a police officer who was following closely behind in his patrol car.

I would step through the sliding door from the balcony as we arrived home, and Finnegan would jump straight into Marie-Paule's arms and nestle his head deep in under her chin. "Did Finnegan have a nice day at LEMSIP today?" would be Marie-Paule's first words. Finnegan would always answer with a sad, drawn-out lament. "No? It wasn't nice at LEMSIP today?" she would respond. "Oh, that must have been *te-rrib-le,*" she would stretch out the reply in her thick French accent, to which Finnegan would respond as if he were about to keel over and die. What these little conversations were about I could not guess, but they held great importance for Finn. Then he would throw himself off of Marie-Paule's neck, land on the countertop of the kitchen island, and pick up an Indian demitasse spoon. With some difficulty, he would scoop banana cereal from a baby jar that Marie-Paule left out for him every evening. And so began the routines that Finnegan came to know for the next six months.

Finnegan roughhoused every night with Angus, pinching him on the nose or grabbing him under the tummy and then running away as fast as he could, the length of the kitchen and back, just as Spike had done when he used to come home with me. As Finnegan got older, Angus would take him on his back to explore the woods. Then Finn would go and spend time with the three children individually, to play with Nathalie and her dolls in her walk-in cupboard, to see what Pádraig was up to with his homework, and to chase Christopher around the house.

* * * * *

We often have distorted impressions of the wild nature of primates because of the conditions under which we keep them in captivity. Could the chimpanzee we see at the zoo—the one who makes what appears to be buffoonish faces and throws his feces at the gawking crowd—truly be our next of kin? Could the capuchin monkey we see making endless repetitive circles, gone crazy from lifelong confinement to a cage, be the same graceful animal we see brachiating through the high forest canopy of the Amazon in *National Geographic* documentaries?

Just as misunderstood is the rhesus monkey, the one primate that has served humankind in the fight against disease more than any other during the last seventy years or so.

Rhesus monkeys living in the wild have quite complex social lives. The so-called alpha male, who makes the rules for the troop, and his second in command, the beta male, who makes sure that the rules are obeyed, are the top-ranking animals of the troop, but only if they are accepted as such by the top-ranking females. Young females stay in their natal groups and learn how to become good mothers by assisting their mothers in the care of younger brothers and sisters, and nephews and nieces. Young males have a harder life. At around 2 years old, they leave the troop into which they were born to form bachelor groups that roam the forest in search of other troops into which they might be accepted. It is estimated that only about 5 percent of the males are successful; the rest perish.

The rhesus monkey, or rhesus macaque as it is also called, is the best known and understood of all the primate species in terms of physiology and behavior. For that reason it is the main species used in the United States for drug testing and toxicology. Rhesus monkeys are also used in drug development of reproductively active pharmaceuticals, such as contraceptives and fertility-enhancing agents.

Rhesus monkeys are used in AIDS-related research as well. They do not have their own version of simian (monkey) immunodeficiency virus (SIV), but being an Asian species they are highly susceptible to the various African strains of SIV. In fact, SIV was first discovered quite fortuitously in 1985 in one of the U.S. National Primate Centers, when rhesus monkeys were injected intravenously with serum from sooty mangabeys, an African species of monkey that carries the virus naturally but does not, itself, suffer from AIDS-like disease. These rhesus monkeys were inadvertently infected with SIV and developed disease within about six weeks and died. Since then, more than forty species of African primates, including the chimpanzee, have been found to carry their own specific subspecies of SIV.

Scientists developed a genetically engineered virus that is composed of both simian and human immunodeficiency viruses known as SHIV, which allows them to carry out AIDS-like studies in the rhesus monkey.

Genetic studies strongly suggest that HIV-1, the most predominant cause of AIDS worldwide, had its origins in the chimpanzee in Africa. HIV-2, the human immunodeficiency virus mostly confined to people living in West Africa, appears to have originated in the sooty mangabey, the species from which SIV had inadvertently been transmitted experimentally to rhesus monkeys. The HIV-2 virus probably jumped from the sooty mangabey to humans through their eating or preparing contaminated bush meat.

The rhesus monkey's greatest contribution to the betterment of humankind, however, has undoubtedly been the role it played and is still playing in the World Health Organization's attempt to eradicate the poliomyelitis virus (polio). Rhesus monkeys were killed by the thousands every year to harvest their kidneys for tissue culture growth of the virus, and they were used to test the vaccine for safety in live monkeys. The disease was almost totally eliminated from the world by 2002, although small pockets of infection remained in Nigeria, India, Pakistan, and Afghanistan. As was feared by the WHO, in many countries where polio had seemed to have been eradicated, the populace lowered its guard and failed to continue vaccination programs, convinced that the urgency had passed. This, together with a fear among many Muslims that western countries were spiking the vaccine with contaminants (antifertility drugs), has led to a resurgence of the disease. Nigeria reported 790 cases in 2008. By mid-2008, the disease had spread to some twenty previously polio-free countries as far away as Yemen and Indonesia.

The rhesus monkey will continue to play its role in vaccine testing.

Typically, the cages for monkeys, like rhesus and Java macaques and squirrel monkeys, in federal primate centers are arranged in two tiers on either side of a central walkway, 30 or more cages per tier, 120 or more cages per room, giving the impression of boring sameness.

The lower tier of cages is plunged into gloom because the room-long metal tray mounted above it, which catches waste, food debris, and the like from the animals in the upper tier, cuts off much of the light coming from the fluorescent strips mounted high on the ceiling. To render it even more austere, one side wall of the cage is typically open metal mesh, while the opposite side wall is solid surfaced to prevent the monkeys from biting each other's fingertips or toe tips as they reach through the bars because the cages are so close together. This means that each monkey in the room is unable to see its neighbors on either side and can clearly see only the monkeys in the cages immediately opposite, on the other side of the central aisle.

Given the seemingly endless double-tier rows of cage upon identical cage, only the most dedicated caregivers will stop to bend down and share a kind word with a monkey, like "How are you today?" or "She's such a good little girl," each time they pass.

Most scientists are likely to have the same misconstrued ideas of the animals they use in the laboratory as the average person has on the street. Rarely do scientists see the animals they work with in their research. They rely mainly on written or telephone reports from the veterinarians, supervisors, or caregivers on the animal staff for information about the health and condition of the animals used in their experiments. Directors of research institutes usually see the animals in the colony only when they show visiting scientists around, like foreign dignitaries reviewing a military honor guard.

It is this lack of understanding of the true nature of animals that led scientists in years gone by to ignore the inhumane conditions that often existed in the laboratory. It is not an intentional cruelty on the part of the scientists. It is a cruelty of omission.

In the early 1980s, around the time that this story took place—before the Animal Welfare Act mandated so-called environmental and psychological enrichment for nonhuman primates—the typical monkey nursery in a medical laboratory comprised incubators and small cages in which knotted white hand towels were hung from the ceiling for the infants to hold onto with one hand. This would be the only soft reminder of a missing mother, while the infants sucked the index finger of the other hand. (Rhesus monkeys rarely suck their thumbs.) I had one particular slide that I used to show at scientific meetings: a 1-year-old male rhesus monkey holding on with both hands to his leg stretched up in front of him while he sucks his big toe. Audiences never failed to let out "Wows!" and "Ahs!" and long sighs of tender appreciation. "I know," I would say, "it's a great picture. But this poor little guy is psychologically ruined. He'll still be doing this when he's 20 or 30 years old."

For the first six weeks after giving birth, mother monkeys hold their infants twenty-four hours a day, hardly ever taking them off breast or laying them down, even for a moment. The mother's constant movement, her jogging the baby up and down, and her frequent grooming of the infant are all essential to the youngster's normal psychological development. It's as if these maternal behaviors somehow unleash important psychological events in the maturation of the infant's brain. In contrast, a young, weaned infant rhesus monkey hand-raised in the typical laboratory nursery is taken out of her incubator for milk feeding with a bottle for around twenty minutes every two hours, giving her a maximum of only four hours of contact with the caregiver out of every twenty-four. As the infant gets older, the frequency of feeding is reduced to four-hour intervals, and then to six-hour intervals as the amount of food per feeding is increased, and the contact time with the caregiver is reduced to zero once the infant is old enough to self-feed at around 4 to 6 months.

This lack of constant, continuous care has severe repercussions on an infant's psychological development. The baby begins to show recurrent abnormal behaviors known as stereotypies. These behaviors range from constant finger or big-toe sucking, to body rocking from side to side or front to back, to screaming uncontrollably when disturbed, to clinging to cage furniture or other infants in an obviously abnormal manner. The bizarre behaviors are often most severe in male infants, and can go on to include constant hair plucking, penis sucking, or feigned and even real self-biting of arms, legs, and ankles. Rarely can the severity of these stereotypies be alleviated once they develop.

I did not want this to happen to Finnegan. Just as with Spike before him, however, I began to be concerned that despite all the efforts my family and Angus were making, we could not provide what Finnegan needed most: the companionship of his own kind to help him learn what it means to be a rhesus monkey and not some human-created freak. After a great deal of soul searching, I realized that only one alternative remained.

Lightly sedating Loretta each weekday afternoon, I would reach into the cage and remove Erin from her mother's arms. *Remove* was hardly the word: it was more like peeling away one obstinate finger and toe at a time while the screaming little spitfire bit and scratched me nonstop. I would then carry Erin in a ski hat under my lab coat to my office, where I had installed Finnegan in his incubator, and place her with him. My goal was to make Erin accept that being taken away from her mother for two hours each day to socialize with Finn was not the end of the world—that she would always go back with her mother—and perhaps one day all three could live happily together.

But that was not to be. Erin squeaked and wailed for her mother the whole time. Finn tried to make friends with her, but she would push him away or even try to bite him. Repeatedly I would try to feed her from a milk bottle, but she fought me every step of the way. Only when the time came to return her to her mother would she calm down and quietly allow me to wrap her in the ski hat. Even then, she would not let me feed her any milk.

As I made my way back to the rhesus monkey room on the other side of the monkey complex, I would talk to Erin, telling her what a good little girl she was and how she was going to see her mama. This was the only time she would not try to bite me, but would nestle quietly beneath my pullover. Only as I reached to open the outer door to the monkey room would she start to scream her little head off, as if I were beating her. By the time I entered the room, all the monkeys would be out of control, shrieking and rattling their cages violently, like the prisoners they were in some penitentiary.

This was not working out as I had planned. For Finnegan's sake, I would have to remove Erin from her mother permanently and raise the babies together. I was not happy with this decision, taking one little creature from her mother in order to save another who had no mother. Was I not just creating another orphan? But I could think of no alternative.

Thanksgiving was coming up in a couple of days' time. That would give me four days in a row at home to concentrate on introducing Erin to a new life without her mother, and give her a chance to develop a bond with Finnegan and, I hoped, find that I wasn't the ogre she thought I was. I crossed my fingers.

As I stepped through the door from the veranda that Wednesday evening, I took Erin from inside my pullover and passed her to Marie-Paule, who tucked her beneath her chin and cuddled her. This was the first time Marie-Paule and Erin had met. I quickly set about making up a warm bottle of milk and gave it to Marie-Paule. To my amazement, Erin took straight to the nipple and sucked. After all my failed efforts to coax Erin to drink during the last month, my wife had succeeded in just a few minutes. Marie-Paule sat for a long time with Erin tucked under her chin, speaking to her softly and getting her used to being rocked up and down.

Finnegan had gone off to eat his banana cereal and then see what Angus was up to. He probably felt a little put out by my wife's paying so much attention to Erin, and he was soon pushing himself next to her so that he wouldn't miss out on the cuddles.

I quickly learned that I had to be cautious about how I approached Erin, especially if I was standing and she was on the floor. I had to be careful not to accidentally trap her in tight spaces that she could not instantly escape from, like the short corridor leading to the washing machine and dryer at the end of the kitchen, or on the stairs leading down to the dungeon-like basement. Erin would immediately panic, as she looked up at me towering above her.

Whereas Erin had been aloof to Finnegan when I had carried out the daily socialization efforts at the lab, she came to look up to him like a big brother. She followed him everywhere. To my surprise, Finnegan acted like a real little gentleman, sensitive to her fears and careful not to leave her behind.

One of the great joys that Erin soon discovered was the morning ritual of the shave and shower. She was quick to jump into the sink and cover herself with lather while Finnegan chewed on the tube of toothpaste. Within moments, they would clamber onto my shoulders and have mock fights as I tried to shave without cutting myself. Then came the shower, which I dreaded most of all. Jumping onto my ankles, they would scramble up my legs and abdomen, their sharp little fingernails gouging my skin, to carry on their roughhousing on my shoulders.

As far as I could tell, Erin showed no signs of missing her mother. She certainly did not pine. I think everything she was being introduced to was so overwhelming that she had no time to mope. By the end of that long weekend, Erin and Finnegan had adjusted to home life together remarkably well.

Most striking of all, however, was the bond Erin developed with Angus. She sort of idolized him right from the beginning, yet you could tell she was a little scared of him at the same time. I happened to witness the breakthrough between the two. Angus was sprawled out on the kitchen floor one afternoon when Erin began to circle him, around and around, as she dragged a washcloth along the floor, chattering quietly to him. I could sense that she was going to make physical contact with Angus, but she was terrified. Suddenly she leapt onto him, landing on his neck, and immediately began to groom the long white hairs of his ears. Angus woke up, stretched, made a great yawn, and fell back asleep. It was one of those wonderful moments that you remember forever. From that point on, without any hint of doubt, Erin trusted Angus.

On the way home from the lab each evening, we would stop to have a chat with two farm horses who stood rooted over the same stretch of fence in a corner of a field by a lake. I would roll the driver's-side window down, and the two infants would clamber out onto the hood of the car and chatter away at the massive horses. I often wondered what they could be saying.

Before Erin came to the house, Finnegan watched the *Muppet Show* every evening after Marie-Paule and I had finished watching Walter Cronkite's *Evening News*. He would nestle beneath Marie-Paule's chin, sucking his first finger (the only time he ever did so), as she lay stretched across the bed, propped on her elbows. Erin never showed any interest in television, however; she simply could not sit still long enough to concentrate on a story. Instead, she would try to drag Finnegan away from Marie-Paule so that they could play together. Finn would get very angry and frustrated by her efforts. Except for a two-hour John Wayne cowboy movie that he watched in its entirety and the nightly *Muppet Show*, Finn showed no interest in any other programs on television.

To see Finnegan and Erin take their first steps in life and to share in their joy was a truly unique and wonderful privilege. We saw their personalities begin to develop. Finnegan was becoming a thinker and a manipulator; Erin, a flighty little girl, was unable or unwilling to take the time to solve a problem, constantly turning to

Finnegan for approval and support. Apart from her need for Marie-Paule's affection, Erin's greatest concern was food, food, and more food. She became a veritable little pig, which in a way was probably a blessing because it may have taken her mind off the mother she no longer had.

Finnegan's greatest frustration in life became the water dispenser on our refrigerator. It worked by a recessed finger-operated rubber pad. Finn would shimmy up the handle of the door, reach in, and press the pad with his tiny hand. It never worked, however: his fingers were not strong enough to press the pad with sufficient force. He would wait for the next person to come to the refrigerator for a cold glass of water, and then he would sidle up the handle and observe even more carefully how it was done. Perhaps it was a little mean of me, but I was in no hurry to teach Finnegan how to operate the water dispenser. He had already discovered how to stick hairpins into electrical outlets, how to stand on doorknobs and twist them open with his feet, and how to pull open bedroom drawers and scatter our clothing all over the place.

This experience with the rhesus monkey infants made me begin to realize to what extent we deprive animals of what they most need when we lock them up in small cages in a laboratory. It is not so much the research, although in many cases it also plays a major role, but the deprivation of their most basic needs: freedom, the facility to choose, the right to be happy, the right to be noticed as unique individuals. Life is just that much worse for them if we don't give them our compassion, our empathy, and try to see through their eyes the emptiness of the artificial world around them that we have created. Finnegan and Erin, along with Spike Mulligan, were the ones who showed me these things, simply because I had the opportunity and privilege to share in their lives, at least for a short while, in a most intimate way.

Now that Erin had become close friends with Finnegan, it was only natural that she would come along on the picnic lunches that Finn and I shared every day at work. During these midday walks in the woods, she developed the habit of grabbing the tips of my fingers of one hand and swinging herself back and forth through the air.

We would make our way to the same spot in the forest that Spike and I used to visit: a huge flat rock with an oak tree growing tight against its tabletop side. It was close by in these woods that Revolutionary troops had mined the iron ore that was used to make two huge chains that they then dragged by horse all the way to West Point, suspending them across the Hudson to prevent the British fleet from sailing up the river. This spot was far enough away from the lab to be assured that I would not catch the distant sound of the paging system: "Doctor Mahoney, you have a call on 2922," or "Please come to Unit Seven." Here I could think and ponder.

During these languid lunchtime picnics, I began to wonder what would become of Finn and Erin. What was their long-term future? Could I allow them to be confined to a laboratory cage for the rest of their lives now that I had given them a taste of freedom? Finnegan, who spent so much of his time climbing trees and shaking the branches in defiance of the world; Erin, who loved to chase butterflies through the woods in graceful bounds of sheer delight. At the same time, just as I had often asked myself about Spike and the other chimps, I asked myself what made Finnegan and Erin different from the other rhesus monkeys back at the lab. I could not hope to save them all.

Having decided that I could not leave Finnegan and Erin in the lab for the rest of their lives, I began what turned out to be a long and arduous search for a suitable, permanent home for them. I would need to find not only a good environment for them but also people who would know how immensely difficult it might be to make such introductions. They would need to have the skill and, more important, the patience to face the challenges that would certainly arise. There was no magic formula for how best to proceed.

Every step of the way was going to be trial and error, with possibly catastrophic consequences brought on by human misjudgment.

Finnegan was around 8 months old by then, Erin 9. The window of opportunity for their introduction into a new group of rhesus monkeys would not be open for much longer, especially for Finn. He would soon reach an age at which he might be seen as an interloper, a challenge to the hierarchical structure of the group. Just as with the 2-year-old males in the wild who leave or are forced out of their natal groups to find another troop to enter and settle down with, the transition can be very dangerous. In Finnegan's case, the switch from the tranquility of our home and the woods of New York to an integrated troop of essentially wild rhesus monkeys might be more than he could take. Rhesus monkeys can be very unforgiving of new male blood.

The managers of several sanctuaries that I contacted made it plain to me that once I brought Finnegan and Erin to them, I would not be allowed access to them again, and certainly would not be given any say in how they were managed from then on. To a certain extent, I could understand their reticence. There is nothing worse than having someone breathing down your neck, a smart aleck who thinks he's a super whiz when it comes to handling rhesus monkeys. Yet I felt I did know these two little monkeys, I had worked with rhesus monkeys and many other species of nonhuman primates in several facilities over the previous fifteen years, and was a veterinarian. Surely my experience counted for something! I realized I would need to find someone with an open mind and the willingness to work with an outsider.

Then one afternoon, I received a surprise phone call from a Ms. Reese, the curator of a small zoo in Davenport, Iowa—the Fejervary Zoo. She explained that she had a small troop of seven rhesus monkeys on an island exhibit that had been created in 1928, the first zoo in the United States to develop the island concept for exhibiting monkeys. The zoo was in the process of reopening after the completion of its newly built and extensively remodeled display. She was concerned about inbreeding among her monkeys and was trying to locate colonies that might be prepared to donate adults that she could use to introduce new genes into an expanded colony of twelve to fifteen.

I explained to her that I had no adults to contribute, but it just so happened that I had two enchanting little infants who would be much better to consider. Introducing adults to a small, established colony could be quite difficult, I said, especially when it was confined to a relatively small space—the outside display was around one-fifth of an acre. Young monkeys would stand a far better chance of being accepted, as the top-ranking adult males and females would be less likely to see them as threats. Ms. Reese thanked me for my suggestions and politely said that she would get back to me. She must have considered my suggestions, because she called me back the next day and we had a long, in-depth talk. Liz, as I soon found myself addressing her, seemed just the very person I could work with, and I have to say, in all the years I did work with her, I never once found myself disagreeing with her decisions.

It took a few phone calls for Liz and me to come to a final agreement, not because of any hesitation on my part about the zoo, but because I was having difficulty saying yes; it meant that Finnegan and Erin would no longer be part of our lives. But deep down, I knew this was the right thing to do, and Liz was the right person to do it.

The reopening of the zoo was planned for a Saturday in July 1982. Marie-Paule was thrilled that the decision had been made, even though I knew she would have emptiness in her heart for these two infants. She immediately set about arranging transportation for me and the monkeys from LaGuardia to Moline, Illinois, the closest airport to Davenport.

The trip to New York City fascinated Finnegan and Erin. They had never seen skyscrapers, or heavy traffic, or tollbooths with people who pass tickets to you through the window. It was not until we had to load them in their small pet carrier, with their teddies in hand, that they realized something not so nice was about to happen. Mama gave each one a kiss, and I put them both into the carrier at the same instant. The carousel took them on its snakelike journey to the freight loading truck. I know how hard this moment was on my wife: she had loved these little things dearly. The fear that overcame Finn and Erin, I can only imagine.

Liz was waiting for us at the airport on our arrival. She drove us directly to the zoo. Monkey Island was atop a small hill surrounded by a broad area of parkland and majestic tall trees. The resident monkeys were out on the island. Macho, the top-ranking male, was sitting on top of one of the dead tree trunks that had been positioned among the rocks, surveying the park. The other monkeys were huddled in two groups, grooming each other. There was something magical about the scene, and a powerful feeling came over me that Finn and Erin would be happy here.

The indoor housing for the monkeys comprised one large pen with perches and climbing bars and ropes, which connected to a much smaller cage to house monkeys separately in the event of illness or injury. This smaller cage would be Finn and Erin's temporary housing until Liz and her assistants, Cindy and Sarah, would start the newcomers' social integration into the resident troop. Finn and Erin took quickly to Liz, Sarah, and Cindy, more or less ignoring me.

Although Finnegan and Erin would not be able to participate in the official ceremonies with the other monkeys the next day, they could at least have the run of the large indoor cage while the other monkeys were out on the island. They would also be able to take turns being on the island when the residents were kept temporarily indoors. It would be a lonely, frightening night for little Finn and Erin, but they had each other for support, and their teddies. I would be back in the morning to take them on the island. It was growing dark, and we all left for the night.

I spent most of the next morning on the island with Finnegan and Erin, while the resident monkeys stayed indoors. They explored every corner and cranny and enjoyed jumping from the top of the tallest rocks into the moat, about a fifteen-foot drop. They showed no fear whatsoever of the height. Finnegan sat astride my shoulders, soaking my shirt with his saturated hair, and Erin swung from my fingertips as we walked around the little island, just as she had done so often when we walked the woods of New York together. The babies would be happy here, I knew.

As I was wandering around the little island with the infants that Saturday morning, I saw the two architects who had designed the display coming toward me. Introducing myself, I congratulated them on the beautiful job they had done. "You must have read up a lot on monkey behavior to have made such a perfect design," I said.

They looked at me quizzically, obviously not understanding what I was talking about. "What do you mean?" one of them asked.

"Well—you know—the way you designed all the visual breaks and the different pathways, the way they divide and then come together again on the other side of the island, the way the paths go up and down. It's fantastic—so three-dimensional, so important for animals, especially for rhesus monkeys, who like to fight and chase each other so much."

I have known architects who tried to design these important features into captive environments and failed. Here were two men who had no knowledge of such things, and yet they had succeeded.

The ceremony was to begin around 2 o'clock. The mayor of Davenport would be in attendance, along with the director of the zoo and, of course, the press. At a certain magic moment, the electrically operated exit doors of the indoor housing opened, and to the delight of the sizable crowd who had come to share in the thrill, seven fun-filled rhesus monkeys burst into the sunlight.

Sunday came all too soon. I would have to return to New York. When I went to say goodbye, I found Finnegan and Erin sitting on the highest perch in their small indoor cage, their arms wrapped around each other, embracing their little teddy bears. I think they knew I was leaving. My camera caught the moment, though not the focus. They both had sad expressions in their eyes, Finnegan's lips pursed into an O as he repeated his lost, forlorn little *whoowh* calls over and over again. It nearly broke my heart. "They will have to be brave, those little ones. But I'll be back soon to see them, I promise," I said.

I did return, three months later, but Liz and I had kept in close contact in the interim. She always had amusing tales to tell me about the infants. Or she would send me their most recent photographs. Liz and her team had been busy trying out different social combinations of two or three of the resident monkeys at a time, with surprising success. While he ate his food, Finnegan liked to sit close to Fruitfly, the beta male of the group, and stare up into his face. Finn also had a cruel fascination for Bunny, an elderly female whose lower jaw was deformed, causing the tip of her tongue to protrude constantly. She also had a pronounced squint of both eyes. Finnegan got carried away with his fascination one day when he reached up and tweaked the tip of Bunny's tongue.

Finnegan had really overstepped his bounds recently, Liz informed me. He had sat in front of Marchette, the alpha female of the troop, eating his food. Apparently such behavior is not tolerated from the low-status monkeys of the group. Marchette reached forward and gave him a sharp slap across the face. Either Finnegan hadn't understood what he had done wrong or he was trying to push the issue, but he proceeded to pick up another handful of food and eat it, still sitting fully square in front of Marchette. Furious with his behavior, she stood up, walked over to Finn, grabbed the scruff of his neck in her teeth, carried him to the edge of the perch they were sitting on, and dropped him below. And didn't Finnegan, the little tough guy from "New Yoik," have the audacity to scurry back up to the same high perch and repeat his performance? Marchette had had enough. She picked him up by her teeth again, but this time carried him down to the floor level (which must have been an immense effort for her), exited through the flap door leading to the island, carried him up, still in her teeth, to the highest rock, and dumped him in the moat. How Finnegan managed to survive that first year in Iowa, I cannot imagine!

The most amazing development, however, involved the Fejervary Zoo's recent acquisition of a young female named Scarlett from a zoo in Louisiana. Scarlett came with the reputation of being "nothing but a troublemaker," but nothing could have been further from the truth. She immediately adopted Erin, whom she adored, and Finnegan, whose face she constantly slapped, presumably to make the point that she was the boss and he'd better not forget it. (Maybe she had witnessed the altercation between him and Marchette and knew he needed some discipline.)

Erin and Finnegan brought something special of their own to the zoo: their love of water and swimming. All the young animals in the troop lined up each day at around 11 o'clock to dive into the moat as fast and as often as they could. Erin had the nicest style, standing on the edge of the highest rock, her feet on the edge, her head facing away from the water. She would actually perform a backward somersault but hit the water so cleanly there was barely a ripple. Finnegan had no style whatsoever. He jumped sideways, forward, backward, hitting the water with an enormous splash. Bonnie, Granellio, and Fooler, Marchette's cocky little baby, joined in enthusiastically. The 11 o'clock diving display, lasting the better part of an hour, became quite a daily public attraction.

I went back to Davenport a year or so later. Erin and Scarlett had each had a baby recently. Along with Finn, they had become an extended family within a family. I am sure Scarlett provided real support to Erin, and she no longer seemed overly bossy toward Finnegan. I could not have imagined a more wonderful outcome for them all.

Liz, Cindy, and Sarah had done a wonderful job, and I was as proud as any father could be of Finnegan's and Erin's achievements. Finnegan would eventually become the alpha male and Erin the top-ranking female. What more could I have hoped for?

7

The Caribbean Trio

Dogs are not our whole life, but they make our lives whole.

—Roger Caras (1928–2001)

What is this pain I have in my heart? What is this emptiness I feel in my soul, like a blanket that smothers me? Why do I keep wondering where you are, when I know deep down you never will be there anymore? How have I allowed myself to think this way?

As I tap away at the keys of the computer, I must be aware at all times not to step on your nose with the toe of my shoe, or kick your side as I extend my leg to ease a cramp, with you lying there stretched out in the alcove beneath the desk. But you are not there: *I know that!* There is just an empty space.

A dollop of melting snow just fell from the roof and plopped on the front doorstep. Is that you coming back from a walk? I didn't realize you were out. The leafless maple branches brush against the roof, caught up in a sudden gust of wind, and I think it is you scratching the front door for me to let you in. I look up every now and then to wonder where you are. Rest peacefully in the frozen earth, my little Pups.

* * * * *

With Pupsie's passing, a wonderful fifteen years came to an end: the end of an era of sharing life with one, two, and then three of the most wonderful dogs you could ever wish to meet. Hardly a day passed when Molly, Ragsie, and Pupsie would not get up to some antic or react to some particular situation without their leaving us speechless with wonder.

Born under the foundation of a tiny wooden house in Jamaica, the runt of an eight-puppy litter, Molly was barely half the size of her brothers and sisters. She was weak and severely anemic from a massive infestation of fleas, her eyelids swollen and gummed together by pus, her breathing labored from bronchitis, and her belly swollen with parasites. She was only $3^{1}/_{2}$ weeks old and did not have the strength to get to her mother's nipples for milk. My wife and I took her back to the house we had rented for our week's vacation and tried to nurse her back to health. I managed to get the bare essentials necessary to give her a transfusion of her mother's blood from a kindly elderly doctor in a run-down hospital in Black River, the nearest town.

During the first two years of her life, Molly was constantly plagued by bouts of illness. Soon after her arrival in America, her eye infection led to rupture and permanent blindness in her left eye and poor sight in the other. She frequently suffered episodes of anemia, sometimes vomiting, other times diarrhea, the cause of which we were never able to diagnose, except to put it down to her having been a runt puppy.

Five years later, we rescued Rags from a mountaintop on the tropical isle of Virgin Gorda, in the British Virgin Islands. She was around 7 to 9 months old. Some of the islanders told us that she had been dumped on the mountain three months earlier to starve to death for having been a "bad dog," as her original owner had described her.

A Border Collie in appearance, her coat was chestnut and white rather than black and white. With an undershot jaw and a nose and muzzle of sooty black, she vaguely reminded me of a baboon. Even from a distance, it was obvious that she was sunken-eyed and emaciated.

How Rags had been able to find enough food to survive for so long, I could not imagine. And what about water? There were no streams or lakes on the steep-sided, 1,400-foot-high mountain, and it hadn't rained since we had arrived three days earlier. It was not the rainy season, meager as the rainfall would be even if it were. Besides, the sandy earth was so porous that any puddle would quickly dry up from absorption or evaporation with the high day-time temperatures. The only conclusion I could come to was that she lived off the nocturnal hermit crabs that passing cars squashed on the road by the score in the early morning hours, and perhaps her only source of water was the dew that she licked off the leaves of the bushes that surrounded her lair.

Just over a year later, we found Pupsie on a garbage dump on the same mountaintop in Virgin Gorda, but at a lower altitude. I'll never know what made me swing the car off the twisting mountain road down the narrow track that led to the dump that day.

A thin pall of blue smoke drifted across the dump. Countless scores of herring gulls squabbled over just-delivered garbage, flap-ping their wings in the air, squawking and screaming. There must have been two acres of Styrofoam, plastic bags, containers, baby bottles, broken beer bottles, squashed soda cans, rotting fruits and vegetables, and an endless variety of unmentionable things—all of it smoldering and stinking.

Just then, a group of four adult dogs jumped over a line of bushes on the far side of the dump and disappeared into the tangled jungle beyond. At the same moment, a brindle-colored puppy rushed out from under an abandoned trailer that was parked off to one side, rolled over onto her back in front of me, her little legs stick-ing up in the air. She said in her silent canine way, "I love you, I love you. Please take me home with you."

I picked her up. Her body was covered in superficial bite wounds, some in various stages of healing, others quite fresh. I could only guess that the other dogs, or perhaps even the gulls, would attack her every time she came out from under the trailer to get some newly delivered scraps of food. We took her back to the little house we had rented for the week and fed her leftovers from the previous night's meal.

There was never a question in our minds of whether we should rescue any one of the three puppies. Even with the blood transfusion, the little Molly would only become reinfested with fleas if we left her behind, and it would be impossible to prevent her from being reinfected with parasites. Furthermore, meningitis could easily develop from the severe infection of her eyes. After three long months, an emaciated Rags was still on her mountaintop, with no hope of rescue. Pupsie was the only one who threw herself at us, begging us to take her home.

Whereas we were able to bring Molly and Pups back with us on the plane to the States—though not without some difficulty—we faced a major problem with Rags: I had not been able to catch her. Three times a day, for five days in a row, I visited her on her steep mountain, bringing her food and water, trying to make friends with her and gain her trust. She was happy to see me every time, bouncing up and down and even yapping with joy, but she remained skittish and would clamber back up to her jungle lair if I came one step too close, dislodging rocks and stones and broken cactus stems as she went.

On the last morning of our vacation, before packing up and leaving for the airport, I made one last visit to Rags. She was her usual happy self, and I came within an inch of touching her nose with my fingertip. The thought of leaving her was almost more than I could bear. Then I remembered meeting a kindly elderly English lady from Yorkshire, a Mrs. Yates, who tended the hotel gift shop in Leverick Bay, the small harbor settlement at the base of the other side of the mountain. She loved animals, that I recalled. Perhaps she could help me with Rags.

I drove as fast as I could to Leverick Bay; time was running out. I explained to Mrs. Yates the situation with Rags and asked whether she could try to carry on where I was forced to leave off—to catch Rags and get her examined by a veterinarian so that she could get the papers and all the other things that would be needed to send her to us in New York. She said that she would be delighted to help.

I remember the deep sadness I felt as the small nine-passenger propeller plane took off and circled back over Ragsie's mountain as it gained altitude. Looking down on the winding road beneath us, I couldn't help wondering whether Rags was sitting on the edge of the road, waiting for me. What would she think once she realized I wasn't going to return to see her? Would she feel that yet one more human being had betrayed her?

"She rolled over for tickle-tum today," the voice over the telephone said in the unmistakable Yorkshire lilt. It was Mrs. Yates calling from Virgin Gorda. "She wouldn't let us take hold of her, mind," she added, "but my friend and I will try again tomorrow."

The next day, Sunday, Mrs. Yates called again to triumphantly announce, "We got her. She's in my kitchen at this very moment eating up a storm. I'm going to take her by ferry in the morning to the humane society in Tortola to get her medical examination and health certificate, and the rabies and all the other shots." (Tortola is the principal island in the British Virgin Islands.) "Then we'll put her on the plane to New York the day after."

We decided that Marie-Paule should be the one to go to the airport and pick up Rags, while I took charge of introducing the two dogs when Rags arrived home. I wasn't sure how Molly would react upon seeing Rags with Marie-Paule.

On hearing the sound of the car turning into the driveway, Molly could hardly contain herself. Mama was back. She rocketed down the balcony stairs as fast as her little legs would carry her, straight into Marie-Paule's arms. At that moment, a whining, hesitant cry came from inside the back of the car, through the open driver's door.

"What's that?" Molly seemed to say, with a snorting-sneezing sort of sound. She parted from Marie-Paule and stood up on the running board, reaching into the back of the car to sniff the wire door of the pet carrier. Rags's ears were drawn back, her head held low, the portrait of submission. Both dogs let out a faint rumbling growl. "That's Rags, Moll," I said, as I ducked my head in beside Molly's. "Rags, this is Molly. I want these two little dogs to be good to each other," I said. "No arguing or fighting, okay?"

"*Fnpp!*" Molly spluttered, with a sharp shake of her head, as she withdrew and stepped down from the car. "*Fnpp!*" she repeated, and then turned, making her way rapidly up the balcony stairs to disappear behind her potted palm tree in the sunroom, her sanctum sanctorum. Molly descended into an inconsolable gloom for the rest of the evening and wouldn't come out except once to go pee.

Come the morning, Molly's spirit had greatly improved. To my surprise, she seemed to have forgotten the uninvited guest's presence in the house. She jumped down from our bed to follow Marie-Paule for breakfast. Passing Nathalie's bedroom at the top of the stairs, Molly heard Rags, who had spent the night with our daughter, scratch at the inside of the door. Suddenly the memory of Rags must have flooded back into her mind. Incensed, she made a mad rush down the stairs, demanding to be let out, and disappeared into the woods, her tail between her legs, her ears drawn back, the very picture of love spurned.

Breakfast was going to present a big problem. As it turned out, Rags behaved in a calm, submissive fashion on Molly's return, showing that she had already accepted her as undisputed leader. Molly, on the other hand, eyed Rags with unbridled suspicion. She let out low, rumbling growls every time Rags moved, making her so nervous she didn't know which way to turn.

Suddenly Molly snapped out of her doldrums. Standing erect, she cocked her ears, straining to make out some sound that only she seemed able to pick up. Forgetting Rags's presence for the moment, she barked and rushed to the front door. It was Whiskey, the Springer Spaniel who lived close by, over the top of the hill. He was on his early-morning walk and had wandered onto our land to sniff the bushes and cock his leg.

Molly secretly doted on Whiskey, but for some reason she never wanted to show it. She exploded with a fury and burst out onto the land to chase him away as Marie-Paule opened the front door. Whiskey, never bothered by these ridiculous displays of uncontrolled aggression, stood his ground, pretending not to care one way or the other how Molly behaved. In the typical stance of a wild creature about to attack, Molly stood in front of Whiskey, almost nose to nose with him, one bent foreleg raised, her ears drawn back, the hair on her neck, shoulders, and back raised into a grotesque mane, like the hackles of a hyena on the hunt, spitting and sputtering, daring him to make the first move. Moments later, Rags shot out the front door to join Molly in combat, standing shoulder to shoulder with her, barking her head off at Whiskey. She gave Molly a fleeting, sideways glance as if to say, "I'm with you." The hapless Whiskey couldn't take any more, and left.

Suddenly, Molly saw Rags in a different light. She was no longer the usurper, the hussy, the one who had appeared in the house unannounced, uninvited. Rags had proved that she was ready to support Molly, come what may. The immediateness of Molly's reaction was something to behold. She and Rags had bonded, then and there.

Rags had a lot to learn about the ways of the upstate New York forests. There would be surprises and dangers ahead. A few days after her arrival, on their morning walk together through the woods behind the house, Molly suddenly stopped dead in her tracks. Her hackles rose, her ears cocked, and she let out a short, sharp, piercing bark. I had never heard her make such a bark before. In that fraction of a second, I was reminded of the alarm call that chimps make in the African forest when they warn each other of impending danger—an eerie, echoing quality to it, a sound that carries far. But

Rags was inattentive and continued on. I strained my ears, but the forest was silent. Moments later, with frightening speed, a large, black mass shot out from the dense undergrowth, like a lightning bolt. It was the Alsatian-Labrador cross, a hulking chunk of a dog, who came from a house some distance away through the forest. Aiming directly for Rags, she smashed her way through twigs and branches, a snarling, salivating banshee, full of fury, intent on vicious attack. Too slow to take adequate evasive action, Rags turned and tried to run away, falling over herself in terror, her bones and joints too weak from her months of undernourishment on the mountaintop to take the sudden strain, yelping and screaming even before the black dog had reached her. Molly stood her ground, continuing to bark, as if issuing instructions to Rags. Just in time, Rags made it over the humpback bridge to safety.

This incident seemed to cement an even stronger bond between the two dogs. Rags looked to Molly for guidance, and Molly seemed happy with Rags's companionship. In fact, like small children often behave with the arrival of a new brother or sister, Molly seemed to revert to puppyhood. She started tearing up newspapers, clawing mats and rugs, and pulling blankets off of beds, just for devilment.

Rags developed some unusual behaviors of her own, one of which was chasing cars and trucks that entered or left the cul-de-sac on which we lived, trying to bite their tires. Fortunately, this dangerous habit was short-lived, thanks to the mailman, who decided to use a bit of reverse psychology. Instead of scolding Rags, he would lean out the open window of his little truck and throw her a biscuit as he passed our house. Molly did not fail to notice this. Between her and Rags, a new tradition started; sitting in the middle of the road like a couple of bandits, refusing to get up, they would attempt to deny right-of-way to any truck entering the dead-end street unless they got a treat from the driver. Whether the truck drivers understood the two dogs' intent, I wouldn't like to say, but Molly and Rags managed to train the FedEx lady pretty fast. They never succeeded with the UPS man, however.

Molly was more than 6 years old when we brought Pupsie home. Though she was not mean or nasty to the new arrival, Molly didn't spare her much love or affection. In her somewhat arrogant manner, Molly expected Pups to fit in and assume her place right away.

Pups's arrival woke the sheepdog in Rags, who took her under her care. Rags allowed her to eat and drink from the same bowl at the same time as she, something that Molly would never tolerate.

Choosing an appropriate name for a dog can be a long and belabored process, a little like trying to determine the best place in your house to hang a new picture. Of course, with Molly we really didn't have to think too hard to come up with a name. The only puppy in the litter to look like her mother, it was only natural that we would name her Mollytoo. She soon became just plain Molly or Mol.

Rags was even more distinctive. Some of the islanders, who seemed to know everything about everything that happened on Virgin Gorda, had told me that her owner had named her Rags. At first I hesitated to call her by this name, fearing that it might bring back unpleasant memories of former days, but then I thought that it might give her a sense of permanence.

With Pupsie, it was different. She chose her own name. "Has anyone seen the pup?" (or "the puppy," or "the pupsie") was an often-repeated question the first few days after we brought her home—so much so that when we said the word *puppy*, her head perked up, and she knew that we were referring to her. Looking back on it, we realized Pupsie had figured this out by the end of the second day. It seemed that by having bestowed that name upon herself, she would from then on have to live up to the appellation: at heart, she remained a puppy.

Pupsie took to a life of thievery during her first year after arriving in New York. It took us a little while to figure out what she was up to and where she was going. She would disappear first thing in the morning and return after an hour or so, prancing in circles like a Virginia quarter horse, her head held high, obviously very proud of herself, wanting to show off her latest acquisition. It was mostly empty beer cans, Budweiser no less (my favorite brew). On two occasions she returned with an unopened can, not a tooth mark on either, leaving me wondering how she could have carried such a heavy weight in her mouth. Her next favorite item was single gloves, one in particular, a rather handsome right-hand leather glove that I still wear after all these years when I split logs. We could only assume that she was raiding house-building sites somewhere off in the forest. Her last swag was an outdoor Christmas decoration, an ugly three-foot-long black plastic chain and lantern with orange panes. Did these deeds remind her of her days at the garbage dump?

The three Caribbean transplants soon formed a tightly knit pack. The first walk of the morning, even before breakfast, included a detailed inspection of the land and the woods to see who had invaded their territory during the night. They progressed in a compact bunch, carefully sniffing the tips of just about every branch of every bush to determine whether the deer or, even more significantly, the bear had been through. Pups was especially terrified of the bear. She would sit and howl to the sky at the first hint of his scent.

As she got older, Rags became the undisputed leader of the pack when she would be called to duty to herd Clinton, the neighbors' dog, when he slipped his leash and ran off into the forest. Described as "difficult," Clinton, a yellow Labrador Retriever, had been ejected from three families during his first eighteen months of life before finally making it to Arnold and Brenda's home (where he found security and unconditional love). On receiving the phone call from Arnold or Brenda that Clinton was loose, one of us would call out, "Rags, she go get Clinton." Instantly Rags would start her terrifying yodel, her way of passing on the alarm to Mol and Pups, and the three would make their desperate dash down the veranda stairway. Off they would set at top speed, soon to disappear deep into the forest. I'm not sure how Rags directed the pack or even how she was able to locate Clinton's whereabouts, but his woofing was a sure sign that she had been successful. Some while later, a sad, contrite Clinton would emerge from the trees tightly surrounded by the Mahoney posse, who would deliver him right to Arnold and Brenda's doorstep, *mission accomplie.*

Pupsie relied heavily on Molly and even more so on Rags, her surrogate mother, for translating human language into dog language. When I would attempt to say something to the three dogs, like, "Dada is going out; he won't be long, he promise," Pupsie would give Rags a fleeting look of entreaty, as if to ask, "What's he saying? What's he saying?"

With the arrival of Pups, Molly promulgated an elaborate series of rules, defining where each dog would sit or stand while Mama cooked the evening meal, and where they could eat it, and where each was allowed to lie around the table during mealtime, and, most important of all, where they could lie on Mama and Dada's bed during the night. Most times, it took Molly just the hint of a short growl or a soft whine to get Rags and Pups into line when they

Tesoro (second from left) joins Molly, Pupsie, and Rags on lookout duty for Clinton, our neighbors' dog.

infringed her rules. She never once, to my knowledge, showed her teeth or behaved as if she might bite or snap. Sleeping positions at night, however, were probably her most important rules to obey. Molly was the only one permitted to lie alongside Mama. Rags and Pups were allowed to get on the bed at bedtime, but if for any reason they had to leave the bed during the night, they could not get back on it. Very occasionally, Molly would find herself breaking her own rule and jumping down onto the floor in the middle of the night. When she would try to return, Rags and Pups would line up, their heads over the edge of the bed, daring her to try and get back on. There was no mistaking the ferocity of their growls. I would then have to get out of bed and carry Molly back on.

We found ourselves having to invest in a king-sized bed. Even so, I would still wake in the morning, my back stiff and aching, my body contorted and twisted, while the three dogs stretched out, relaxed and comfortable.

Rags would sometimes get fed up with being "good" and having to follow Molly's every rule. Chimpanzees and rhesus monkeys, especially young juveniles, often have tizzies, especially when one of their playmates steals something from them, but Rags was the only dog I have ever known to have them. Her nose would quiver and twitch, reminding me all the more of a baboon. Sometimes her tizzies would burst into full-blown tantrums, as when she destroyed a bouquet of flowers that I had placed in the well of the car's passenger seat with her slashing paw because I had told her it was too dangerous to have tickle-tum while we were driving.

Molly's greatest concern of all was that I would forget to make dinner for the three dogs on Thursday nights. That was the one night of the week when I was on cook duty, the night Marie-Paule attended staff meetings at her school long after classes had finished for the day. She usually would not get home until around 7 o'clock.

Molly would start to get distraught if I hadn't begun the procedures by five fifteen, just about on the dot. After all, I had potatoes to peel and boil, and a roast to set in the oven, and I had to cook whatever meat Mama had taken out of the freezer for the dogs that morning before she left for school.

I often found myself suddenly thinking of a perfect word or phrase to use in the health report I was preparing for some primate sanctuary, dropping the potato peeler and rushing off to the computer in the library before I forgot it. One thought would lead to another, of course, and I would soon be deeply engrossed in the report, the potatoes long since forgotten.

The scrape of claws on carpet would bring me back to reality. Looking down from my computer chair, I would see Rags and Pups staring up at me, tentatively wagging their tails, a flick of the muzzle from side to side in agitation. A tense Molly sat out in the hallway, looking through the panes of the French doors, making sure that Rags and Pupsie had delivered her message as instructed: that I should get back to cooking the din-din.

Pupsie was a consummate flirt, making people think that they were the most special in the world. Take, for example, the day the chimney sweep came. After much struggle and blinking of the eyes, with soot falling all over his face, he tried to wriggle outward to free his shoulders from the hearth in order to extract his brush from the flue. Pupsie, who had sat watching the man in fascination throughout the process, seized her chance. She stepped up on him, straddled his chest with her legs, and began to lick his soot-covered face. "Nice—do—doggie," the chimney sweep tried to get the words out between licks of her tongue. "Nice doggie." The more he struggled, the more Pupsie licked his face, until the poor man started to laugh uncontrollably. Had I not intervened, he would have been stuck in the flue for I don't know how long. "For some reason dogs really like me," he said with pride, as he finally freed himself and sat up. I didn't have the heart to tell him that Pupsie was just a flirt.

These are the wonderful memories that still hurt so much to recall.

* * * * *

Over the years, the deer who resided on our land had never taken
our three dogs seriously. The deer looked upon them more as a
nuisance than as a threat. As Molly, Rags, and Pupsie pushed past
me as I went to open the back door giving out onto the balcony one
day, Rags let out her ludicrous, bloodcurdling ululations, like a
Comanche warrior riding into combat. Down the stairs and onto
the grass they exploded. Rags and Pups had already devised a military plan of attack on the deer, the signal indicated by a fleeting
sideways glance into each other's eyes. As usual, Molly made her
wide circle and then broke off to pee and sniff the bushes, as if she
was convinced that the other two were just being puerile.

This time, Rags decided to take the neighbors' bridge to cross
the stream into the woods. Pups would use our bridge, the two cutting the deer off in a pincer movement, as I think military strategists
would call it.

They chased the small herd all the way across our land and to
the farthest border of our neighbors', Don and Sally's land, a distance of maybe 130 yards, purposely running out of steam and slow-
ing down before reaching the deer. I watched the three of them
saunter back, shoulder to shoulder, long flapping tongues hanging
out the sides of their mouths, ridiculous grins on their faces as if to
say, "Aren't we great?"

To get an unimpeded view of what was going on, I went upstairs
to look out the windows of our bedroom and bathroom. This van-
tage point gave me a 180-degree view of the rear of the land and a
partial view of the front of the house.

One of the does had broken away from the herd as it entered
the woods, and she circled around to begin a quiet chase of the dogs.
Suddenly realizing that they were being pursued, Rags, Pups, and
Molly broke into a desperate run. This had never happened before,
and I think, for a moment at least, they were scared. Reaching the
limits of the other side of our land, they came to a halt, breathing
heavily from the effort. The doe had peeled away twenty yards short

of the dogs and made her way back toward her herd in a light trot. This behavior was an affront to the dogs, who immediately broke into a full-scale dash after her.

And so a most remarkable game of hide-and-seek or tag developed. The dogs broke up and independently stalked the doe. She, in turn, hid behind bushes or sneaked around corners of the neighbor's house, craning her long neck to see where the dogs had gone, stepping smartly backward if one suddenly appeared. The game went on for an hour or more, ending only when the dogs became exhausted.

What was the meaning of what I had observed? It was a game, I am sure. Did it involve a certain communication between the two species? It certainly must have involved a sense of humor.

It takes such a long time to establish a deep bond with a dog, much longer than most people realize. To forge that bond, you have to talk to the dog constantly—"intellectualize" with him or her, as I like to call it. You've got to give dogs opportunities to make decisions for themselves, to choose what they'd like to do next. "Would those little dogs like to go for a walk in the woods or a walk in the car?" I would ask them as they sat before me in a semicircle on the floor, tails wagging, the sparkle of expectation in their eyes. (The dogs didn't know the word *ride*.) "Well, let's go then!" Molly would almost invariably veer to the right as we stepped off the balcony steps, which meant that she wanted to cross the bridge and go for a walk in the woods. Rags and Pups would peel off to the left, which took them to the garage and the chance to hang out the open windows of the car as we toured around the ponds in the village and bark at all the civilized dogs being taken by leash on their morning walks—Molly included. In the end, they were always equally happy to take either option. Even asking a dog a meaningless thing like, "Did you see what that chipmunk just did?" will make him feel included.

People often ask me, "How long do you think it will be before my dog stops being a puppy? I've had him over a year now; I got him when he was six months old. He still chews the carpets and the legs of the piano, and he doesn't even listen to me when I tell him off." "Not until he's about four," I reply. "What? You mean four *years*?" the enquirer usually answers in near apoplectic consternation. But there will be no end to the depth and maturation of the relationship once you start.

In the beginning, you suspect that it is never going to be special like it was with your last dog, whom you loved so dearly and who knew just about what you were thinking and what your next move was going to be. Recent behavioral studies carried out on dogs and chimpanzees by Brian Hare of Harvard University indicate that the dog—far better than the chimpanzee—has an inherent ability to understand human beings and that the trait is exhibited as early as 9 weeks of age. Molly was only $3^1/_2$ weeks old when we took her into our care for her many health problems: she had a good head start.

As Molly got older, she picked up a great deal of what we talked about, listening from under the kitchen table for keywords. As I said earlier, she secretly doted on Whiskey, the dog who lived over the hill. At the mention of his name, or a similar-sounding word that she would catch from snippets of our conversation, like the "whi" of *wishful* or *which* or the "skwee" of *squeaky,* her favorite rubber hedgehog toy, or *squirrel,* Molly would immediately perk up her ears and bark or whine.

Our daughter, Nathalie, is a good example of someone who intellectualizes with her dog, Tesoro, and her two cats, Chateau and Shaggy. Her nonstop babble must drive her husband to distraction.

Tesoro, or Tessie, as we usually call her, is a diminutive Cocker Spaniel, the runt of her litter. What didn't go into her as muscle, bone, and fat certainly went into her as brain. She is the most intelligent little dog that I have ever come across.

"Tessie," I said to her one day, "she go get her blue ball." It's known as her blue ball, even though we are aware that she is color-blind. When she comes to visit us, she retrieves this favorite toy from a plastic laundry basket full of stuffed animals and other play items that we keep in a corner of the kitchen. This time, though, she seemed not to hear or understand me. "She go get the blue ball," I repeated.

Tesoro stood stolidly, staring into space, her face wholly expressionless, her mind somewhere else. *Oh well,* I thought; *I guess the light's been turned off.* But suddenly Tessie shot off, heading into the kitchen from the sunroom, through the short corridor to the library. I followed her as fast as I could, taking giant strides, trying not to make noise, doing my best to keep up with her. There she was, all excited, the stump of her little tail wagging furiously, her head raised in the air, the blue ball in her mouth. The light must have been on all the time: she remembered where she had last seen her ball.

Tesoro likes to talk to me over the speakerphone. She lets out a continuous string of howls, growls, and soft barks, interspersed with occasional yowls and yaps. She has a lot to say, if only I could understand the words.

Having brought this pack of three into our lives, I would often sit and ponder the origin of dogs. The dog is known as man's best friend, yet we have no idea how this special bond developed between the two species. I can't help thinking that it was the personality of dogs that naturally attracted ancient people to them—dogs made people feel good, providing them with dependability and loyalty in an otherwise hard and thankless world.

Results of comparative DNA studies in dogs and wolves by a team of American and Swedish scientists, published in a 1997 paper entitled "Multiple and Ancient Origins of the Domestic Dog," strongly indicate that dogs evolved from a common ancestor of the gray wolf more than 100,000 years ago.

Yet the oldest archeological remains of dogs found at human sites are only 12,000 to 14,000 years old. In other words, it would appear that the dog had already evolved long before it first came into contact with people. What happened during the 86,000 years in between? What role, if any, did human beings play in the dog's emergence?

The archeological evidence goes against the once-popular theory that humans were responsible for the development of the dog through controlled breeding of wolf cubs kidnapped from their lairs. A variation of that theory, given by Roger A. Caras in his book *A Perfect Harmony: The Intertwining Lives of Animals and Humans Throughout History*, is that wolf cubs were taken and reared as future sources of food, a sort of live meat on the paw that could be killed at some time in the future when required. However, now and again, some wolf cubs may have turned out to be especially friendly and gentle toward their human captors, licking rather than biting the hand that fed them. People wouldn't have had the heart to kill these gentler cubs when the time came. As the theory goes, breeding between these pet-like wolves would give rise, over time, to what we now know as dogs.

With tongue somewhat in cheek, and without a shred of personally gained evidence to support my contention, I would opt for the theory that dogs split from wolves a very long time ago, long before humans got involved. Dogs saw people coming and said to themselves, "There's a bunch of suckers. Let's rush out and greet them, roll over on our backs at their feet (just as Pupsie did with me on the Caribbean garbage dump), stick our legs up in the air, and faithfully promise them our love, devotion, and protection if they give us food and tickle-tum in return, and let us lie by the fire at night. When they finally get around to inventing proper beds with sheets, pillows, and blankets, we'll amend our contract."

Selective breeding by human beings for most of the breeds we know today did not begin until around 500 years ago in China. In fact, recent studies carried out by British researcher Matthew Binns on a special type of DNA found in dogs and all other species—the so-called mitochondrial, or "junk," DNA—strongly suggest that 95 percent of today's more than 400 breeds of dogs originated from three females, the Eves of the dog world. Interestingly, this DNA has no known function and may well represent remains of bacterial and viral DNA, which became incorporated into the genetic material of all animal and plant cells—a sort of inert leftover of infectious diseases that occurred millions of years ago.

Furthermore, if human beings had been responsible for domesticating wolf cubs and eventually obtaining dogs or dog-like variants through selective breeding, one would expect that archeological evidence of such variants would have been found at human archeological sites. Certainly the striking skeletal differences between the wolf and the dog or any hybrid in between would be readily apparent. For example, dog brains are 30 percent smaller than wolves'; there are also notable differences in the teeth and pelvis, the latter of which results in a dog's gait being different from that of a wolf. These features would be readily discernable in skeletal remains.

Yet, the power of selective breeding for a genetic trait such as friendliness toward human beings (a measure of domestication, in other words) cannot be denied, as was demonstrated in the case of the silver fox. Dmitry Belyaev, a respected scientist in the Russian Academy of Sciences, theorized back in the 1950s that if a species is selectively bred for a particular behavioral trait, such as tameness, changes in expression of certain physical and physiological traits, referred to as *phenotypes*, might also be expected to occur.

That is exactly what did occur, when, in 1959, Belyaev and his colleagues began what has to be the most remarkable, long-term (fifty-year) study in genetics ever undertaken: the so-called Farm-Fox Experiment. They selected breeding stock from an existing colony of silver foxes based on four categories of tameness: the lowest being outright viciousness toward human caregivers, and the highest marked by extreme affection in the form of tail wagging, licking, and playfulness. (They forgot to add tickle-tum to the list, however!) By the tenth generation of breeding, close to 20 percent of cubs fell into the highest category of tameness—that is to say, the friendliest. By the thirtieth to the thirty-fifth generation, the number had increased to 70 to 80 percent of puppies being in the friendliest category, as well as being the most dog-like in physical appearance: their tails no longer had a brush shape, their ears were floppy rather than peaked, and their coats were variably marked and colored. In other words, the animals became more dog-like in appearance and less like foxes. Physiological changes, such as becoming sexually mature at an earlier age, and behavioral changes, such as dog-like wagging of the tail to express happiness, also emerged. (Foxes don't wag their tails when they are happy.)

My theory of how the dog's association with humans came about is quite different. I believe it was dogs, not people, who initiated the partnership. When I was a child, I pictured our ancestors sitting around their fire, cooking the buffalo that they had hunted that day. Attracted by the mouthwatering aroma of the cooking meat, wild dogs collected at a distance from the fire, their eyes shining in the darkness. Feeling sorry for the dogs, the chief would toss scraps of meat to them, and little by little the dogs shuffled closer and closer to the people. In return, the dogs warned the people of approaching danger, just as American and British troops have reported dogs doing in Iraq when soldiers are out on street patrol.

My latest theory is that dogs were born twisters, able to convince people that they were the greatest things, and that the dogs would love them faithfully forever and ever, if the people would only let them join the group. After all, isn't that exactly what Pups had done when she ran out in front of me at the garbage dump that day and rolled over on her back at my feet?

"Oh, but that's the classic canine submissive gesture," the true scientist would say. In a dog-meets-dog situation, I would agree that this is a primitive response of submission: one dog has only a fraction of a second to convince the other dog that he is no threat. In a dog-meets-human encounter, however, I think it is a cunning ploy on the dog's part, a feint to make the human being feel good and special, allowing himself to be twisted around the dog's paw, just as Pupsie did with the chimney sweep. On the garbage dump, Pupsie had only a few seconds to get the message across to me that I was the greatest thing since Boomer Balls and long walks in the park; this might be her one and only chance of rescue, and she'd better not miss the opportunity.

One thing I know for sure: dogs often use people as passports to get them through other dogs' territories. I first discovered this in the Gambia, in West Africa. The common village dog of Africa, known as the *bush dog* (or by non-Africans as the *pariah*—a term I really dislike because of its demeaning definition), is, to me, your basic, true dog, free of any genetic defects that human tampering might have installed. Bush dogs don't have hip dysplasia, tears of their cruciate ligaments, or dropped eye lenses like so many purebreds suffer. These dogs usually belong to the village, but they are free to roam and free to breed. On the whole, people are kind to them.

Bush dogs do not follow people or their goats or chickens in a menacing fashion; quite the opposite. They trot along behind you and somewhat off to one side, tongues lolled out the sides of their mouths, a wag of their tails every time you look back at them. This dog, taking to you, a total stranger, so readily makes you feel quite special. After a while, you say the odd word to him, tell him how nice he is, and ask him his name. Then you notice savage eyes looking out at you through the bushes lining the path or riverbank: you are in another dog's territory. No doubt your new acquaintance assumes that you are going to turn around eventually and return to where you came from, just as he would plan on doing to get back to his home territory. If you don't turn around, the dog is left in a precarious situation. No longer supported, he will surely be bitten on his return journey alone, or maybe torn apart, if more than one irate dog attacks him.

The most remarkable example of the bond between human and dog that I have ever seen occurred in Sierra Leone, also in West

Africa. I received an urgent request to go to the Tacugama Chimpanzee Sanctuary, near the capital, Freetown. There had been an outbreak of disease, and several chimps had died, some within twelve hours of the first symptoms being observed. From the description of the symptoms, I was sure we were dealing with an epidemic of meningitis. Everyone feared that the infection would spread through all the chimps, and even the sanctuary staff might be at risk.

The timing for an outbreak of disease could not have been worse: Sierra Leone was in the middle of a brutal civil war.

I contacted veterinarians I knew in the Nairobi office of the World Society for the Protection of Animals (WSPA), who offered to have sufficient antibiotics and antimeningitis vaccines available for me by the time I arrived in Freetown, at no cost to the sanctuary. (The cost of the antibiotic alone was more than the sanctuary's total annual expenditures.) I set off as fast as I could, my usual six cardboard boxes of medical supplies in tow. The first leg of my journey was without incident: I flew Air France to Paris and on to Accra, in Ghana. After an overnight stay, I went to the airport the following morning to take the last leg of my journey to Freetown on Air Ghana. I was told that all civil flights into Freetown had been canceled for the day but was assured that if I came back the next day, I would get a flight.

Three mornings in a row, I turned up at the airport at 7 o'clock only to be told the same thing: the flight to Freetown had been canceled. (I later found out that all Air Ghana flights to Sierra Leone had been canceled for the previous two weeks because of the extreme security situation.) I began to panic: I couldn't just give up. Telephone communication with the sanctuary in Sierra Leone was erratic at best, and I had difficulty apprising everyone there of my situation.

By sheer chance, I ran into an inebriated Scotsman who told me of a pilot for a Bulgarian airline who would probably fly me into Sierra Leone. He jotted down the name and address of the hotel at which the pilot was staying, somewhere on the other side of Accra, and suggested I take a taxi there. This sounded like the makings of a shady deal, but I was desperate.

The taxi dropped me off outside a small, dilapidated motel. As I walked up the path toward the office, I noticed a late-middle-aged white man stretched out on an old-fashioned deck chair by a green algae-covered swimming pool, his portly belly overhanging his boxer shorts and a half-empty bottle of vodka by his side.

"Excuse me," I said. "Are you a pilot?"

He answered me in a coarse Russian accent that, yes, he was.

"Would you fly me into Freetown?"

"How much you vant to pay?" he responded.

"That's for you to decide," I answered. He gave me a figure in U.S. dollars, which, I said in shock, was way above what I could afford. He immediately halved the price, and we made the deal. He told me to be at a given terminal gate at 4 o'clock the next morning, and not to be late, because the control tower might not let us through later.

I took a taxi to the airport the next morning, arriving a little before 4 o'clock. It was still dark.

The terminal was deserted except for one solitary security guard. There were no swarms of young boys waiting to carry your baggage, whether you wanted them to or not; just a vast, empty silence. There were also no flatbed dollies available that I could use to load my luggage and the half-dozen cardboard boxes of medical supplies and equipment that I had brought. I had to carry or kick everything along, a few items and a few feet at a time, until I finally made my way down to the hall to where the pilot had instructed me to meet him. The place was empty—no pilot waiting for me, no customs agents working in the little emigration kiosks, no one.

The pilot arrived at around 5 o'clock, but there was still no one else in sight. It wasn't until about 7 o'clock that a customs and immigration officer appeared and cleared our papers.

An old Russian Ilyushin-18, a 125-passenger, four-engine propeller airplane, stood alone on the tarmac. Apart from the crew, which comprised the pilot, a copilot, a flight attendant, and a Russian engineer ready to fix any mechanical problem that would arise during the flight, I was alone.

"Where are the rest of the passengers?" I inquired.

"You are the only one," he replied.

She must have been a beautiful plane in her heyday. Her bathroom alone must have been sumptuous. But now the huge mirrors were cracked, the elegant cabinetry split, the ornate hand basins chipped, and the luxurious carpet in tatters. I actually got stuck in the loo during the flight, the door lock jamming on me. I was sure I would be marooned there for the remainder of the flight, but I finally unjammed the lock after much panicked forcing.

We ground our way steadily over the 900–odd-mile flight to Lungi, in Sierra Leone, passing over the endless forest of the Ivory Coast and Liberia.

As I stepped through the forward door to exit the plane onto the attached stairway, the deafening roar of just about every type of military aircraft imaginable hit me all at once. The scene was chaotic. Huge Russian transport planes (Antonov 124s), their nose cones tilted up into the air, their long ramps sloping down toward the ground as if they had been split open by monstrous prehistoric creatures, were being loaded and unloaded. Personnel carriers and small tanks were being offloaded through the tailgates of the planes. Gigantic Russian helicopters carried mobile gun units, their long barrels sticking out from heavy nets suspended beneath their bellies.

Planes took off and landed moments apart. Companies, platoons, and squads of soldiers in sky blue berets dotted the taxiways and aprons of the airport: Nigerian, Jordanian, British, and Indian troops of the United Nations peacekeeping forces.

Then I noticed small packs of dogs, ranging from half a dozen to twelve or more per group, scattered all over the airfield, sitting calmly in empty areas among the planes or along the edges of the runways. I asked a British soldier what the dogs were doing at the airport. "Waiting for their pilots to return from their missions," he replied. There must have been a hundred or more all told, mostly African bush dogs, each one waiting to tell his or her pilot that he was the greatest in the world. Twisters, the whole lot of them, just like Pupsie.

I couldn't help wondering if I was looking at a replay of evolution. In a figurative sort of way, I might have been seeing how it all began, this bonding with man: a point where the two species so needed each other. The man was a long way from home, in a dangerous and unfriendly environment; the bush dog presented with what might be the best opportunity he would ever get for his next meal and a bit of love.

On the way from the airport at Lungi, I heard the Russian pilot of the huge military-style helicopter that ferried passengers to and from Freetown ask in English over his radio, "Has anyone fed the dogs yet?" I think if humans would stop interfering with nature, dogs would stop evolving: they have already reached the point of perfection, and there is no need for them to go any further!

Every time I saw examples of dogs' abilities to bond with human beings and fellow dogs, like I had seen in Sierra Leone, I couldn't help thinking of Pupsie. I have described her as a flirt, yet she was no philanderer. Pupsie was a peacemaker. On the very rare occasions when Molly would growl at Rags for breaking one of her cardinal rules, Pups would rush in between the two to quiet things down. With an expression of deep concern in her eyes, so hard to describe in words, she would push Ragsie's muzzle to one side as if she were silently saying, "It's not worth getting upset about it." In this way, she gave Ragsie solace while respecting Molly's dominance, a sophisticated level of diplomacy, which I saw rivaled in only the more socially sophisticated chimps.

But Pupsie was more than a peacemaker; she was also an angel of mercy in the most remarkable sense. She had an extreme sensitivity and compassion. I am almost loath to use the term *empathy* to describe Pupsie's behaviors—not because she was a dog, and therefore a nonhuman animal incapable of empathy, as some might argue, but because the term is incredibly difficult to define and easily misused even when applied to human beings.

As Molly got older, she began to have brief bouts of sudden, sharp abdominal pain that would cause her to collapse. Physical examination, ultrasonography, and repeated blood tests failed to reveal the cause, although Dr. Rothenberg, our vet, was sure it was related to the severe illnesses she had when she was a very young puppy. During these episodes, Pupsie would rush to Molly and nudge her gently with her nose all over the body, as if she were trying to alleviate Molly's pain. The expression of anguish in Pupsie's eyes was something to behold. She would continue to give Molly attention until Molly was able to rise from the floor on her own.

Ragsie's syncopes first became apparent when the three dogs were playing together in deep, freshly fallen snow. Like most dogs, Molly, Rags, and Pups loved to burrow their heads in the snow and snort and sniff. One day Rags suddenly collapsed. Pups desperately set about trying to dig her out of the snow. Tests would later show that the syncope was due to sudden deprivation of oxygen in the blood flow to Rags's brain. Pups became very sensitive to Ragsie's medical condition, which rapidly worsened, and she seemed always primed and ready to respond to Rags's next seizure. Pups would try to get to Rags while she was still in an upright standing position, burying her head in Ragsie's chest and neck, spinning with her while she was on the spot, pressing her muzzle or head into Ragsie's neck or shoulder, trying desperately to support her body so as to prevent Ragsie from collapsing. Even more distressing was to watch Pups's futile efforts to raise Ragsie's body once she had fallen, trying to scoop a crooked paw under Rags's shoulder and lifting with all her might. Pupsie was never successful, of course; Rags was far too heavy to lift.

The best testimony of the extent to which some dogs are willing to go in order to save another dog's life at the risk of their own has been shown on television news and on the Internet.

In one example, caught on video on the Major Deegan Expressway in the Bronx, New York, a dog is struck by a car during the early-morning rush hour and lies in the middle of the road with a broken leg and internal bleeding. Another dog, sidestepping the traffic, comes to the rescue, a German Shepherd mix who turns out to be the injured dog's son. He circles his prostrate mother continuously, trying to keep attending police officers at bay, not wanting them to touch his mama, but wagging his tail in great sweeps to let them know that he doesn't wish to hurt them, either. Finally, the police are able to get both dogs to safety and the amazingly non-horn-honking commuters on their way to work.

An even more amazing, if grainier, example caught on a traffic camera in Santiago, Chile, shows a dog finding itself on a congested, high-speed, multilane highway, where it is struck by a car. Moments later, another dog jumps over the barrier and dodging the traffic, reaches the injured dog. With the greatest of difficulty, it drags the hurt dog by its shoulders, inch by inch, using its front paws, constantly looking up at the oncoming cars, finally reaching the comparative safety of the roadside, where a group of highway workers removes the injured dog. The rescue dog runs off on its own.

Mol and Ragsie passed on six months apart. Despite her own loss, Pups tried to fill the gap by staying extra close to us, doing her best to understand our language when we talked to her.

We started taking her on weekend mini-vacations in the Catskill Mountains to try and get her mind on fun things. When we opened the cabin door, she would rush in, jump on the bed, stretch her legs forward and back, and look at us intently. You could imagine her saying, "Not bad!" She loved the long walks along the deeply wooded Willowemoc River, using the rocks as steppingstones. She and Rags would have had a lot of fun together there.

The unexpected occurred just a few months later.

Who would think that constipation could be the first sign of a life-threatening condition in a dog? Following a brief period of straining and abdominal discomfort at 7 o'clock one morning, Pupsie quickly returned to normal activity.

Then, at around 11 o'clock, she stumbled and almost fell. Her lips and gums took on a sudden pallor, which lasted for only a few seconds. Within a few minutes, she was back to normal. Yet that was an alarming sign, suggesting a serious state of shock.

I immediately called Dr. Rothenberg. "Bring her in around three this afternoon, when the office is less busy, and we'll do some scanning on her," he said.

"If she has another one of these turns, I don't think she'll be alive at three," I replied.

After a moment's silence, he said, "Bring her in right away."

Poor little Pups was the perfect patient, lying still on her back, without any form of restraint, in the V-shaped groove of the special table that Dr. Rothenberg used for abdominal ultrasonography examinations. Several blood samples were taken, and we were awaiting the results from the lab in the room next door. The vet slowly and methodically scanned her abdomen while I kissed her ear every now and again to tell her everything would be okay.

"Doesn't look good," Dr. Rothenberg said as he stared intently at the computer screen. "Seems like she's got some masses in her abdomen."

At that moment, the first of the blood test results was in. Pups had extreme anemia. "She's hemorrhaging internally," the vet said. "Let's get her into surgery right away."

Pups was riddled with small cancerous masses affecting almost all of her abdominal organs. The largest mass, however, was located in her spleen: It had ruptured, causing a massive hemorrhage into her abdominal cavity. Pupsie died that night, at around 7 o'clock, just twelve hours after I had observed her first symptom.

"But I saw her only the day before, running with the deer. I gave her a bone; she seemed fine," said Alicia, the young mail lady, in shock when we told her of Pupsie's passing.

Poor little Pups, she was such a trooper.

8

The Gang of Four

Youth is all the glad reason of life; but often only by what it hopes, not by what it attains, or what it escapes.

—Thomas Carlyle (1795–1881)

I used to like to walk into the animal rooms in the evening at around 6 o'clock, when most of the other people at the lab had gone home for the night. This was the quiet period of the day, when the 300-odd monkeys and 250 chimps bedded down for the night in their cages of galvanized wire or aluminum bars. Unlike their breakfast of hard chow biscuits or their midday meal of fruits and vegetables, both of which they scoffed down with frantic avarice, most of them would eat their late-afternoon meal of biscuits at a more leisurely pace. Some of the chimps might still be munching on a biscuit or two that they had set aside earlier. Others would be absorbed chewing their last biscuits into an even, pasty mash. This was a long, drawn-out process that required careful mixing of each mouthful of biscuit with tiny sips of water that they sucked from the containers on the sides of their cages. Once all was blended into the final perfect consistency, the chimps would extrude the wads from their mouths

Cynthia tends to her second kindergarten class in the nursery: Arden, Regis, Gordo, Kareem, and Digger.

and store them on the ledges of the horizontal cage bars within easy reach of the suspended rubber tire hammocks they slept on, so that they could consume them later in the evening, a little snack before finally falling asleep.

Since we had figured out ways to modify some of the cages, linking them by short tunnels, we were able to keep some of the monkeys and an increasing number of the chimps in small social groups. The rhesus monkeys and baboons would huddle together for their end-of-the-day grooming sessions. This was their way of reaffirming friendships and burying grudges of earlier in the day, so essential in maintaining the social harmony of the group.

As I entered the room, I would often catch them lip smacking and muttering in soft, whimpering tones as they sifted through each other's coats, searching for imaginary fleas and lice. The chimps would do the same, but in a much noisier fashion, some forcing air through tightly closed lips to produce loud, repetitive raspberry sounds. Sadly, the singly caged animals, still the majority of the colony, had only themselves to groom, but even that effort showed their resolve not to be brought down by the boredom of captivity.

The luckiest of all the animals were the marmosets, from the jungles of the Amazon. Tiny as they were—an adult male weighs no more than sixteen ounces, a baby barely one ounce at birth—it was easier for us to provide them with a larger, more complex space. The marmosets lived mostly as extended families, older children assisting their parents in caring for the younger babies, learning in the process how to become good parents themselves for some day in the future.

This was the only time of the day when I could hope to escape the constant demands of the paging system and spend a bit of time with the animals, especially the chimps. Lost to the world behind closed doors, I would squat on my haunches before the cages or crouch on one knee, whiling away the time, talking to each animal in turn. I would whisper to one, "How's his little nose tonight?" as I wiggled it with the tip of my finger, or blow gently into the ear of another as she pressed it against the front bars of the cage.

I'd stare into each animal's face and marvel at its uniqueness, so full of architecture and sculptured lines, so much more complex, by comparison, than our own human visage. After a while, I'd find that my mind had drifted off into space as I contemplated life, wondering what it was all about, asking myself if I really believed in what I was doing—this use of animals in research for the betterment of mankind. There was a time when I would have answered with a resounding yes, but I was less confident now, increasingly plagued by doubt, seeing our use of animals no longer as an incontestable right, but more as an unavoidable necessity.

One of these days, I vowed to myself, I would take my camera—the one with the good 100-millimeter macro lens—and get some close-up pictures of each animal. Then I'd sit down and write a book about them, showing a picture of each, with a little story underneath describing their individual backgrounds and personalities, what types of research they had been used in, and how each animal had stood up to the burden. But there was always something to distract me from my resolve.

Each animal had a story to tell, I knew, like the old Chelsea pensioners my mother used to take me to see along the Thames Embankment when I was a young child. Veterans of the Great War—some even of the Boer War—they sat chatting or just staring vacantly into space on the park benches in their tight, smart uniforms of black trousers and scarlet tunics, their brass buttons closed to the throat, their white mustaches waxed and twirled, their knobby, liver-spotted hands clutching canes. *Did they ever reminisce about King and Country and deeds of valor?* I wonder to myself now. And, as with these old soldiers, would anyone care to pause and ask about the sacrifices the chimps and monkeys had made? Certainly not most of the scientists I knew.

Once you've had a little experience, you can often read what a chimp is thinking by the expression on his face or the glint in his eye. A few softly spoken words, just loud enough for the animal in front of you to hear, give depth to the intimacy of the moment. "Did I ever tell him that I loved him?" I would whisper to one. To another I'd say, "She's so beautiful, that girl."

That's not to say that you can't make a mistake, of course, but that's usually because you haven't been paying attention, or you allow your mind to wander or get distracted. The consequences of such a miscalculation can be devastating: you could end up losing a fingertip or several digits all in one go in the blink of an eye. Most times, accidents occur because you move in an erratic, unpredictable fashion, or somebody unseen slams a door unexpectedly, taking the chimp by surprise and giving him a fright, or you just don't see the warning he has been giving you to cease and desist in your behavior. Whatever the reason, we shouldn't be quick to judge; chimpanzees are wild animals, after all.

It's hard to adequately describe the lives of individual primates in research—what they have been subjected to, what the outcomes of the studies have been, and how they handle their sometimes-difficult loads. This is not to say that the research procedures are always hard on the animals in a physical sense, as some might assume. Chimps, especially, are quite tough physically and to a certain extent, emotionally, ready to give as much or more than they receive. They almost dare you to destroy their moral fiber, but in the end, even the toughest can succumb. There is only so much an animal can put up with when he has to face the same soul-destroying procedures day after day. It is often the biggest, toughest, most physically robust chimpanzee who comes crashing to the ground, demolished by the weight placed upon him: one procedure too many, one day too much.

His greatest suffering often comes not from the physical aspects of the research so much as from the psychological and social deprivation that the research imposes upon him. For many types of research, especially in the fields of disease investigation and vaccine development, the strict rules of biocontainment—the prevention of inadvertent disease transmission—dictate that the animals must be singly housed.

At LEMSIP, we housed all the animals in open-barred cages that gave them an unimpeded view and a chance to communicate openly with their friends and neighbors in the room; we never used so-called metabolic cages. These cages, mainly solid-sided, are used when urine and fecal material must be collected around the clock, or in infectious-type studies. We made every effort to assign all the members of a social group to the same study so that they could go through the project together and finish at the same time. They would not be allowed to touch or groom each other, however—an essential component of normal primate behavior.

In many research facilities, animals on infectious studies could find themselves in near or complete isolation, tucked away in some back room at the end of a long corridor or in a remotely located hut, away from the mainstream of human traffic, unable to see each other, like shipwrecked hulks cast upon a deserted beach.

Assigning chimps to research projects at LEMSIP was always a difficult task, especially when it came to the juveniles. The old rule had been that no chimp who weighed less than ten kilograms and was under 2 years of age could be assigned to a study. But even at this size and age, they are still infants.

The dilemma I constantly faced was whether it was more humane to use fewer animals in more studies, which would require limiting breeding to produce fewer babies, or whether it was better to increase breeding so that there would always be more animals from which to choose the psychologically fittest for a particular study. The former approach would not only be more cost effective, but would also keep the number of animals needed in research to a minimum. It would, however, mean that each animal would have to carry a heavier workload, with shorter breaks between studies. Carried to the extreme, this approach could result in working animals from infancy to old age like slaves in a diamond mine.

During one of Jane Goodall's visits to LEMSIP, she suggested during a tour of the nursery that I should consider hiring someone to develop a sort of kindergarten for the young chimps so they could learn how to do fun things like solve puzzles and perhaps use computers, which might help them deal with the boredom of cage life as they got older. Not a bad idea, I thought, but this was 1990, a bit before universities had reached the stage of hiring people solely to play with chimps for the sake of their psychological enrichment.

A few weeks later, we interviewed an applicant for an animal caregiver position that we had advertised in the newspaper. Cynthia was her name. I showed her around. She obviously enjoyed the tour of the nursery and the time spent talking and playing with the infant chimpanzees, but she clearly had hoped to find a full-time position, whereas we required only a half-time candidate. Yet she was just the sort of person Jane Goodall had been talking about. I could offer her only a part-time position at this moment, I told Cynthia, but I would do my best to expand it to full-time later. She said yes.

I put Cynthia in charge of organizing the kindergarten program. Her first class would be Josh and his friends Sabina, Ewok, and Alexis. This bunch of no-good juvenile delinquents—this "Gang of Four," as I used to label them—was rather special in LEMSIP's historical development. These young chimps would be the first students to graduate from the kindergarten program that Cynthia created in the nursery.

I was never able to make up my mind whether Josh was less intelligent than the other chimps or just downright lazy. He didn't delight in drawing and painting like Sabina did. In fact, he used to try to pull her pictures away from her or sit on them, which would make her really mad. Sabina took to wrapping her arm around her paintings to protect them as she lay stretched out on the floor, like a little first grader, or lowered her head over them as a way of hiding them.

Unlike his classmates, Josh refused to operate the puzzle boards or the cash register, as if it were beneath his dignity. But he always made sure he was in position to grab the treat rewards that were due the others on the successful completion of their tasks. He was the boss, there was no denying that.

Some months later, I was able to make Cynthia's position full-time and put her in charge of our fledgling volunteer program, which I had started three or four years earlier. Over the next seven years, until LEMSIP closed, this program contributed greatly in enriching the lives of the young animals and provided many undergraduate and graduate students opportunities to follow careers in primate studies.

When they reached the age of 5, Josh and his gang were put on a trial to test the effectiveness of a nasal spray vaccine against a common virus that causes respiratory infections in very young children and infirm elderly people. This was the simplest of studies. It lasted only six weeks and required no more than a single spray of vaccine up the nose, and later a similar spray of virus suspension, weekly blood samples and nasal and throat swabs, all carried out under sedation. Josh did not mind the procedures, but he could not bear being caged alone, even though he was in the same room as his friends and could readily see and communicate with them. The only barriers between him and Sabina, Ewok, and Alexis were large transparent sheets of Plexiglas hung between their cages to prevent them from sneezing or coughing directly on each other. Sabina and the rest of the group showed no anxiety whatsoever, but, to our surprise, Josh started to whimper and rock from side to side every time Roxanne, Darlene, Cynthia, or any of the other people working in the nursery stopped by to give him extra-special attention. He wanted out, he was trying to tell them.

Josh had never shown this type of behavior before. Being separated from his friends was obviously painful to him. His one and only mission in life—to boss the rest of the group around, benign dictator though he was—had been taken away from him.

He did settle down eventually, but his initial reactions were a sharp demonstration and reminder of how delicate the psyche of these animals can be.

One comfort was that the research rapidly led to the marketing of an effective human vaccine.

Each member of the Gang of Four had a unique story to tell. Barely 6 weeks in age separated the youngest, Ewok, from Josh, the oldest of the group.

Josh's mother, Missie, had loved him dearly from the moment he was born, but she hadn't the faintest idea how to look after him. She held him on her ankle hour after hour, patting him gently on the back and squeezing him lovingly every time he cried in hunger. She literally did not know how to take him to her breast and feed him.

Missie's lack of normal maternal behavior was almost certainly due to shortcomings in the way she herself had been reared, although we did not have the information to prove it. (Records of chimp histories were often spotty at best back then.) She had most likely been taken from her own mother at birth or shortly thereafter, either purposely, so that she could be human reared for the circus, or because her mother could not care for her adequately. Whatever the reason, the deficiency almost certainly spanned two, and possibly three, generations.

Mike, Dave, and I took turns sitting by Missie's cage, trying to coax her into taking hold of the baby properly. After twenty-four hours of agonizing observation, we had to admit defeat and remove Josh from his mother, at least temporarily, and place him in the nursery to be cared for by Roxanne and Darlene. Tomorrow would be another day, we told ourselves; we would try again.

Over the next three or four weeks, we persisted in our efforts, returning Josh to his mother first thing in the morning in the hope that Missie's maternal skills would have magically gotten better overnight. With a growing sense of disappointment, we would have to separate him again twenty-four to forty-eight hours later when it became obvious that Missie's behavior showed no sign of improvement. In the end, we had no alternative but to take Josh away permanently from his mother, who, as you might imagine, was disconsolate from her loss.

Ten days after Josh was born, Sally, an unusually large chimpanzee who cared hardly a fig for human beings, gave birth to a female, whom we named Sabina. Sally was one of those unique and special types of animals who love babies. The very sight of someone else's baby would turn her into a quivering jelly as she fretted and humped, trying to find a way to take possession of this latest potential prize. I'm sure Sally would have adopted fifty babies all in one go had we given her half a chance.

Sabina's birth gave Mike an idea. "Why don't we try to adopt Josh to Sally?" he suggested to Dave and me. "I bet she'd take him in a flash."

We weren't the least bit happy that Josh had ended up in the nursery. Even though Roxanne, Darlene, and all the other ladies were doing their best to raise Josh with lots of TLC, they knew, as we did, that there is no substitute for a real mother.

"Let's give it a try," I said.

Mike and Dave set up the special transfer cage that we had built to safely introduce babies back to their mothers after health examinations. Sally knew the score. She was already peeking through the little window in the front wall of the baby cage and could clearly see Josh huddled there on the floor where we had placed him, wrapped in a soft towel. When we opened the first and then the second door of the cage, Sally gently reached into the box, picked up Josh by his chest, and brought him out to place him on her breast. Josh must have felt the brush of her nipple against the side of his face, because he immediately latched onto it and started to suckle. And big tall Sally looked down with an expression of obvious pride as she studied Sabina and Josh, clung contentedly together on her chest. It had worked! Mike and Dave, Roxanne and Darlene, we all felt the rush of excitement, the thrill of success, the realization that something beautiful had just occurred right before our very eyes.

Sally reared the two babies for the next three months, but, as good a mother as she was behaviorally, there was one problem we couldn't overcome: Sally's milk, though plentiful, was poor in quality. Sabina and Josh began to lose weight. In spite of our efforts to give the two infants supplemental feedings, we came to fear for their survival and were forced to wean them when they were about 4 months of age.

In the meantime, two other babies had been born: Alexis, by Caesarean section to Andrea, and Ewok, born naturally to Mona.

During a routine obstetrical examination of Andrea under anesthesia, which we performed on all the chimps in the late part of pregnancy in an attempt to detect and correct any abnormalities that might arise, Mike, Dave, and I found some highly abnormal fetal heart rate patterns. I had never seen patterns quite like this; they weren't what are called late decelerations, an indication of placental insufficiency, nor could they be described as variable decelerations, which point to strangulation of the umbilical cord, most often caused by a twist. Both conditions, indicating interference with the normal delivery of oxygen to the fetus, constitute the most common causes of perinatal infant mortality in chimps and human beings alike. There was something amiss in Andrea nonetheless, although I could not determine exactly what it was.

We performed a fetal stress test on Andrea. Setting up an intravenous drip, we began to deliver an extremely dilute solution of oxytocin, the hormone responsible for initiating uterine contractions to induce labor. The principle of the test is to measure the fetus's heart rate response during artificially induced uterine contractions that are too mild to actually put the patient into labor. In a normal pregnancy, as a uterine contraction begins to develop, the fetal heart rate begins to drop from around 120 beats per minute to a low point of around 90 beats at the height of a contraction, and then slowly returns to normal as the contraction gradually wears off. This pattern, known as early deceleration, lets you know that although the fetal heart rate slows during the mother's uterine contractions, there is enough oxygen reserve in the placental blood not to put the fetus at risk of fatal oxygen deprivation. In Andrea's case, the Doppler trace of the fetal heart rhythm became so bad that I knew the baby would not survive being born naturally. We immediately scheduled Andrea for an emergency Caesarean section without allowing her to wake from anesthesia. This was a true emergency.

I always felt so proud of the technicians at LEMSIP for the way they responded to emergencies. They needed no instruction, forming small teams to see to every aspect of what had to be done. In this case, Mike and Dave would continue the fetal heart monitoring until the latest possible moment; Terry and Nick set up the surgery;

Bill was in charge of anesthesia and intravenous therapy; Roxanne, Darlene, and Dr. Raymond Hayes, my veterinary colleague, set up an incubator, ready to take charge of the infant once it was delivered; and Ray and Tom, supervisors of animal husbandry, would arrange for the mother's needs once she came out of surgery.

As I incised the wall of the uterus to deliver the fetus's head, I knew right away that something was dreadfully wrong. The baby was blue from lack of oxygen. A fleeting glance at the infant's tiny face suggested features of a human child with Down's syndrome. As I delivered the baby into a warm, sterile towel, I saw that there were no pulsations of the umbilical vein, which feeds oxygen-rich blood from the placenta to the fetus, and the tiny heart was beating with no more than a faint flutter. This was a crisis; we needed to act fast.

I clamped the umbilical cord with two mosquito forceps and severed it with my scalpel. Holding the limp, wet body upside down by the ankles, I knelt on the floor by the side of the surgery table, pulled down my facemask, and gently began to give her mouth-to-nose resuscitation. Terry, my chief surgical assistant, was already filling a hypodermic syringe with a respiratory stimulant, ready to drip it into the baby's nostrils. I squeezed the baby's chest roughly between finger and thumb in a desperate effort to resuscitate her. With a sudden spluttering cough and a gush of birth fluids from her nose, Alexis began to breathe. This was encouraging, but not the end of the crisis.

I passed the baby wrapped in the towel to Roxanne and Darlene, who, under the direction of Dr. Hayes, would have to take care of Alexis and give her all the supportive aid she needed. In particular, they would have to make sure she did not lose body temperature, a high risk for any newborn, especially after being delivered by Caesarean section. They would also have to make sure her lungs did not fill with fluids and that her heartbeat remained strong and steady.

After delivering the placenta, I began to close the uterus and then the abdominal incision. Although I had to concentrate on Andrea, the mother, I could tell that things were touch and go with the baby. Roxanne, Darlene, and Dr. Hayes were mumbling comments to each other, a sure sign that they were having difficulty keeping the infant going. The baby's respirations frequently became irregular and shallow, and her heart was barely beating.

"Hey, Jim," Dr. Hayes called out loudly in alarm, his stethoscope dangling from his ears. "The baby's got a terrible heart murmur, and she doesn't seem to have any use of her left arm and leg; it's like she's paralyzed. The joints of her fingers are all enlarged and swollen, too, like they're infected. I've never seen anything like this," he exclaimed.

I stopped what I was doing and stepped away from the surgery table to glance over Dr. Hayes's shoulder. The baby's little body seemed lost in the incubator, her chest pumping up and down rapidly like a miniature bellows. She was struggling for life.

"Better get an endotracheal tube in her," I suggested, "and give her some oxygen directly."

Dr. Hayes, with the help of Roxanne and Darlene, immediately set about trying to insert a kitten-sized endotracheal tube, the smallest we had in stock, into the baby's tiny windpipe—a difficult procedure in the best of times. He disconnected the oxygen tube from the incubator wall and held it closely to the tip of the endotracheal tube hanging from the baby's mouth.

While Dr. Hayes and his two assistants struggled with Alexis, Terry and I concentrated on finishing Andrea's surgery as fast as we could.

The struggle to save this little baby continued for several hours. As she began to overcome her breathing problems, other abnormalities affecting her started to become more obvious. Dr. Hayes had been right; the joints of Alexis's fingers were severely swollen and taut. Her heart murmur was so loud that it sounded like a little steam engine inside her skinny chest. And there was no doubt that she was paralyzed down the left side of her body. Her arm and leg hung limp on the soft blanket. Her eyes were now open, but I realized that every time I moved her in the incubator to where the light shone on her face, her eyes reflexively rolled up into her head. She must surely have brain damage, I realized.

I called through to the front office to speak to Fred Davis, the lab's assistant director. "Hey, Fred," I said into the phone, "I've got a real problem here. This little baby we've just delivered by C-section seems to have brain damage. We need some special diagnostics here. Any way you could pull a few strings and get a hold of some specialists at NYU Medical Center who might be able to help me on this?" Fred got on it right away. I'm not sure who he got a hold of or what he said, but over the next couple of hours, he managed to line up a neurosurgeon, a neurologist, and a pediatrician at the Medical Center in Manhattan.

The pediatrician called me later that afternoon. "Better bring the baby down to the city tomorrow," he said, "and we'll see what we can do. Oh, and by the way," he added as an afterthought, "could you also bring a normal baby with you, about the same age? That'd give us a good comparison with your problem child."

Fred, the bean counter with a big heart, still had a lot of organizing to do. You can't just take a baby chimp to one of the biggest hospitals in New York City and expect to walk into a doctor's office without causing a stir, or at least raising a few eyebrows. Fred would have to alert his pals in the security department, a bunch of hardcore Irishmen like himself, and make sure that everything could be arranged in such a way that I would be able to sneak Alexis in without having some bystander call the *New York Post* or, worse, the *National Enquirer.*

The next morning, I drove the fifty miles down to Manhattan, along with Roxanne and the two babies, Alexis and Hulk, the latter so named because he was the largest baby we ever had birthed at LEMSIP—a normal, bouncing bruiser if ever there was one. I parked the car in the underground parking lot, and Roxanne and I cautiously made our way up the ramp to one of the side-door entrances into the Medical Center, each with a baby chimp clothed in a little hooded jumpsuit—one pink and one blue—tucked inside our coats. It's times like these that you become aware of your own heartbeat, sure that everyone around you can hear its pounding. *Say someone stops me and asks what I've got stuffed inside my coat?* I pondered. *Please, God, don't let anyone realize what we've got here.* I could picture the lurid headlines in the newspapers the next day: "Eminent doctors fired from New York City hospital for treating monkeys in their clinics," or "Veterinarian sneaks apes into New York City hospital for treatment."

One of the security officers greeted us on our arrival, just like Fred had said he would. The burly Irishman had been keeping an eye out for us all morning. "Come on," he said in a Boston drawl as he led us by the shoulders to a bank of elevators. "Everyone's been waiting for yous guys."

He pressed the button for the neurology department on the fifth floor, and up we went. Luckily, no one else was in the elevator.

As we got off, two other security guards waved us down a long corridor to an open door at the end. The secretary of the department rose from her desk as she saw us coming, a big smile on her face. "Let me see, let me see your little bundles!" she squealed in excitement. "I'll take you in, the doctors are expecting you."

We entered a long room with all sorts of medical equipment lining one wall. The three specialists were standing around an ultrasound machine. After friendly introductions, I filled them in on the babies' histories. Then the doctors got to work examining the babies, trying not to upset them or make them cry. This was not the first time the pediatrician had helped me with chimps, but it was a new experience for his two colleagues. Each one listened carefully to the babies' chests with stethoscopes, performed a battery of neurological reflex tests, and then examined first Hulk and then Alexis by ultrasound. They also obtained blood samples to determine red and white cell counts and some of the critical serum chemistries that would be needed to help make a diagnosis.

After a good two hours of testing, the doctors came to the unanimous conclusion that Alexis had contracted meningitis while in her mother's womb. She had then developed septicemia, a bacterial infection of the bloodstream, which resulted in bacteria settling in her brain. The septicemia had caused the neurological symptoms I had seen in her eyes and the paralysis of her left arm and leg, as well as the murmur of her heart valves and the swelling of the joints of her fingers.

"The mother probably contracted placentitis," one of the doctors explained—an infection of the placenta. "Then the infection would have spread along the umbilical cord to the fetus. You'd better check the mother again and make sure she doesn't have an infection of her uterus, otherwise she's going to be in big trouble, too," he added earnestly. The prognosis was guarded.

We examined Andrea the next day, taking a blood sample and a uterine bacteriological culture from her to determine whether she might have had a persistent infection of the uterus. She was already being treated with a broad-spectrum antibiotic as a precaution against post-surgical infection. The sample came back negative.

And the good news continued. All signs of Down's syndrome had disappeared from Alexis's face by the following morning: a false alarm, thank goodness.

Alexis had received her first massive dose of a broad-spectrum antibiotic there in the doctors' office, which we continued for another three weeks. Based on the specialists' recommendations, Roxanne and Darlene began an exhaustive program of physiotherapy for Alexis in the hope that she would regain normal function of her left arm and leg. Several times a day, they would take her out of the incubator and work her arms and legs up and down, trying to get her muscles to respond. Alexis hated this exercise, of course, and would cry out in rebellion every time. Little by little, though, she began to respond to treatment, first with momentary and then, later, with more sustained contractions of the muscles of her limbs. After six months, Alexis's pupillary response to light was normal, she had developed normal control of her left arm and leg, her heart murmur had disappeared, and the swelling in her finger joints had gone down. Amazingly, Alexis turned out to be one of the most intelligent chimpanzees we ever had at LEMSIP.

Then there was Ewok. He was born two weeks after Alexis to Mona, a highly sophisticated and intelligent chimpanzee who was also one of the most loving of mothers.

A most unfortunate accident occurred one day. The tab broke on the security lock that closed off the door in the tunnel system that led from Mona's cage to a group of chimps who lived in the neighboring cage complex. Mona must have slipped the padlock from its tag, slid the door open, and entered the tunnel, presumably to have a little chin-wag with the other chimps. Ewok, probably still in his mother's arms, may have stuck his leg through the bars of the tunnel, or one of the other chimps may have reached through and grabbed him; either way, Ewok's foot had been bitten badly.

I caught the frantic tone of Mike's voice as he put out an emergency call over the paging system: "Dr. Mahoney, come to Unit 5! Dr. Mahoney, come to Unit 5, stat!" I dropped what I was doing and ran as fast as I could to the chimp room on the other side of the building complex.

At first, it was difficult to see what had happened. Mona was sitting quietly in her cage, Ewok tucked in under her chest. I could see blood all over the floor of the cage, but I couldn't figure out where it had come from. Ewok seemed comfortable enough in his mother's arms, and for the moment all seemed normal. Then I noticed flaps of skin hanging from his foot. The bleeding had already stopped.

As fast as they could, Mike, Dave, and Terry helped me load two syringes and needles with anesthetic, and we tranquilized Mona so that we could remove Ewok and take him to the clinic to examine his foot. It was a mess! All but his big toe, the little toe, and the stump of his first toe had been bitten off, and only flaps of skin remained. The most important thing to do was to clean his foot thoroughly, bandage it, and put him on high levels of broad-spectrum antibiotics. I didn't want to operate on him straightaway to remove the remains of broken toe bones because I was scared that given his young age and his present state of shock, he might not be able to handle the anesthetic. It would be better to keep him in the nursery overnight and determine whether we could operate on him the next day.

As it turned out, he did not require a great deal of surgical attention. Apart from snipping off a few odd flaps of skin under local anesthesia and removing tiny splinters of crushed bone with a pair of forceps, we were able to bandage his foot after placing just a few sutures to bring the broken skin loosely together. The greatest tragedy of all, however, was that we would not be able to return Ewok to his mother because he would need to be given antibiotics every six hours, and his bandages would have to be changed once, if not twice, a day for the next several days.

Of course, Roxanne and Darlene had no trouble feeding Ewok and giving him his oral antibiotics; all the animals, from the tiniest marmoset to the brawniest chimp, seemed to trust them instinctively. I was the ogre; I was the one Ewok grew to hate with a passion. No matter how gently I tried to speak to him as Roxanne or Darlene held him in their arms, or however slowly I moved when unwrapping the old bandage from his foot and replacing it with a new one, Ewok would make a grab at me any chance he got, nipping my fingers or swiping me hard across the face.

This miserable state of affairs went on for two long months. I had long ago accepted as a fact of life that animals would not always appreciate what I was trying to do for them. Imagine my intense joy, therefore, when one day, as I was changing Ewok's bandage, he reached out from Roxanne's embrace, wrapped his arms around my neck, and gave me a great big, wet kiss on the lips. I have no idea what caused him to change his mind about me, but from that moment on, Ewok and I became bonded, the greatest of buddies.

* * * * *

At 9 years old, and still looked upon as babies by all of us at the lab, Josh and the rest of the Gang of Four made it to sanctuary in California in 1996, along with Herbie, a wise and socially very sophisticated 43-year-old male.

While Josh and Ewok were vasectomized to avoid unwanted pregnancies, everyone somehow forgot Herbie. As a consequence, Alexis gave birth to Shauri in 1999. Unfortunately, Alexis was unable to take care of her infant, who had to be hand-reared. Sad to say, Alexis died suddenly of unknown causes less than three years later, at 15 years of age.

Sabina immediately assumed the role of adoptive mother to Shauri upon Alexis's death. Although she was unable to feed her, she proudly carried her around in her arms or on her back. Dear old Herbie, who turned out to be a wonderful father to Shauri, died at 54 years of age from heart failure.

Ewok is still delighted to see me when I visit the sanctuary. Sabina immediately tries to look up my nose as she clambers over Ewok's side to get to me—a very annoying habit that she had developed at LEMSIP. Josh still thinks he is the leader of the group, although Ewok doesn't seem quite convinced of that.

9

Three Wild Mice

TO A MOUSE, ON TURNING HER UP IN HER NEST
WITH THE PLOUGH

Still thou art blest, compar'd wi me!
The present only toucheth thee:
But och! I backward cast my e'e,
On prospects drear!
An forward, tho I canna see,
I guess an fear!

—Robert Burns (1759–1796)

The close relationship between human beings on the one hand and mice and rats on the other is thought to have begun between 4000 and 1000 BC, when the ancient Egyptians came up with the idea of long-term storage of grain in silos to cover years of poor harvest, drought, and famine. Rats, of course, have a notorious reputation for causing deadly disease in human beings. At least twenty-five million people, one-third of the population of Europe, died of bubonic plague, better known as the Black Death, in the Middle Ages, and severe outbreaks still occur around the world every now and then.

Mice, with a less noisome reputation, have nonetheless been associated with the spread of human disease also. The deer mouse was identified as the vector of the hantavirus, a nasty respiratory disease, when an outbreak occurred in the southwestern United States in 1993. There is evidence that this disease may have occurred as far back as around 1,000 years ago in China. A complex biological relationship established among white-tailed deer, deer ticks, and deer mice has led to the spread of Lyme disease, caused by the bacterium *Borrelia burgdorferi*, from the northeastern United States, where it was first identified in 1975, to practically the entire lower forty-eight states today.

Deer mice are pretty little things with lustrous chestnut brown coats; prominent white underbellies, chests, and throats; and large ears. When they are frightened or stressed, their eyes bulge prominently from their sockets, as if they were on stalks.

Unlike the ubiquitous house mouse (*Mus musculus*), which colonizes households year-round, deer mice (*Peromyscus maniculatus*) establish temporary living quarters during the winter in houses like ours that are in the middle of forests or on the edges of woodlands. I recall only one winter in the thirty-plus years we have lived in this house when they did not invade us. That was last year, after I tried to mouse-proof the garage and other access points into the house.

Invariably, the first evidence we see of mice having moved in is their droppings. We find them in one particular drawer beneath the kitchen countertop in which we store unused ashtrays, matches, and rubber bands, but never food. The perplexing thing about this drawer is that there is no connection between it and the rest of the kitchen cabinetry. How, then, do the mice get into it to use it as a bathroom? This has caused me indescribable frustration over the years—something akin, I would imagine, to what Finnegan, the little rhesus monkey, must have experienced when he couldn't figure out why everyone in the house except he could get water to flow out of the dispenser on the refrigerator door. For the zillionth time,

I rechecked that particular drawer just before typing this part of the story: *there ain't no access hole!*

With the first sign of mice, I would set a humane trap in the cupboard under the kitchen sink. Rarely would I be successful the first night; in fact, it might take me a week or more to catch the first mouse, and maybe several more days before I would be able to satisfy myself that I had trapped all the mice that were living free in the house.

In the past, if I managed to catch the mice during the January thaw, I would release them into the forest that night or the following morning, but I came to realize that doing so was not very humane: often the weather would take a sudden turn for the worse, and the mice might not have had time to construct a warm nest for themselves.

It was just before Christmas when this particular family of deer mice moved in. After a few nights of trying, I managed to catch two young females at the same time. I presumed they were sisters. The next night, I caught an adult female, much larger than the two from the night before. Judging by the friendly interactions among the three when I put them together, I assumed this adult female was the mother. There were no traces of other mice in the kitchen cabinetry after that. I had obviously caught all the members of the family, and I proceeded to transfer them to a typical laboratory cage.

The cage was made of a transparent plastic dish and a stainless steel wire grid on top, fitted with a small water bottle and spout, a food tray, and a deep litter of wood shavings. I suspended an infrared lamp four feet above the little cage to provide not only heat, but also light that would not interfere with the mice's diurnal rhythm. This design was specifically intended for tame laboratory mice, not wild hooligans like I was soon to discover we were dealing with.

The transfer of mice from trap to cage is tricky, and I am always careful when dealing with deer mice—or any species of wild animal, for that matter. I wear disposable rubber gloves and avoid contaminating myself with urine or feces while handling soiled bedding, when aerosol spread of virus particles and bacteria is most likely to occur.

To catch the mice, I use a tongue retractor designed for newborn human infants. It looks like an instrument of torture, a relic of the Inquisition, with its long handles and long, narrow blades with large, serrated metal loops at one end, yet it is extremely gentle on delicate tissues. With a little care, I can guarantee no breakage of bones or damage to the skin.

Having completed the transfer, I realized I would have to invest in winter-long living quarters for the mice. The laboratory cage was far too small for three, and it was only December; spring was months away. I would have to invest in a two-house unit joined by a connecting tunnel so that I could not only provide adequate space for the mice, but also close them off in one unit while I cleaned the other each day. This was becoming a very expensive undertaking.

Each house, twice the size of the laboratory cage, comprised two short towers with removable pepper pot–like lids for air ventilation, and an arched ventilated roof. I added a six-inch length of cardboard core from a depleted paper towel roll, lined with a double layer of paper towel. This provided the mice with a warm, easy-to-clean bed, which they liked to squeeze into, side by side, their little heads poking out the other end like a tiny bouquet of flowers. A fresh facial tissue each night provided them soft material that they could tear up and pack in the sleeping tube. Again, I rigged up the infrared lamp.

Arnold, our neighbor from the other side of the pond, saw the warm glow from our sunroom windows and phoned the next morning to ask whether I had started up my own red-light district.

Unlike Molly and Pups, who seemed utterly bored by the mice, Rags loved helping me with the cage cleaning. The mice must have appealed to her sheepdog nature. (Rags had once raised a small litter of abandoned wild rabbits.) She would stick her nose right up to the transparent wall of the cages. I was surprised at how quickly the

Rags found our family of mice endlessly fascinating.

mice became fearless of Rags's pestering, often sitting upright, side by side in a line, as close to her nose as they could get, munching pieces of food they held between their hand-like paws.

I was always impressed by the cleanliness of the mice. They never soiled their sleeping tube or food dish, and they seemed to make quite an effort to be clean with the wood shavings in their sleeping cage. The other cage, which they seemed to use mostly for playing and exercise, was a different matter altogether: I had to clean that cage daily.

These three mice looked quite different from each other in the face and had quite different personalities, as I would eventually find out. The mother seemed easygoing and unperturbed, while one daughter was more likely to get stressed and anxious. The other daughter, whom I soon began to refer to as Minnie, was the most independent of the three and the most likely to attack my fingertip if she got the chance. I would also find in time that she had delinquent tendencies.

On their first night residing in what I thought of as their castle, I was awakened at around 1:30 in the morning to what sounded like the gnashing of teeth, alternating every now and then with the noise of heavy banging or tapping. *What on earth could that be?* I wondered as I lay there in the dark. It seemed to be an awfully loud noise to be coming from three little mice. Were they playing wildly with each other, or were they up to something more sinister?

Trying not to disturb Marie-Paule, I crawled out of bed and carefully made my way down the stairs in my bare feet. I remembered to avoid the creaky sixth step down the staircase, which was especially noisy in winter and would certainly alert the mice to my approach. It was dark and bitterly cold.

I stopped at the entrance of the hallway into the kitchen. At the other end of the kitchen, through the French doors in the sunroom, I could vaguely make out in the red glow of the heat lamp what looked like a Ping-Pong ball bouncing up and down in one of the mouse cages. It was Minnie, I was certain. *What the heck is she doing?* I wondered.

I should have thought to bring my glasses with me or, better still, have my binoculars standing by.

As I was about to take my first step into the kitchen to take a closer look, all suddenly became quiet. Minnie had obviously heard me, in spite of my efforts to be quiet, and had sounded the silent alarm bell: "Stop! It's him. It's him! Just act normal." The three mice were going about their business in a quiet, nonchalant manner, all innocent-like, grooming whiskers, scratching bellies, munching on morsels of food.

I must remember to keep my binoculars on the island countertop in the kitchen, within easy reach from the hallway, I told myself. I could view the cages through the French doors of the sunroom, about thirty feet away at the other end of the kitchen, without having to step into the kitchen at all.

I made my way to the sunroom to take a closer look. The mice looked up at me as if to say, "Oh, it's you!" They had eaten all of the Cheddar cheese, none of the Munster, all six of the red dog-treat strands, and two of the six brown strands, as well as almost all of the black sunflower seeds but none of the black-and-white-striped sunflower seeds. Deer mice are very picky eaters.

Everything seemed normal enough, and I went back to bed.

The next day was Christmas Eve. Pádraig, our older son, had come home to spend a few days with us over the holidays. Rags, who adored Pádraig, seemed to find great delight in showing him the mice, reaching up to their cages with her paws, looking back to see if she had gained his attention. It was late at night when he arrived, and the mice were already asleep in their cardboard tunnel.

That night, again at around 1:30, I was once more wakened by the loud noises of gnawing teeth and banging. I had remembered to place the binoculars on the countertop of the kitchen island before going to bed. This time I was determined to get to the bottom of what was going on. It was Minnie who was bouncing up and down, all right, while her mother and sister chased each other in circles.

I had barely gotten the binoculars to my eyes, however, when they must have sensed my presence and froze. I was no further along in solving the mystery than I had been the night before.

When we got up at around 8 o'clock that morning, Pádraig mentioned over breakfast that he still hadn't seen the mice. I immediately went to look. "They're still in bed asleep," I assured him. "They had a pretty hectic night last night," I added, relating to him what had transpired the night before. Wads of carefully arranged interlocking pieces of chewed tissue paper plugged both ends of the cardboard roll.

A little later, Pádraig came to me with a big grin on his face. "I think the mice have escaped, Dad."

"What makes you think that?" I said.

He pointed silently to one of the pepper pot towers. The center of the blue dome had been eaten through. How could I not have noticed? It must have been Minnie, of course. Now I knew what all her bouncing had been about: she had no other way to reach the perforated dome, so she jumped and wedged her body up inside the tower so she could reach out and grab the tower, get a grip on the dome, and chew through it.

I checked one of the other pepper pot domes for comparison. The ventilation holes were arranged as a single hole in the center, surrounded by six holes in an intermediate ring and twelve holes in an outer ring. Minnie had concentrated all her efforts on eating through the plastic material between the middle and outer rings of holes of just one of the four available domes, leaving a somewhat jagged-edged hole measuring three-quarters of an inch in diameter. It had taken her two nights. What incredible determination! You would hardly imagine the mice being able to squeeze their bodies through such a small hole, especially the mama mouse, who was decidedly larger than her two daughters.

I couldn't help thinking of Steve McQueen and the movie *The Great Escape,* in which Allied soldiers plan their escape from a German prison camp. It really makes you feel humble when an itty-bitty animal like a mouse can so easily outsmart you. Of course I was somewhat used to that, having worked for so many years with chimps and monkeys, as well as with elephants like Loki.

I came up with a simple solution to stop Minnie from causing further destruction of the pepper pot towers: wedge the perforated dome upside down in the tower. *Who's the smarter one now, Minnie?* I felt like saying.

Back to the drawing board! I would have to set the humane trap again. I managed to catch all three of the mice, one at a time, during the remainder of Christmas Day and into the following Boxing Day morning.

Several days went by during which all seemed normal and uneventful. Then one morning, there was no sign of the mice. *Not again!* I sighed. I quickly checked the pepper pot towers: all were in place, upside down, and whole. I checked the side doors, thinking that maybe I had accidentally left one open when I cleaned the cage the day before: but, no, nothing was out of place. Certainly there was no one asleep in the paper-filled cardboard tube. I checked everything again, but all was normal. The red tunnel connecting the two house units was secure, and—wait a minute! There was a neat little pile of psychedelic blue plastic dust beneath one end of the tunnel. When I looked more closely, I could see that the half ring attached to the end wall of the house into which the tunnel fitted had been chewed away. A quarter-inch slot designed into the retainer rim had been chewed into an irregular space that had opened up, through which, *quod erat demonstrandum,* three little mouse bodies could fit. Minnie's little jaw was distinctly more pointed than her mother's or her sister's. It must have given her just enough room to get the tip of her chin in so she could gnaw away at the plastic. Minnie had done it again!

This was serious damage, much worse than eating the pepper pot lids out of the ventilation towers, as Minnie had done before. Buying a new house to replace the damaged one would do no good because Minnie would just eat through the plastic rim again. The house had an inherent design flaw: it could never be "Minnie-proof." I would have to keep the tunnel doors closed off each night and hope that Minnie didn't try to make a break for it during daylight hours, when the tunnel would be open. But first I would have to capture the escapees again.

To my surprise and amazement, the next morning I found that I had caught all three in the humane trap beneath the kitchen sink. This escaping and being caught again was becoming a habit, a normal part of life for them. These three had certainly earned their freedom, but they would have to stay cooped up a little while longer until there was a significant break in the weather. The mice undoubtedly saw our house as part of their natural domain, yet I could hardly leave them to roam free in it.

In late March, along with Rags, I took the three mice in one cage to a secluded spot I knew in a state forest close by. I placed the cage beneath the broad trunk of a maple tree and began to cover it in a deep layer of dried leaves. There was enough food and water in the cage to last twenty-four hours: I'd come back tomorrow. I closed off the doors because I wanted them to spend their first twenty-four hours together in safety. The following evening, I went back with Raggie. The mice had eaten the food, which I replenished, but this time I opened all the doors and towers of the cage. They did not move. I went back the following night to find that all the food I had left had been consumed. The next night it was untouched, and I assumed they had left the house and made their way into the forest.

I'm sure it was my imagination, but I remember that as I placed the house among the deep bed of leaves on the forest floor, Minnie had looked up at me and seemed to say, "Why are you doing this to us?" No matter how much we profess to care, we cannot coexist in harmony with creatures of the wild. Our worlds will always clash. How can we preserve their freedom?

I couldn't help thinking of a section of Masson and McCarthy's book *When Elephants Weep*. In chapter 6, in the section entitled "Reveling in Freedom," the authors muse: "Whether an animal without freedom to choose its own environment, no matter how small, can be happy is a question that needs to be asked. Is not freedom of choice basic to the meaning of happiness?"

10

Great Escapes

Those who deny freedom to others deserve it not for themselves.

—Abraham Lincoln (1809–1865)

Igor is 53 years old. That's pretty old for a white-handed gibbon. He's a funny little guy, all black except for the white tops of his hands and feet, and an irregular narrow band of white hair outlining his face. He sometimes twists his lips into a knot as he looks at you with an expression of, "What are you looking at?" He was one of a dozen or so gibbons that LEMSIP had in the late 1970s to early '80s as part of an international primate blood-grouping program for the World Health Organization.

He had been injected in the muscle of his upper arm with a substance known as Freund's complete adjuvant, a preparation that boosts the immune system, in this case for the production of antibodies that can then be used to detect the various types of blood group factors that gibbons possess. Igor had reacted badly to this injection, the muscle at the injection site becoming highly inflamed and irritated. Some while later, he developed a psychological stereotypy, that is, a psychotic behavior. He began to mutilate himself whenever he became distressed, biting repeatedly at his arm, at the very spot where he had been injected. So much did he damage himself that the muscle at that point became completely atrophied.

Igor self-mutilated only when he saw other gibbons. We had to hang a thick black-painted Plexiglas sheet between his cage and his neighbor's so that he couldn't see any of the other gibbons, although hearing them vocalize and sing caused him no problem. This was not the sort of existence that an elderly gibbon, who had already given many years of his life to research, should be subjected to. I managed to talk Dr. Jan Moor-Jankowski, the founder and director of LEMSIP, into donating Igor, along with some of the lab's other gibbons, to the International Primate Protection League's sanctuary in Summerville, South Carolina, the organization founded by Dr. Shirley McGreal. That was more than twenty years ago, and Igor has never once bitten himself again.

Shirley McGreal is a petite, feisty English lady with a rich Yorkshire accent. She has probably done more than any other single person to protect primates living in the wild and to stop, or at least curb, their illicit trade and smuggling. When she lived in Thailand with her husband in the early 1970s, she was horrified to discover the appalling conditions under which primates, including gibbons, were being captured from the wild and smuggled to the United States and other countries. It was this experience that prompted her to create IPPL in 1973.

Through the efforts of concerned students working undercover at the Bangkok airport, Shirley was able to document the lucrative nature of the primate trade in the first issue of the IPPL newsletter that she launched in 1974. Sad to say, the newsletter is still going strong. Now, however, it deals not only with the continuing smuggling for research and the pet trade, but also the bush meat crisis, unlawful habitat destruction, and countless other issues. Shirley's life has been threatened more than once.

The National Institutes of Health and biomedical researchers soon learned that they would have to take Dr. McGreal seriously when, in

1977, she exposed the United States' breach of a treaty with India by importing rhesus monkeys for neutron bomb testing. The treaty specifically stated that the monkeys could not be used in warfare-related research. This exposure led to an immediate and total ban on exportation of rhesus monkeys from India to the United States, no matter what the scientific purpose. The price of a rhesus monkey in the United States skyrocketed overnight from around $30 to $2,000, if the monkey could be obtained from China, the only immediately available nondomestic source after the Indian embargo went into effect.

The price of rhesus monkeys never went down again. Although this, in itself, did not lead to a curtailment in the use of rhesus monkeys in research as primate advocates had hoped, it did make scientists more careful and precise in how they used them, and funding agencies more circumspect in which research proposals they funded.

Shirley finally received the official recognition she had long deserved for her years of unrelenting dedication to the cause of primate protection worldwide. She was awarded the Order of the British Empire by Queen Elizabeth II in 2008. I think Shirley was equally thrilled to have a private chin-wag before the investiture with Prince Phillip, Duke of Edinburgh, who has long been an admirer and supporter of her accomplishments.

Once or sometimes twice a year, I get together with IPPL's local veterinarian, Dr. John Ohlandt, to carry out physical health examinations on the gibbons. John and I have known each other for many years, and we work well together.

As soon as I arrive from the airport, I go straight to the little cottage where I stay, unpack my bags, ready my medical supplies for work the following morning, change into work clothes, and make a tour of the animals.

Health examinations, unfortunately, necessitate sedating the gibbons by hypodermic injection, something they all hate, as you can imagine. Of course, I need the assistance of all the staff to achieve this, but the animals blame me, not the caregivers or Dr. Ohlandt, for doing all the nasty things. And gibbons have long memories for unpleasant experiences.

The gibbon colony is divided into two low-fenced areas, each of them two to three acres in size. Michelle and Louie-Louie's cage is the first one I have to pass, something I dread doing. They see me coming from quite some distance, no matter how hard I try to hide myself, and they immediately start to shout, as if to say, "He's back, he's back!" This gets the whole colony riled up. The sanctuary staff thinks the pandemonium is hilarious; even Dr. Ohlandt is amused. The gibbons no doubt remember me and think of me only as evil incarnate.

Fortunately, the chimps and monkeys at LEMSIP did not resent me like Michelle, Louie-Louie, and the rest of the gibbons at IPPL did, although that's not to say some of them didn't dislike me. That was more of a personal dislike, for reasons I often could not determine, than a consequence of my having to stick needles in them or do other unpleasant things. Most of the animals at LEMSIP I saw daily, and some several times a day. This gave me the chance to talk to them, groom them, give them a tickle, or slip them one of the peppermint candies that I always carried in my pocket.

The basic pattern of housing for the gibbons at IPPL comprises large, well-lit indoor houses with heat and air-conditioning for sleeping quarters or daytime confinement during severe inclement weather. The gibbons are kept in their houses at night to reduce their being bothered by mosquitoes.

The outdoor housing consists of various designs and sizes of corncribs, which are tall, round, or oblong galvanized, heavy-duty wire structures with cone-shaped roofs. (As the name implies, corncribs are usually intended for use by farmers to store Indian corncobs.) Extensive systems of overhead open-wire tunnels or runways, suspended eight feet above the ground and fifty to one hundred feet long or more, connect the indoor housing to the outdoor corncribs and provide the animals the opportunity to go visit friends for a chat or have little vocal arguments with them, if they feel so inclined.

I am always amazed by the speed and grace gibbons can muster in brachiating, arm over arm, in the exercise areas, performing their acrobatics eighteen to twenty feet above the ground as if they were in the high canopies of their native forests.

Gibbons are equipped with exceptionally long arms, hands, and fingers, which enable them to be artistes of the trapeze. Their short legs and relatively short feet make them feel uncomfortable and unsuited to terrestrial living, although, when they are on the ground, they run bipedally, with arms and hands stretched above their heads like ballerinas about to perform pirouettes.

Gibbons also love to sing. Each morning at around 11 o'clock, and again at about 4 o'clock in the afternoon, they hold their concerts, the sound carrying far. It begins with one gibbon slowly cranking up, *whoo-ah, whoo-ah,* each bar getting higher in tone and a little faster in rhythm. One or two others will join in at this stage, but there is nothing terribly musical about it yet. Little by little, more gibbons join in until, suddenly, they are all in synchrony, *whoo-whahh, whoo-whaahh, whoo-whaaahh,* reaching the climax of the rhythm and then tumbling down, *whoo-wha-wha, wha-wha-whooo,* like a kettle boiling over, ready to begin again. This goes on for half an hour or so, and then it is all over.

There is something very therapeutic, almost spiritually relaxing about the atmosphere of the sanctuary. I like to sit out on one of the many benches hidden among the vines and heady blossoms, the soft shades of the setting sun and the quieter tones of the gibbons as they attend to the last details of the day sending me into daydreams.

On one particular afternoon, I was making my way through the outdoor runs, quietly speaking to the gibbons as I passed them, when I found Hardy, one of the caregivers, crouched down by Blackie's cage, tickling his belly through the wires of the corncrib.

Like Igor, Blackie is also a white-handed gibbon. He's a particularly handsome, youthful-looking little guy for his 50 years of age, but he is utterly deaf as far as we can tell.

Except for Finnegan and Erin, the two little rhesus monkeys I had spirited away to Iowa in 1982, Blackie and Penny, along with their offspring, E.T., were the first primates to be sent legally into retirement from LEMSIP. Penny had died recently. She was in her late forties; her organs just got old and slowly gave up. She was the sweetest gibbon you could ever imagine. Blackie was sometimes a little mean to her—he would poke her in the back now and again, not to hurt her, just to annoy her.

Gibbons are truly monogamous, sticking to their mates all their lives. This faithfulness causes a bit of a problem because the one left behind after the death of a mate is unlikely to accept a new social partner, especially in Blackie's case, his being so old and a bit arrogant.

Hardy has an extra-special relationship with Blackie, who likes to roughhouse with Hardy. Blackie tries to give him toothy mock bites in return for Hardy's tickling his sides roughly. It was during

Blackie is a handsome 50-year-old gibbon.

one of these rough-and-tumbles that Hardy accidentally slammed his foot down hard on the concrete floor of the corncrib. Blackie, not seeing him do so, jumped in fright, presumably feeling the vibration through his feet. He let out a series of *whoop* alarms, setting off all the other gibbons in the colony in similar fashion. Because of the dense curtain of grapevines and small fig trees that shielded Blackie's corncrib, none of the other gibbons could see Blackie or Hardy and me standing there.

Blackie immediately jumped to the conclusion that the vibration had come from within a large plastic toy igloo that was positioned on the concrete slab of the corncrib. With one hand holding onto a hanging climbing rope, he reached forward with his other long arm and flicked the back of his hand at the tunnel entrance to the igloo, as if there were an evil spirit inside. Step by step he got closer until, overcoming his fear, he was finally able to flick the igloo off the floor a couple of inches at a time. By now, the rest of the gibbons in the colony were in an uproar, and Blackie was out of control.

Hardy tried to calm him down by repeatedly telling him, "Everything is all right," but no words of comfort would ease him. I became concerned that Blackie would go into hypoglycemic shock from severe, acute stress and told Hardy to go and get some bananas and glucose water to feed him.

After Hardy left, I decided that maybe I should leave also, because my continued presence as a relative stranger might only add to Blackie's discomfort. I made my way around Blackie's corncrib and proceeded toward a small gate in the grapevine-enshrouded fence.

As I emerged through the gate, I was suddenly in full view of all the other gibbons, who burst into screams and whoops. "It was he," they were undoubtedly shouting. "It was he!" I made my way as fast but as smoothly as I could across the fenced-in grassy area containing the gibbon runs to a small gate on the far side of the compound. As I exited, suddenly all became quiet. The hobgoblin was gone!

* * * * *

By 1995, LEMSIP found itself once again in financial distress. The lab was not in compliance with amendments to the Animal Welfare Act, which had been passed in 1986 and put into effect in early 1993. Many of the lab's cages for adult chimpanzees, although larger in floor area than the minimum legal requirements, were seven and a quarter inches too short in height, less than the finger span of an average man's hand. The minimum seven-foot height requirement was to ensure that all chimps would be able to swing from the roofs of their cages without their feet touching the floor. Our chimps could do this quite comfortably.

Dr. Moor-Jankowski thought it ridiculous that for the sake of a few inches, we would have to carry out major construction and purchase new cages. "Why don't you take your video camera and film the chimps swinging from the roofs of their cages, and we could send it to the USDA, and perhaps that would give us clearance on the ruling once they could see that the chimps are not being deprived?" he asked.

All very fine for him to say, I thought as I left my meeting with the director. You can't just walk into a chimp room and expect to film the animals swinging happily on command. My pointing the camera directly at them would be enough for them not to want to cooperate. I opened the doors of the first chimp room that I came to, still deep in thought, wondering how I could achieve this. As I entered the room, I saw Midge swinging back and forth from the ceiling of his cage. I couldn't believe my eyes. When Midge saw me, he jumped down to the floor of the cage and came over to greet me. "That was very good, that Midge, swinging like that," I said to him. "Would he do that again for me, please?" He looked up at the roof of the cage, stood up, started to bounce up and down on his heels, and leaped into the air, grabbing hold of the bars of the ceiling.

I went straight away to get my video camera. Unfortunately, the USDA wouldn't accept the evidence: "Rules are rules," they proclaimed.

The cost to construct sufficient new cages, at $9,000 per cage, and enlarge and modify the existing buildings to house them would have been on the order of $2 million, a sum that the lab would never be able to raise. Faced with its own financial deficit, New York University, the mother institution, announced that it could no longer support the primate laboratory and would seek another lab to take it over.

Already the largest chimpanzee colony in the world, the Coulston Foundation of Alamogordo, New Mexico, stepped up to the plate and offered to take over LEMSIP, gratis, after a six-month trial period, beginning in mid-September 1995. The agreement further stipulated that in the event the foundation decided not to take over LEMSIP, the university would give it a minimum of approximately one hundred chimps free of charge.

Dr. Moor-Jankowski was fired, and I was made acting director, captain of the sinking ship, until the foundation would take over.

In the first week of September 1996, I got a call from the dean of the NYU Medical School. Would I come down to Manhattan the next day and meet with a lawyer from the Coulston Foundation to arrange the transfer of all the young chimps at LEMSIP (the most valuable of the chimps because of their young age and the many years ahead they might have for potential use in research) to New Mexico? "Bring Kathy with you," he said.

With the announcement of LEMSIP's takeover, Kathy, who had worked at the lab for eighteen years and knew its operation well, had been promoted to the position of business manager. Furthermore, the dean of the Medical School trusted her.

In the meeting the next day, I received clear instructions to make arrangements without delay for the babies' transfer, no exceptions.

Kathy and I left the medical center and walked out onto First Avenue. We were in a state of shock. We had known for months that this day would come; we often asked ourselves why it hadn't come already. Yet the sharp order was like the slam of a sledgehammer to the head. How could I send the twins, Amber and Alyse, to a strange place and risk their being split apart when Amber depended so much on her sister's comforting when she went into one of her seizures? What about little My-T-Fine with his devilment and cockiness; and Shake, who was suffocating at birth because the placental membranes would not split away from her face?

I couldn't help thinking of each and every one of the thirty-two as I went down the list in my mind. I knew they would be doomed.

Dr. Frederick Coulston was well known for his less than compassionate attitudes concerning the use of chimpanzees in research. In a *National Geographic* television special entitled "Chimp Rescue," he gave a very revealing definition of sanctuary, which summed up all his previous views:

"Let's look at the biggest sanctuary in the world: prisons for human beings. Hey! That's a sanctuary, isn't it? They're fed and they're cared for, but they also work. They're in prison, in a sanctuary. We put people in prison: we don't ask them whether they want to go or not. We put them in. I don't see the difference."

To date, we had already sent twenty-nine chimps to the Coulston Foundation on demand, although we had managed to smuggle out thirty monkeys and forty-six chimps to sanctuary.

"What on earth are we going to do?" I said to Kathy as we stood out on the busy street.

"Would Martine be able to take the babies?" Kathy asked, knowing full well that it was a ridiculous question.

"We'd have to get the babies out within the week if there was any chance of smuggling them out secretly," I countered. "How on earth could we expect the WayStation to build cages for thirty-two chimps in that short a time?"

"Well, at least give her a call and ask her," Kathy suggested.

I called California from a sidewalk phone booth and posed the question to Martine Colette, the founder and director of the Wildlife WayStation. "Phone me back in an hour," she told me.

I called back. "We'll take them," she simply said.

Martine was true to the motto of the Wildlife WayStation: *Deeds, Not Words*. She had accepted an enormous responsibility by agreeing to take the babies. The WayStation, in fact, was to give refuge to 50 of the 109 chimpanzees that we eventually got out of LEMSIP, as well as several baboons. Initially, the WayStation got no money from the NYU Medical School for support of the animals: I could hardly ask the dean for money when I was smuggling the chimps.

And so began "Mission Impossible." We were about to smuggle out the largest convoy of chimpanzees ever to hit the road at one time, on a near-3,000-mile journey across the continent, all in utter secrecy. I spent the week making arrangements to get the babies out. They would all need physical examinations, tuberculosis tests, and blood work to verify that they were in a good state of health. My colleague, Dr. Doug Cohn, and I would have to get cracking. They would need import permits to enter the state of California, as well as all the requisite United States Department of Agriculture papers. Because of wild chimps' endangered status, we would also have to get Convention on International Trade in Endangered Species of Wild Flora and Fauna (CITES) papers for the U.S. Fish and Wildlife Service to prove that the chimps were domestic born and not wild caught.

On such short notice I couldn't get the truckers we normally used and trusted implicitly to do a good job. I found another group, however—truckers I had never heard of before.

"It's going to take two trucks to transport that number of animals with their cages," I was informed. "We've never transported chimps before, so you will have to provide your own cages and build wooden frames around them, once they are in the trucks, to hold them in place so they don't slip and slide all over once we're on the road."

That's a problem right there, I thought. *How can I instruct the LEMSIP maintenance department to construct frameworks to hold the cages when I don't know the size or internal configuration of the trucks?* This job would have to be done quickly during the darkness of night in order to maintain secrecy. I had a gnawing feeling in the pit of my stomach that things might not turn out well.

The plan was that the two trucks would arrive after dark on the coming Sunday night. The LEMSIP maintenance crew would be waiting, ready to get to work measuring the insides of the trucks and constructing the frameworks for the cages. Then, at around 2 o'clock Monday morning, the technicians would arrive at the lab and start loading the chimps into the cages, now securely fastened in the trucks. The older, larger, immensely strong juveniles would have to be anesthetized, of course, to allow them to be carried from their home cages into the transport cages on the trucks. At the last moment, Roxanne and her nursery crew would carry the babies fully awake in their arms to the transport cages, arranged according to their social groups, once all the older chimps had fully recovered from anesthesia. It would be a hard night's work, no doubt about it.

I instructed Terry, the supervisor of the research technicians, and Ray, the supervisor of the husbandry technicians, to call me as soon as they heard the trucks roll down the driveway, and I'd be at the lab as fast as possible.

I fell into fitful sleep, the telephone beside me. But by two o'clock in the morning, I had received no call from LEMSIP. I called and spoke to Terry.

"The trucks haven't shown up, Doc, and we've had no phone call from the drivers to indicate what might have gone wrong." The drivers had no telephone with them; I knew that, so there was no way we could call them. I told the technicians and the maintenance crew to give the trucks one more hour and then go home; there would be no point in their waiting any longer at the lab. This was turning into a disaster.

The phone rang, jarring me out of a deep sleep. It was 7 o'clock in the morning. "Hey, Doc!" the gravelly voice boomed into my ear. It was Nick, one of Terry's research technicians, calling from the lab.

"The two trucks've just arrived," he announced, "but you won't believe it, they're covered in buffalo shit!"

"What on earth are you talking about?" I replied as I shook my head, trying to stir myself from torpor.

"I'm not kidding, Doc," Nick chuckled. "There's buffalo pat splattered all over the inside of the walls, the floors, the ceilings, every nook and cranny you could possibly imagine. That's why they were so late getting here," he added, referring to the four drivers in charge of the trucks. "Apparently, they were delivering two shipments of buffalo from one zoo to another and got held up. Trouble is, we're going to have to clean the trucks thoroughly before we can even begin to load the transport cages for the babies, and it's going to take us hours."

"They never told me anything about transporting buffalo," I said in consternation. "It's not just how clean the trucks must be," I continued, "you're going to have to sterilize them as well. There's no knowing what diseases buffalo might carry. They could've had tuberculosis or brucellosis—all sorts of things, for all we'd ever know. See if you and the guys can start the cleaning right away, and I'll get to LEMSIP as fast as I can."

One more thing sprang to mind: "Nick!" I shouted into the telephone, hoping I could stop him before he put down the receiver. "If you think this job is going to take a long time, you'd better ask Roxanne to lightly feed the older juveniles, like the twins and Terry and Cy, maybe even Tequila and the like, all the ones who are going to need anesthesia later. The younger babies will be no problem; they can be fed according to their normal schedule."

This was unbelievable. Not only were the trucks twelve hours late, but we were also going to lose additional time cleaning and disinfecting them. Then we'd still have all the problems of loading the transport cages and constructing the wood frames.

By the time I arrived at LEMSIP, Nick, Terry, Bill, Tom, Ray, and all the other guys were busy sweeping, scrubbing, scraping, and hosing the insides of the trucks. I climbed up into one to inspect it and was immediately assailed by the deep, musky aroma of buffalo feces. Fond memories came to mind of days long gone, when I was a young veterinarian attending cows on the small farms of Ayrshire in the uplands of southwestern Scotland.

I looked closely into the corners and grooves, recesses and holes, and every other conceivable irregularity of the internal surfaces of the truck. The manure was semiliquid, and I imagined the buffalo must have gotten instantaneous diarrhea from fright as they were being loaded into and out of the trucks the day before. Ray was hosing down the inside of the other truck, and the liquefied manure was pouring out the back, as thick and dark as beef broth.

It took the technicians a good two hours to sweep, hose, and then disinfect the insides of the two trucks. The fumes of the bleach almost choked me as I climbed into each truck to double-check that everything was perfectly clean.

Everyone broke for coffee and donuts, courtesy of Kathy and the other ladies in the front office—a chance to give the disinfectant time to work before the guys climbed back in to give the trucks their final hosing-out.

It was now almost 10 o'clock, and you could already tell that the day was going to be hot and steamy. Any chance there might have been of carrying out this mission in secrecy had long since gone. By now, for all I knew, the dean of the Medical School in Manhattan was already aware of the capers we were up to. Maybe even Dr. Coulston had gotten wind of it out there in the New Mexico desert, not to mention the animal rights groups who would jump at the opportunity to create trouble. After all, if they somehow found out about the shipment, they would naturally assume that the babies were on their way to the Coulston Foundation, not to a sanctuary, and were therefore fair game for interception.

And the hardest part of the job was yet to begin. Carl, Pete, and the rest of the maintenance crew, with the assistance of Terry and his technicians, would have to figure out how to get the required number of cages into the trucks to house all the chimps in their respective social groups. Then the cages would have to be secured within their wooden frames. It was like playing with a Rubik's Cube, trying to figure out how best to arrange the cages. There were so many irregularities to the internal surfaces of the trucks—wheel boxes, ventilation manifolds, window ledges, and the like—that it was difficult to avoid wasting space through poorly configured arrangements.

As the day grew hotter, everyone's patience grew thinner. Lifting the cages on and then off the trucks, as the technicians found themselves repeatedly having to do—laying them this way and that in order to conserve every square inch of space—was making everyone grouchy. We all knew that time was of the essence. What had seemed like a difficult task at the beginning of the day was turning into an insoluble conundrum. The maintenance guys couldn't even begin their work of building the wooden frames until the technicians had solved the problem of how best to arrange the cages. Enough space for walkways had to be incorporated into the maze of cages to allow Terry and David, the two technicians who would accompany the chimps, easy access to feed and care for them during the long journey ahead.

I don't know how they managed it, but by 3:30 that afternoon, the job was done.

The saddest part of the operation was about to begin: carrying the babies from the nursery and loading them into the cages on the two trucks. It was a heart-rending exercise. Some of the technicians must have felt deep down that they might never see these "babies" again, never hold them in their arms, never kiss them and tell them how much they loved them. They had reared them since birth or since they had been weaned from their mothers, had known them almost as intimately as a human mother knows her baby. Back and forth they went, Roxanne, Cynthia, Nancy, and Jennifer, from the nursery to the trucks, carrying small bundles of chimps in their arms, two to five at a time, or the older anesthetized animals one at a time, slung across their shoulders, making sure they were put in the right social groups, in the right cages, their names clearly marked in indelible ink on the front of each cage feeder. Eyes became redder and cheeks more scalded as tears continued to flow.

Although we had always tried not to have favorites, each one of us had bonded more closely with certain of the young chimps than others—it was only natural. For me, that included the identical twins, Amber and Alyse, who were now 7½ years old (no longer babies, I had to keep reminding myself!), born so premature that none of us had expected them to survive. Then there was My-T-Fine (along with his brother Mousse and sisters Mocha and Vanilla, all named after desserts, because their mother was called Pudding). Small for his 4 years of age, he was an adorable, mischievous little monster, constantly getting himself into trouble with the other chimps because he couldn't resist playing pranks on them, like pinching their bottoms and then running away as fast as his little legs could carry him. Billy and Maudie, the real babies of the group at just 11 months of age, were too absorbed in wrestling with each other to realize what was happening.

For Cynthia, the heartbreak of separation would be felt most strongly for Cy, her namesake, and Terry, the philosopher of the group, both 6½ years old.

It was ten past five in the afternoon by the time the two trucks with the thirty-two young chimps and Terry and David on board rolled out the front gates of LEMSIP. We all felt that this was a historic moment: the largest single shipment of chimpanzees ever to be transported from coast to coast in the United States had hit the road. But none of us felt like celebrating.

The whole staff of the lab turned out to bid their sad goodbyes. As the trucks disappeared from view, everyone made their way back to their various posts. It must have been devastating for Roxanne and the rest of the women under her to return to the empty silence of the nursery, which only minutes ago had resounded with the happy noise and clatter of chimps at play.

I left LEMSIP at around 6 o'clock that evening. It had been a long, emotionally grueling day. I just wanted to go home, sit with little Molly, our Jamaican bush dog, have a cold beer, and try to dispel all the sad thoughts that flooded my mind.

As I slowly drove out the gates of the laboratory, the young security guard, who had just begun his night shift, said in a matter-of-fact tone, "Funny, the police coming like that in their squad car to ask about the chimps."

"What are you talking about?" I asked him as I leaned out the car window.

"Oh, you didn't know?" he replied. "I guess I forgot to tell anyone." He seemed to reflect on this a bit as he gazed at the ground and then continued, "Yeah, two cops came along and asked me if I knew whether those trucks that left had baby chimps in them."

I couldn't believe my ears. Why on earth would the police want to know if there were baby chimps on the trucks? And why had the young security guard not telephoned from his security station or walked down to the front office to alert someone right away?

I immediately turned the car around and drove back to the parking lot. I jumped out and ran as fast as I could to Kathy's office. "You won't believe this," I said, out of breath, and began to relate to her what the guard had just told me.

Kathy looked at me, nonplussed. "I think we've got trouble," she said, aghast. "I bet you it's the animal rights people up to no good. Tell you what," she said, "let me call the police and make some inquiries, see what's going on. I'll get back to you."

"You'll never believe this!" Kathy said when she called me back in my office half an hour later. "Apparently, a woman phoned the police department at around 5 o'clock this afternoon from somewhere in Pennsylvania, saying she was some sort of federal agent and asking if they would help her by stopping two trucks that had just left LEMSIP loaded with baby chimps. She told the police some story about how she had received a complaint that a Dr. Mahoney was stealing baby chimps out of the laboratory in the dead of night to sell them on the black market. The woman apparently said she would get there as fast as she could if only the police would stop the trucks on the road and impound them. The chief said it wasn't within his jurisdiction to do so."

Kathy continued to fill me in on the rest of her conversation with the police chief. He finally had given Kathy the name and beeper number of the woman who had claimed to be an investigator for the U.S. Fish and Wildlife Service.

I felt sick with fear wondering what this could possibly mean. Was the woman a genuine federal agent, as she claimed, or was she just out to create trouble? Say she was an animal rights activist and she and her cronies were out to intercept the trucks and somehow kidnap or waylay the babies. She would have no way of knowing that the babies were on their way to a sanctuary. She would certainly think they were going to the Coulston Foundation in New Mexico. What if she managed to convince the police that the trucks should be turned around and sent back to LEMSIP with their live cargo? The cat would certainly be out of the bag then. New York University, and probably even the Coulston Foundation, would find out about this by the morning. Then the game would be up. There would be no freedom for the babies.

Who had tipped the woman off? I wondered. Somewhere within our ranks was a traitor, someone who could quite happily destroy the babies' chance of freedom for some malevolent personal gain: someone who perhaps looked me straight in the eye each day, with nary a blink. But who? I could not think of a single person at LEMSIP who would be capable of such evil. I now realized that without meaning to I had put the babies in the worst possible jeopardy. They might never make it to freedom in California if the Fish and Wildlife Service impounded them.

Once I got home, I tried several times to call the federal agent on her beeper, but without success. Then, at around 7:30 that night, Martine Colette from the Wildlife WayStation in California called. "Jim," she said in her gruff voice, "I just got the weirdest telephone call. I had a Fish and Wildlife agent inquire whether we were expecting two truckloads of chimps from New York. As far as I can make out, the trucks have been stopped somewhere on the interstate highway and your two technicians have been arrested."

My heart just about stopped. "What are you saying?"

"Well, I'm not sure," Martine replied. "The best I can make out, someone reported you to the Fish and Wildlife Service with a tip that you were engaged in smuggling chimps. Of course, I told her we were expecting the chimps and everything was legit and above board. I told her we even had the import permits issued by the California State Department of Health to prove it."

This was turning into a nightmare. My brain was shot; I could hardly think straight. *How could something get blown so out of proportion?* I asked myself. *How could Terry and David have been arrested, and for what reason? And where had the trucks been stopped?*

I told Martine what Kathy had learned from the police and explained that I had already tried several times to reach the agent on her beeper without success. "I don't know whether I should jump in the car and just drive along one of the interstate highways and see if I can see the trucks parked on the side of the road. The trouble is," I said, "I don't know which route they would have taken."

There were at least three routes the trucks could have followed: Interstate 84, a few miles north, off Route 17; I-80, a few miles south of Tuxedo; or, the most likely, I thought, I-78 through Allentown, Pennsylvania.

"Do you have any idea what time the trucks were stopped?" I asked Martine. She had no information on that. Without some time parameters, I'd have no way of guessing how far the trucks might have made it.

"I wouldn't try chasing the trucks if I were you," Martine advised. "It's already dark in the east," she said, "and you could easily miss seeing them on the side of the road. Better to keep trying the agent on her beeper. If I hear anything more in the meantime, I'll let you know."

I couldn't help thinking of Louis XVI and Marie Antoinette being stopped on their road to freedom because they were six hours late leaving the Palais des Tuileries. For sure, my head would roll once the dean found out about what we were doing!

I went to bed that night a nervous wreck, the telephone drawn up beside me, a road atlas of the United States open on the bedspread. Why hadn't Terry or David called to let me know what was going on? I wondered. Why hadn't the federal agent called? For God's sake! I continued to contact the agent on her beeper every half hour or so, but to no avail. At around 7 o'clock the following morning, after a fitful night of sleep, I stirred, bleary-eyed, my back aching, to the clangorous ringing of the telephone. It was David calling from somewhere in Ohio.

"Why didn't you call me earlier?" I barked, cutting him off in midsentence. "I've been worried sick."

"First of all," he replied somewhat defensively, "I did try calling you, but they wouldn't let me. Second, I didn't know you would have even been aware of this situation, and I didn't see the need to disturb you in the middle of the night, especially when there was nothing you could have done about it."

David was right, of course; I would have to calm down and get a grip on myself. He began to describe to me in detail what had happened the evening before. The two trucks had reached the western border of New Jersey, and when they crossed over into Pennsylvania, a dozen federal agents and a slew of Pennsylvania state police troopers stopped them at the first tollbooth. The truck drivers, together with Terry and David, were escorted to the state trooper command post and interrogated for the next four hours. The federal agents questioned Terry and David separately as to the purpose of the shipment and its destination. So closely watched were they that they could not even go to the bathroom without being escorted by an agent, nor were they permitted to get back on the trucks to feed the younger chimps, like Billy and Maudie, who required milk in bottles every two hours. David suggested that the agents call me at home, because, in my position as acting director of LEMSIP, they could get the information straight from the horse's mouth, as it were. But the agents refused to do so, and wouldn't allow Terry or David to phone me, either. Instead, they called the Wildlife WayStation. That's how Martine had found out about all the problems.

On hearing that the chimps were indeed expected in California and that all the relevant state and federal forms and permits had been filled out appropriately, the Fish and Wildlife agents released Terry and David. The state troopers then stepped in. After an intense search of the two trucks from top to bottom, what should they find in the glove compartment of one of the trucks but a small bag of marijuana and a pistol. Based on further investigation, one of the four truck drivers was arrested for possession of an illegal substance and a supposedly stolen firearm, but at least the trucks were freed and everyone else was allowed to go on their way.

The one thing I now feared most was that whoever the miserable person was who had undertaken this dastardly act might try again with the police in other states as the trucks continued to cross state lines on the long journey west. I phoned Martine straight away to bring her up-to-date. She, too, shared my concerns.

"Let's try and keep in touch with each other and with the trucks at least twice a day," she suggested, "and see if we can guide the drivers to make little detours here and there, and hopefully foil any attempts someone might make to intercept the trucks again."

Martine and I stayed glued to the telephone over the next two and a half days, maps of the United States spread out before us. Ike's invasion of Europe had not been better planned. Once the trucks reached the New Mexico–Arizona state line, I jumped on a plane and flew to Los Angeles, as previously arranged, ready to meet the babies upon their arrival at the WayStation.

Poor David and Terry; they looked exhausted and totally washed out when I met them that evening. They hadn't shaved or showered for three and a half days. The babies, on the other hand, were bundles of energy, jumping up and down in their cages, performing somersaults and having their usual intrafamily squabbles. They seemed totally unaware of the drama and risk that had marked their epic journey across the continent from New York to California.

Off in the distance, in the deepening twilight, I could see Martine directing her construction crews, the welders, carpenters, electricians, and others, as they feverishly worked under floodlights to put the finishing touches on the temporary housing for the babies. Their safe arrival in California had taken a mere eight and a half days, start to finish, from the time I had phoned Martine that afternoon in New York City to ask desperately for her help.

A bright, golden moon was already ascending over the canyons, and the mournful howl of coyotes echoed through the heavy air. I felt a certain peace wash over me; the babies had finally made it to freedom.

11

The Last of the Sparrows

There are hundreds of sparrows, thousands, millions,
They're two a penny, far too many there must be;
There are hundreds and thousands, millions of sparrows,
But God knows ev'ry-one and God knows me.

—John Gowans (1934–)

E very chimp at the lab had a story to tell. I had known many of
them for twenty years. Some of their stories were humorous,
some touching and sad, and others so amazing they are difficult to
believe. Yet they all left indelible impressions on my mind.

Despite their muscle and brawn, I couldn't help seeing the
chimps as helpless and fragile, totally at our mercy. They brought
back memories of my favorite story in the Bible, and I came to see
them as "the last of the sparrows." As I remember it from early
childhood, the story goes something like this: "And Jesus said to the
multitude [Jesus was always talking to the multitude, that much I
recall], 'Think of two sparrows in a tree. They cost only a farthing
each, yet not one shall fall to the ground without God, our Father,
knowing about it. Imagine, then, how much he must care about you
and me.'"

Picture how crestfallen I was when, as an adult sitting down to write this book, I discovered that according to the Rheims New Testament, AD 1582, the Gospel according to St. Matthew 10:29–31 actually reads:

> [29]Are not two sparrows sold for a farthing? and not one of them shall fall on the ground without your Father. [30]But the very hairs on your head are all numbered. [31]Fear not therefore: better are you than many sparrows.

I had remembered nothing as a little boy about God counting the hairs on our heads or our being better than many sparrows. I prefer my version.

The saddest and most painful duty I had to perform during the days leading up to LEMSIP's closure was to select which chimps should go to the Coulston Foundation and which, with any luck, might make it to sanctuary. I didn't do this entirely on my own: I sought the opinions of many of the technicians who knew the animals well, like Mike and Dave, my two breeding technicians. I always carried the responsibility for the final word of judgment, however. Once the decision was irrevocably made, I would cringe at the thought of facing the animals I had selected to continue on in a life of research. I could hardly look them in the eye, certain they somehow sensed that I had been a traitor to them. I couldn't help thinking of the cows in Scotland I had diagnosed as not pregnant, and how my diagnosis would have sent them to their deaths.

In many cases, the research histories of individual animals determined for me what their fates would be. Of all the viruses we dealt with at that time, the hepatitis B virus was perhaps the most readily transmitted from chimp to human being. It could be transferred not only through bites or scratches and blood-to-blood transmission, but also through contamination of body wounds from infected surfaces, such as cage materials. In terms of the number of virus particles required to set up infection, hepatitis B is significantly more transmissible than the viruses for hepatitis C or HIV (fifty to one hundred times more so than in the case of HIV). One would not be able to rely on every person who would have contact with infected chimps being vaccinated against hepatitis B; secondary, unvaccinated personnel or visitors to sanctuaries might unknowingly find themselves exposed.

Two sanctuaries openly welcomed HIV-infected chimps: the Wild Animal Orphanage in San Antonio, Texas, run by Carol Asvestas; and the Fauna Foundation in Carignan, Quebec, founded by Gloria Grow. The Wild Animal Orphanage observes careful protocol in handling primates of many species infected in research or naturally with potentially dangerous viruses, such as herpes-B virus in macaques (not to be confused with the hepatitis B virus), HIV, and the monkey equivalent, SIV. The cofounder of the Fauna Foundation, Dr. Richard Allan, is a veterinarian who is qualified in the safe handling of chimps infected with HIV.

I had to take into account other equally important criteria in my decision making. First, I knew there was a legally binding agreement between the Coulston Foundation and the NYU Medical Center that the foundation would receive, gratis, approximately one hundred chimps, even if it decided in the end not to take over LEMSIP. This meant that for every chimp I would set aside for inclusion in the sanctuary list, I would have to select one for Coulston. I had to accept that there was no way for me to undo this agreement, and any attempt on my part would almost certainly put in jeopardy my being able to find sanctuary for *any* of the chimps. More to the point, I would be fired; then I would be powerless to save a single one.

I vowed to do my best to keep social groups of chimps together and not allow them to be split. However, I knew that I might have to part with chimps who were friendly to humans, which would almost certainly include some of the favorites of the caregivers and the volunteers, because these animals might find the transition to another research facility easier than the shyer animals would. And what about the "babies"? I had to ask myself. How would I ever be able to break them up and send them away to New Mexico? A lifetime of research ahead of them, they were worth their weight in gold!

Melilot

Melilot came from Sierra Leone, in West Africa. He had been imported into the United States in 1969 as a youngster, around 3 years of age, when LEMSIP was gearing up for its hepatitis B studies. Like so many other infant chimps taken from the wild during that period, Melilot was almost certainly ripped from his mother's breast after she fell dead on the forest floor from gunshot wounds. Perhaps other chimps in the group had come to her aid, and they may have been injured or killed in the mêlée as well. What terror Melilot may have experienced, and what memories of horror might have lain deeply embedded in his mind, we will never know.

Poor Melilot, the strangest looking chimp I ever saw, was also one of the sweetest, most wonderfully natured I'd ever known, a sort of hairy angel, all soul and heart. I doubt he was capable of biting or harming anyone, no matter what the provocation. He was long and lanky, with gangly arms and legs that never seemed to coordinate properly with each other. His bony fingers were slender; his huge ears protruded like a flying Dumbo's; and his great flapping lips constantly smacked with liquid splats or juicy raspberry sounds as he obsessively groomed the hairs on the back of your wrist with opposed thumbnails whenever you came by to talk to him. His most outstanding feature, however, was his distorted, twisted face.

In most instances, baby chimps pop out of their mothers within a few seconds, the mothers barely, if at all, giving any outward sign that they are about to give birth. Melilot's delivery, however, was almost certainly a long, painful affair, his head squeezed by the powerful contractions of his mother's uterus, the great plate-like frontal and temporal bones of his skull, the smaller bones of his zygomatic arch and supraorbital rim, which fit together like the pieces of a jig-saw puzzle, pressed out of alignment. You sometimes see this happen in children, but within a few months after birth, the various inter-locking bones shift, like the great tectonic movements of the Earth's crust, and take on a proper alignment. Not so with Melilot; his twisted face remained a permanent feature. It was as if a steamroller had run over his head, making the right side of his forehead and cheek protrude and giving his face a distinctly lopsided appearance.

Mel, as we used to call him, was transferred to the Coulston Foundation when LEMSIP closed in 1997. I agonized for a long time over what was the kinder thing to do with him—try to get him to sanctuary or send him to Coulston. Not only was he infected with HIV, but he was also a carrier of the hepatitis C virus, and therefore was not a suitable candidate for retirement in any of the sanctuaries that existed at the time. My hands were tied.

Mel was caged with a small group of females in an indoor-outdoor pen when he arrived in Alamogordo. You would have thought this, and the exposure to the New Mexico sunshine, would have been a welcome change from his mostly single-cage existence at LEMSIP. But Mel had never been exposed to a concrete floor before—he had spent all the years since his capture from the wild on aluminum cage bars—and the feel of the concrete on the soles of his feet terrified him. Who would ever have guessed such a thing? He constantly hung at the top of the indoor cage, not coming to ground even for food or water.

My colleague Dr. Doug Cohn, who had accompanied Melilot in the truck to New Mexico, came up with an idea. He and several of the technicians and maintenance men at LEMSIP got together with some of the Coulston animal care staff over the phone and devised a solution. They would make a piece of aluminum barred false floor. They constructed it so that it could be collapsed through the aid of a series of hinges and fitted through Melilot's cage door and then opened out to be used for him to sleep on. The upper management of the Coulston Foundation took umbrage at this and told me to ask my staff to refrain from meddling in the foundation's affairs.

Melilot died a year or so later. I was never informed of the cause.

Shirley the Heroine

Shirley, unwitting heroine that she was, blazed the trail to the conquest of hepatitis B by demonstrating early on that chimps were unique models for developing a vaccine. She was found to be a symptomless chronic carrier of the hepatitis B virus. How she had acquired the disease was never determined. Nonetheless, Shirley contributed a great deal of early information about the immunological characteristics of the virus, important in the development of a specific diagnostic blood test, one of the most important first steps in producing a vaccine. It would take scientists almost fifteen years to isolate the virus for hepatitis C, thanks to the high virus load found in the chimpanzees Don and Rodney. With Shirley's help, hepatitis B was conquered in only ten years, from first isolating the virus to having a vaccine on the market.

Shirley died recently at the ripe old age of 42. Her last days were spent in the confines of a laboratory cage, all alone—no longer at LEMSIP but back at the Holloman Air Force Base in New Mexico, where she had started out as part of the aerospace program. She never made it to a sanctuary, but her daughter, Chance, did, at the Fauna Foundation in Quebec.

Jaybee

Jaybee did not like me one bit. I have no idea why this was so; I cannot recall a single incident when he might have thought that I had been bad to him. Yet he was quite friendly to just about everyone else.

Jaybee wasn't the only chimp who spat on me, not by a long shot, but for him it was a mission in life, an intellectual challenge, a matter of honor.

I had a particularly notable run-in with him once, when he fooled me into believing that he had made a remarkable turnaround in attitude toward me.

I had been kneeling and talking to another chimp, Jojo-M, on the other side of the room, directly opposite Jaybee's cage. As I quietly talked away to Jojo, I suddenly realized the position I had taken in relation to Jaybee. I turned toward him, amazed that he had not yet spat on me. To my surprise and happiness, I saw that Jaybee had a mellow, pleasant expression on his face, as he held the bars of the cage in front of him. It was as if he were pleased to see me. "Well, how is that Jaybee?" I called across to him. He started to sway from side to side and shake his head up and down, all signs of a happy chimp. Jaybee was being nice to me; I couldn't believe it. "He's such a good boy, that Jaybee, such a good boy," I cooed.

Suddenly Jaybee looked sideways, toward the doors at the end of the room, which contained a small Plexiglas window, as if someone were there looking in from the anteroom. "There's no one there," I said to him. Jaybee shook his head up and down and looked across at me with a smile on his face. *Remarkable,* I thought. Keen to take advantage of the situation, I continued to speak to him in a friendly manner. "He's such a good boy." Jaybee nodded his head enthusiastically, and then suddenly turned his gaze once more to the door at the end of the room. "There's no one there, Jaybee," I assured him. Again, he shook his head up and down, an ever-sweeter expression looming on his face.

This interchange between us continued for a little while until it suddenly dawned on me what Jaybee was up to. Each time he had turned his attention to the door at the end of the room, he had leaned sideways, a little bit more, a little bit more. He was now within easy reach of the water container mounted on the front of his cage, a stainless steel box containing a gallon of water. Too late, I realized Jaybee had fooled me into allowing him the opportunity of a royal spit on me like he had never had before. Before I could get up from my knees, he had filled his mouth with water and let go at me with all his force. Full in the face he got me, cold water running down the inside of my shirt. The power of the deluge left me unable to open my eyelids.

Jaybee had been on an HIV vaccine study. One day short of a year after we had been given the word that the Coulston Foundation was taking possession of LEMSIP, he, along with nineteen other chimps, were loaded into two trucks in the middle of the night, to be shipped to Alamogordo in New Mexico. I checked on all the animals frequently to make sure they were recovering from the sedative we had given them to enable us to load them into their transport cages. Jaybee was already sitting up, obviously fully recovered. As I leaned close to the front of his cage to observe him carefully, he squeezed his two hands out through the bars and took hold of my two hands very gently. He looked up into my eyes and cried, a pathetic, lost cry like I had never heard before. It was one of the saddest moments I ever experienced with a chimp. I was nearly overcome by the urge to unlock the padlock on his cage, raise the door, and tell him to come with me. Under normal conditions, I would never have dreamed of allowing Jaybee to hold, or even touch, my hands: it would have been too dangerous. But now I squeezed his hands, looked into his eyes, and told him that everything would be all right.

I have thought many times since about that moment. What was he thinking when he pleaded with me not to allow him to be taken away? Was he telling me that he hadn't really hated me, that it had only been a game?

Jaybee and a number of other chimps whom we had to send to the Coulston Foundation are in a sanctuary now, taken over by the late Carole Noon, founder of the New Mexico sanctuary Save the Chimps. Who could ever have believed that possible back in those dark days?

* * * * *

Billy Joe and Sue Ellen

Billy Joe and Sue Ellen were two chimps cast off from the circus. Their teeth had been punched out by hammer and chisel so that they wouldn't be able to bite anyone in the crowds they mingled with during their performances. When their circus days were over, their only alternative besides euthanasia was to be given up to research.

Billy Joe and Sue Ellen's journey from circus act to research subject began with a young man. I don't think his name matters anymore, except to say that he lived in a beautiful area deep in the Adirondacks. He had gotten to know Billy Joe and Sue Ellen through working for the owner of a small chimpanzee circus act. Times were getting tough, business was not good, and the owner decided he had no alternative but to sell the two chimps for as much as he could get. Nobody wanted them, apparently—certainly none of the zoos did—and the only sanctuary that existed at the time was the Primate Foundation of Arizona, which was having its own problems surviving.

The only option the owner had left was to have them "put to sleep." The young man could not accept that alternative. He bought them from the owner with whatever cash he could scrape together. He built a neat little hut just for the chimps in which he constructed a fairly large cage that was bedded down in deep, fresh straw each day, with a large electric heater to keep them warm at night and during the winter.

The heating bills during the long, harsh mountain winters were more than he could bear, however, and he was forced to consider research as the only alternative to euthanasia.

He asked me whether I would mind giving him a few minutes to say goodbye to the chimps before I loaded them in the transport cage I had brought in the truck. He undid the lock to their cage, and they quietly walked out, each taking him by a hand. I shall always remember the scene as the three of them walked away from me, up a long, gentle slope of a field toward a copse of pine trees on the crest of the hill. Sue Ellen looked up into the young man's face and then sprang up to wrap her arms around his shoulders, her feet clinging to his side. With one step more, Billy Joe did the same, the two chimps now hanging one off each side of his body, his arms scooped under them to hold them in place. Within a few more paces, the young man turned to make his way back toward me. Even at a distance, I could see the glint of tears cascading down his cheeks. I could feel the pain he was going through. I felt rotten, like a cheapjack. One day, I vowed to myself, I would find sanctuary for these two animals.

This incident had a profound affect on my way of thinking. Maybe we could create our own sanctuary at LEMSIP. Over the years, we looked into three options for such a venture, but funding such projects is a constant challenge.

Fourteen years later, Billy Joe and Sue Ellen were saved when the Fauna Foundation in Quebec stepped in and offered them, and thirteen other chimps, sanctuary.

Sammy and the Twins

The most profound caring behavior I have seen in chimpanzees was in the identical twins Amber and Alyse, who were born at LEMSIP. They were eight weeks preterm (which is incredibly premature for chimpanzees, who normally have a seven-and-a-half- to eight-month gestation period), and their chances for survival were very low indeed. Unfortunately, because of their extreme underdevelopment and weak physical state, we could not allow the twins to be reared by Andrea, even though she had proven herself to be a doting, loving mother in the past. The twins would require round-the-clock intensive care in the nursery for quite some time.

Thanks to the skills and dedication of Roxanne and Darlene and their wonderful team, Amber and Alyse did survive. However, when Amber reached about 18 months of age, she started to have occasional seizures. I consulted with pediatricians I knew at the New York University Medical Center in Manhattan. They had helped me often over the years with pediatric problems in chimps. Apparently, petit mal seizures are not uncommon in premature human twins because the birth of the first twin often holds up that of the second. The second twin to be born is likely to suffer not only severe oxygen deprivation but also micro blood clots to the brain, which can lead to seizures later in life.

Over time, the seizures increased in frequency, and we had to put Amber on medication permanently. Trying to get to Amber when she was having a seizure became increasingly difficult for us because her sister wanted to hold her and give her special attention herself. She would actually try to bite us for intervening. Amber's psychological development became stunted. She was not able to make friends with other chimpanzees, and she became more and more reliant on Alyse.

Since their arrival at the Wildlife WayStation in 1995, Amber has never had another seizure, and we were able to gradually withdraw her daily treatment. Most incredible of all, she fell in love with another chimp—through the bars of her big cage and his—and started to blossom. The male, named Sammy, was the worst self-mutilator I have ever known in my more than thirty years of working with chimps. He must have developed this severely abnormal behavior from his days in a so-called roadside zoo—a trailer where tourists paid a couple of dollars to go in and "see the ape." He desperately needed psychological help, but that was easier said than done.

Martine Colette, the founder of the WayStation, and Darlene, the woman who had reared all the young chimps back at the lab in New York, were able to integrate Sammy and Amber, along with Alyse and four other chimps, and neither Amber nor Sammy has looked back since. Sammy rarely bites himself now, and even when he does, he does not show the same intensity for self-abuse. Equally remarkable, Amber has come out of her shell and is much more apt to socialize with other chimps. She and Sammy, the two desperately needy chimps, continue to help each other out. And the friendship between Amber and Alyse is still as strong as it ever was.

Mystery

There were three reasons for naming the baby Mystery. First, he was the only chimp—or other primate, for that matter—to be born at LEMSIP without a single written record ever being made of his birth. This was to hide his existence in case the Coulston Foundation made a special request to obtain him. Second, no one knew that his mother, Lulu, was pregnant, including me, the veterinarian and Chief of Reproduction, Perinatal Growth and Development Program, with twenty years of hard-earned experience working with chimps. And third, the most remarkable of all, was that the man who discovered Mystery's birth had one of those impossible Polish names that was about thirty-six letters long but contained only one or two vowels, making it almost impossible for all but a Polish tongue to pronounce. His name started with the letter E, so we called him Mr. E.

On August 10, 1995, on the day he announced the takeover of LEMSIP by the Coulston Foundation, the dean of the NYU Medical School ordered that all breeding of primates at LEMSIP be stopped immediately. Examination of Lulu's records seven and a half months later indicated that she had been impregnated within the twenty-four hours preceding her separation from Conrad, the male she had been living with.

That Lulu was not noticed to be pregnant was doubly mystifying because she was an unusually long, slender female. By the time she reached late pregnancy, if not way before, the swelling of her abdomen should have been obvious even to someone completely unfamiliar with chimpanzees, yet not one of us had raised any suspicions.

The first time anyone at the lab discovered that Lulu was pregnant was when Mr. E., who had been hired only recently, was

Molly became Mystery's adopted mother.

performing his morning cleaning of the room where Lulu was caged along with nine or ten other chimps. As he swept the mop back and forth across the wet floor, he heard a sudden strange noise behind him, like the sound of a large, tense rubber balloon being deflated. He turned and saw a flood of yellowish bloodstained fluid discharge onto the floor. Lulu had deposited a very wet-looking, helpless baby on the floor of her cage. Instantly recalling that Lulu had acquired a reputation in her previous colony of killing her infants at birth by trying to push them back into her birth canal, Mr. E. barreled out the door, grabbed the first person he saw, and ordered that person to make an announcement over the PA system, "Lulu has just given birth in Unit 5. Come quick!" before returning to the room. Everyone at the lab immediately recognized the urgency of this announcement, even the secretaries in their offices. This was as much a crisis as any life-threatening emergency could be. One of the research technicians happened to have a syringe and needle loaded with tranquilizer solution with him. He rushed into the room and coaxed Lulu to the front of her cage, where he was able to inject her in the bottom by hand. Mr. E's sharp memory and quick action had saved the day.

Poor little Mystery found himself in an almost identical predicament as Spike Mulligan had been when I delivered him by Caesarean section some sixteen years earlier. Mystery was motherless, and there were no other infants even close to his age with whom he could socialize. The situation became even more critical when some five months later, all the other young chimps at LEMSIP were sent to the Wildlife WayStation, leaving Mystery entirely on his own.

He was far too young to face the three-and-a-half-day journey to California. It would also have been very hard on Terry and David, the accompanying caregivers, to provide the required feeding every two hours around the clock, when they already had thirty-two other infants and juveniles to care for.

So Mystery stayed at the lab during the day, just like in the old times, before we had built the nursery, and I took him home with me every evening to be reared by Molly, our Jamaican bush dog.

I flew with Mystery to California a month or so later, first class on a jumbo jet, compliments of Continental Airlines. The captain took him in his arms and walked him along the aisles, introducing him to all the passengers. Mystery loved every moment of it.

As the plane began its descent into LAX, an announcement was made over the intercom: "We've had the pleasure of a very special passenger with us tonight: a little chimpanzee named Mystery who has been rescued from research and will spend the rest of his life in a sanctuary here in California. We wish him the very best." The passengers clapped heartily.

Little Mystery had represented all 109 chimpanzees and more than 100 monkeys who finally made it out of the lab to freedom.

Tomaish-Mór and Termite

Tom was a great hulk of man with a belly on him the size of a beech-wood keg. He had a soft, kindly face that usually bristled with a three-day-old five o'clock shadow. His hair floated around him in thin, wispy gray strands that he constantly had to swipe to one side to keep under control, and he had the habit of pushing his glasses up the bridge of his nose every few seconds as he stood over you talking. His voice was booming, with the faint crackle at the end of each breath that you often hear in overweight, large-chested men. If his gait became jaunty as he strode along a corridor, he was likely to hit the top of his head on the next doorjamb. Tom was a gentle giant.

"Thomaish-Mór"—pronounced something like *Tomosh* (with a soft *T*) *Mower*—was what I used to call over the intercom when I needed to speak to him. Meaning "Big Thomas" in Irish, this nickname was my way of differentiating him from our other, more normal-sized Tom, "Thomaish-Beag"—pronounced *Tomosh Beeog* ("Little Thomas"). Big Tom always got a kick out of this. Somewhere in his genes was a bit of Irish—I'm not sure exactly how much, but he was very proud of it. On many a Monday morning he'd greet me with, "Hey, Doc! I watched *Braveheart* on television again over the weekend." I don't know how many times he must have watched that movie. "Had a wee drop of the Tullamore Dew you gave me for Christmas, too," he'd add with a wicked wink, "then sat back and rooted for the Irish when they lifted their kilts to moon the English." Then he would roar with thunderous laughter.

Thomaish-Mór loved his animals, and they him. As with the other technicians at LEMSIP, he worked with all the chimps, but his main responsibility was toward his own two rooms of ten adults each. Like a homeroom schoolteacher, Tom had a special sense of bonding with his "guys," as he called them. Among them was Termite, a huge, 180-pound, 30-year-old Buddha of a male chimp, who was all folds and wrinkles and oozing belly.

Termite had a hormonal problem when he was young and had been castrated long before he came to LEMSIP. He too had probably come from a circus background (records were often incomplete, or even missing altogether, in those days), because his front incisor teeth, top and bottom, had been extracted, and root canals had been performed on the cut-off stumps of his canine teeth. For all that, Termite was an unusually happy chimp, always smiling and laughing, wagging his head from side to side when you sat down to talk to him, saliva drooling from his chin in great long strings because of his lack of teeth, as he reached forward to groom your wrist.

Termite had been on a hepatitis C program for many years and had become a chronic carrier of the virus. Whether or not that had any effect, I don't know, but he developed a condition known as thrombocytopenia, where a life-threatening drop occurs in circulating levels of blood platelets, which control clotting mechanisms in the blood. An extensive diagnostic work-up, including bone marrow biopsies, indicated that he had the idiopathic form of the disease, meaning its cause, or perhaps multiple causes, are unknown to medical science but may, in some way, be related to the chronic effects of an ever-present virus such as hepatitis C. Instead of the usual 200,000 to 300,000 platelets per milliliter of circulating blood, Termite had only 7,000 to 15,000. Every so often, he suffered tiny pinpoint hemorrhages all over his gums, lips, and the skin down the front of his chest and under his armpits. But more serious, his tongue would sometimes swell up alarmingly because of a sudden leakage of blood into the tissues. We took him off research, of course, but his future was bleak. Steroid therapy was the only treatment available that could relieve his condition, but we all knew it wouldn't work forever. Termite's condition was terminal; one day he would suffer a sudden, fatal hemorrhage, and we would be powerless to save him.

Termite didn't seem to realize he had a fatal illness, however: He remained his usual happy self. Nonetheless, as the lab's closure loomed ever closer, we had to decide what to do with him. I couldn't allow him to go to New Mexico to continue on in a life of research, nor could I send him to a sanctuary where there might be little available in the way of emergency support treatment, not to mention the danger to untrained sanctuary staff given his status as a carrier of hepatitis C.

These were somber times. I brought the staff up-to-date on Termite's condition and what the latest diagnostic tests indicated.

But the writing was on the wall, everyone knew that. Somehow, I had to convince everyone that the only humane thing to do would be to put Termite "to sleep." I could hardly term it *euthanasia* because Termite was not actually suffering yet. I didn't want a majority opinion; I wanted a unanimous decision, especially to include Thomaish-Mór. Over a series of three meetings, everyone finally agreed that there was no alternative.

The effect on Thomaish-Mór was devastating. I'd often catch him, when he didn't realize I was standing behind the door, hunkered down on his heels in front of Termite's cage, talking quietly to him, the two of them holding their huge hands together. Termite would bounce his head up and down every now and then, in obvious agreement with whatever Tom was saying to him, a big, silly smile on his face, his voice coming in soft panting grunts.

We put Termite to sleep on the morning of December 16, 1997. This was the day the rest of the animals in his research group, the last chimps remaining at LEMSIP—the last of the sparrows—were sent out to another laboratory. This one was located in Texas, where they would continue on in research for a few more years before going into permanent retirement.

Tom's heart was broken, I know. He never seemed to recover from the loss of Termite. It was a bleak Christmas for us all, and an even bleaker New Year, when the lab finally closed. Thomaish-Mór died less than two years later, without a job and unable to face the future, I suspect. He had developed pneumonia and, having no health insurance, didn't seek treatment until it was too late. He passed away the morning after he was taken to the hospital.

Every time I think of Tom, the words come to mind of an old Irish song my mother used to sing to me in her cracked, out-of-tune voice when I was a little boy:

This life's a weary puzzle, past finding out by man,
So I'll give the day for what it's worth, and do the best I can.

Epilogue

When I was 4 years old, my parents and I lived in the upstairs apartment of a house owned by a Mr. and Mrs. Williams, whom I would visit every afternoon at around 3 o'clock. My mother was concerned that I would make a nuisance of myself and would forbid me to go. I found a way around that, though: I would stamp my feet hard as I made my way down the stairs, creating so much noise that I could honestly say to my mother that I hadn't heard her telling me to come back.

Mrs. Williams used to make a most wonderful mug of hot, sweet cocoa, with delicious slices of toast and jam.

Mr. Williams was a very tall, dear old man, with silvery white hair and moustache, who always carried a knobby cane with a worn silver head. He had worked in Africa and India, probably for the British Colonial Office. He would mesmerize me with tales of vast herds of wildebeests crossing broad rivers in Africa, huge elephants stomping through the wilds of India, and the tallness of giraffes, as well as Rudyard Kipling's Rikki-Tikki-Tavi, the mongoose.

"If a lion were to meet a tiger and have a fight with him, who would win?" I would ask Mr. Williams. (I secretly wanted the lion to be the victor.) "A lion and a tiger would never meet" was his constant reply. "Yes, but if they did meet and had a fight, who would win?" I would insistently repeat. "Lions live in Africa and tigers live in India"; that was all he would say. I think he was trying to tell me, "Animals are what they are, not what you may want them to be."

Mr. Williams imbued me with a fascination for animals, but many decades later I am still asking questions of myself that I cannot fully answer. Apart from their obvious difference in size, elephants and mice, and all the other species of critters in between, share a great deal in common: their capacity to surprise and amaze us, their ability to leave us in awe and demand our respect. Who would guess that a huge elephant could be brought almost to his knees, yet at the last moment pull himself together and refuse to give in to his captors even though they beat him? Who could imagine the extent to which a little mouse might be prepared to go to seek freedom for herself and her family?

Animals can only be their true selves if they are part of nature, where they can show off the skills that they have mastered in the environments in which they evolved over thousands, and maybe millions, of years. Animals were on the face of the earth long before us: The human being, *Homo sapiens,* is a relative newcomer.

In the late 1980s, I attended a keynote address given to the American Society of Primatology by Dr. Marian Diamond of the University of California–Berkeley that left an indelible impression on my memory. One of the most famous neurophysiologists of all time, Dr. Diamond is also a great speaker. The lecture was entirely about rats—nothing to do with primates at all. *Why on earth would she be chosen to lecture to primate researchers about rats?* I wondered. I was soon to learn why.

Dr. Diamond had studied the effects of environmental enrichment and a little tender loving care each day on brain development in three age groups of rats—young, middle-aged, and seniors. She compared them to control groups of rats who received no enrichment or special care, just the usual laboratory fare. Not only was the enriched rats' lifespan increased by more than 30 percent over the controls', but a particular area of their brains—the neocortex, the most recently evolved part—had increased in thickness by 6 percent. "That's not much," you might say, but the thickening of the cortex was due to a marked increase in the number and complexity of the dendrites of the neurons—the spidery connections linking the nerve cells together in the brain. This is a direct measure of increase in brain capacity and activity. None of the rats in the control groups showed such changes. All it took was a little TLC. Who would imagine that a lowly little rat would respond in such a fashion?

Yet rats and other rodents are not even considered living creatures in the eyes of the Animal Welfare Act, nor are birds. In theory, you can be as cruel as you like to a mouse or a bird and fear no reprisal from the law.

"There is no reason to believe that the human brain is not equally capable of responding in a similar fashion, even in old age," Dr. Diamond said. "And if this is the case for rats," she concluded, "what do you think you are doing to your primates sitting in their sterile, boring cages day after day?"

In chapter 6 of their book *When Elephants Weep*, Masson and McCarthy comment a great deal on the meaning of freedom to captive animals. Their overriding conclusion is that animals cannot be truly happy in captivity unless they are given some opportunity to choose their environment. They challenge the scientific community to answer the question, "Can an animal be happy without the ability to choose its own environment?" I can think of no better question to ask.

In my experience of working with primates, I would say that, crudely speaking, captive animals might experience two types of freedom: one where they literally escape and take off into the sunset and the other where they explore their surroundings, at first with a little trepidation and then, once they have overcome their initial uncertainty, with the effervescent joy of novelty. I have never seen chimps, for example, try to make a real break. Given the opportunity, they prefer to go back to their cages or at least to the room from which they came.

Does the lack of freedom mean perpetual unhappiness? No, the lack of freedom is not the most deleterious effect of captivity on animals. The failure of their caregivers to give them love and recognize their individuality is far more detrimental, as Dr. Diamond's research has shown. Of course, nothing could ever replace the unbound freedom they would experience in their native habitat. A cage is a cage, no matter how big; even a three-acre island is a form of captivity, as the late Carole Noon, founder of the Save the Chimps sanctuary in Florida, never failed to emphasize. To imagine that a seven-foot-tall, twenty-five- to thirty-square-foot laboratory cage could ever be acceptable indicates a total lack of understanding of the chimpanzee's most fundamental needs.

Animals in research are our captives, but often so are animals in the wild, like the deer and the bears of the East, the prairie dogs of the Plains, the manatees of Florida, and the wolves of the Alaskan wilderness, who live and die at our mercy because of our often heartless and selfish destruction of their habitats. Animals are losing ground at a meteoric rate. Maybe we can no longer avert the clash between their environments and ours. We must never fail to bring into play our compassion, however—one of the emotions we selfishly claim as uniquely human—and go beyond ourselves to embrace all living creatures.

I once stood on the edge of a purple glen overlooking a long, narrow loch. The sun was setting in a warm, golden glow. I was suddenly overwhelmed by a desire to reach out and embrace all that was before me, hug it to the point where nature and I would become one. But you must already be one with nature to have such a deep feeling. And even when you have it, it is easily lost. I lost it once myself, and it disappeared for several years. I had let nature down, had failed to defend her in a moment of need. But that's another story.

With Gratitude

On behalf of the more than 100 monkeys (rhesus and Java macaques, baboons, cotton-eared marmosets, and red-bellied tamarins) and the final 109 chimpanzees rescued from LEMSIP, I give grateful thanks to the animal sanctuaries listed below. I also recognize the dedication of the staff of the laboratory through the trying and very sad two and a half years leading up to the lab's closure on December 31, 1997. I especially extend my thanks to my colleagues, Dr. Doug Cohn and Cynthia Kirby (head of the volunteer program at LEMSIP), for their tireless efforts to find sanctuary for many of the monkeys, and to Darlene Kuhn, assistant supervisor of the monkey colony and the chimpanzee nursery, who followed the "babies" all the way to California to continue looking after them at the Wildlife WayStation.

—James Mahoney, November 2009

Black Beauty Ranch
P.O. Box 367
Murchison, TX 75778
903-469-3811
www.blackbeautyranch.org

Fauna Foundation
P.O. Box 33
Chambly, Quebec
J3L 4B1 Canada
450-658-1844
www.faunafoundation.org

Pacific Primate Sanctuary, Inc.
500-A Haloa Road
Haiku, Maui, HI 96708
808-572-8089
www.pacificprimate.org

Primarily Primates, Inc.
26099 Dull Knife Trail
San Antonio, TX 78255
830-755-4616
www.primarilyprimates.org

Primate Rescue Center, Inc.
2515 Bethel Road
Nicholasville, KY 40356
859-858-4866
www.primaterescue.org

Sanctuary for Animals, Inc.
38 William Lain Rd.
Westtown, NY 10998

Trevor Zoo
Millbrook School
131 Millbrook School Rd.
Millbrook, NY 12545
845-677-3704
www.trevorzoo.org

Wild Animal Orphanage
Animal Sanctuary of the
    United States
P.O. Box 690422
San Antonio, TX 78269
210-688-9038
www.wildanimal
    orphanage.org

Wildlife Rescue &
    Rehabilitation, Inc.
P.O. Box 369
Kendalia, TX 78027
830-336-2725
www.wildlife-rescue.org

Wildlife WayStation
14831 Little Tujunga
    Canyon Road
Angeles National Forest, CA
    91342
818-899-5201
www.wildlifewaystation.org

Suggestions for Further Reading

Chapter 1. The Power of Dignity and Courage

Alter, Stephan. *Elephas Maximus: A Portrait of the Indian Elephant.* Orlando: Harcourt, 2004.

Fowler, Murray E., and Susan K. Mikota, eds. *Biology, Medicine, and Surgery of Elephants.* Ames, Iowa: Blackwell Publishing, 2006.

Mahoney, James. "A Plea for Freedom (2/15/99)." India Project for Animals and Nature (IPAN). Available at www.gcci.org/ipan/loki/plea021599.html.

Masson, Jeffrey Moussaieff, and Susan McCarthy. *When Elephants Weep: The Emotional Lives of Animals.* New York: Delacorte Press, 1995.

Schmidt, Michael. *Jumbo Ghosts: The Dangerous Life of Elephants in the Zoo.* Xlibris Corporation, 2001.

Chapter 2. A Life in Captivity

BBC News. "African Chimps Decline 'Alarming.'" BBC News World Edition, October 17, 2008. Available at http://news.bbc.co.uk/2/hi/science/nature/7673914.htm.

Burns, Robert. "The Twa Dogs." 1786.

Goldman, Russell. "Bushmeat: Curse of the Monkey's Paw—The Illicit Trade in Wild Animal Meat Could Spark a Public Health Crisis." ABC News Health, March 15, 2007. Available at http://abcnews.go.com/Health/story?id=2952077&page=1.

Golub, Edward S. *The Limits of Medicine: How Science Shapes Our Hope for the Cure*. New York: Times Books, 1994.

Salt, Henry S. *Animals' Rights Considered in Relation to Social Progress*. New York and London: MacMillan & Co., 1894.

Singer, Peter. *Animal Liberation: A New Ethics for Our Treatment of Animals*. New York: New York Review/Random House, 1975.

Chapter 4. Humor in Animals

Clarke, Alastair. "Mechanism and Function of Humor Identified by New Evolutionary Theory." EurekAlert, June 27, 2008. Available at www.eurekalert.org/pub_releases/2008-06/ph-maf062708.php.

de Saint-Exupéry, Antoine. *The Little Prince*. New York: Harcourt Brace Jovanovich, Inc., 1971.

Greenberg, Idaz and Jerry Greenberg. *Guide to Corals and Fishes of Florida, the Bahamas and the Caribbean*. Miami: Seahawk Press, 1986.

Chapter 5. Personality in Animals

Britt, Robert Roy. "It's No Joke: Even Animals 'Laugh.'" MSNBC, March 31, 2005. Available at www.msnbc.msn.com/id/7348880/.

Dethier, Vincent. "Microscopic Brains." *Science* 3611 (1964): 1138–1145.

Mather, J. A. and R. C. Anderson. "Personalities of Octopuses (*Octopus rubescens*)." *Journal of Comparative Psychology* 107(3) (1993): 336–340.

Siebert, Charles. "The Animal Self." *New York Times*, January 22, 2006.

Chapter 6. A Story of Love

Voice of America, "Nigeria Still Fighting False Rumors About Polio Vaccine." VOANews.com, February 17, 2009. Available at http://www1.voanews.com/english/news/a-13-2009-02-17-voa48-68672337.html.

World Health Organization (WHO) Global Alert and Response (GAR). "Poliomyelitis in Nigeria and West/Central Africa." June 18, 2008. Available at www.who.int/csr/don/2008_06_18/en/.

World Health Organization (WHO) Global Alert and Response (GAR). "Poliomyelitis in Nigeria and West Africa," January 13, 2009. Available at www.who.int/csr/don/2009_01_06/en/index.html.

Chapter 7. The Caribbean Trio

Babyboomerqueen.com. "NY Bronx Dog Protects Injured Mother Dog On Deegan Expressway." Available at http://babyboomeradvisorclub.com/ny-bronx-dog-protects-injured-mother-dog-on-deegan-expressway/. For video, see youtube.com/watch?v=2rWP1O3HbAs.

Belyaev, D. K. "Domestication of Animals." *Science* 5 (1969): 47–52.

Caras, Roger A. *A Perfect Harmony: The Intertwining Lives of Animals and Humans Throughout History*. New York: Simon & Schuster, 1996.

Dinets, Vladimir. "The History of Dog Domestication." Course paper for Systematics class at the University of Miami, 2007. Available at http://dinets.travel.ru/dogs.htm.

Hare, B., M. Brown, C. Williamson, and M. Tomasello. "The domestication of social cognition in dogs." *Science* 298 (2002): 1634–1636.

McGourty, Christine. "Origin of Dogs Traced." BBC News World Edition, November 22, 2002. Available at http://news.bbc.co.uk/2/hi/sci/tech/2498669.stm.

Spady, Tyrone C. and Elaine A. Ostrander. "Canid Genomics: Mapping Genes for Behavior in the Silver Fox." *Genome Research* 17 (2007): 259–263. Available at http://genome .cshlp.org/content/17/3/259.full.pdf.

Trut, Lyudmila N. "Early Canid Domestication: The Farm-Fox Experiment." *American Scientist* 87 (1999): 160–169. Available at www.floridalupine.org/publications/PDF/trut-fox-study.pdf.

Vilà, Carles, Peter Savolainen, Jesús E. Maldonado, et al. "Multiple and Ancient Origins of the Domestic Dog." *Science* 276, no. 5319 (1997): 1687–1689.

Index